A SHEARWATER BOOK

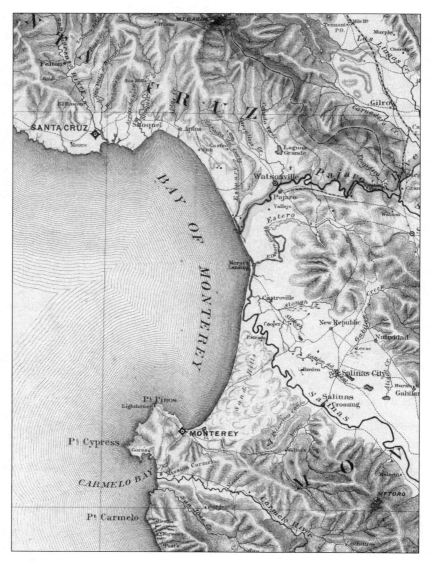

Topographical map of Northern and Central California, 1873. (California Geological Survey, David Rumsey Map Collection)

THE DEATH AND LIFE

OF MONTEREY BAY

A Story of Revival

The Death and Life of Monterey Bay

A STORY OF REVIVAL

Stephen R. Palumbi
and Carolyn Sotka

◖ **ISLAND**PRESS | Shearwater Books
Washington | Covelo | London

A Shearwater Book
Published by Island Press

SHEARWATER BOOKS is a trademark of The Center for Resource Economics.

Library of Congress Cataloging-in-Publication Data
Palumbi, Stephen R.
The death and life of Monterey Bay : a story of revival / Stephen R. Palumbi and Carolyn Sotka.
p. cm.
"A Shearwater Book."
Includes bibliographical references and index.
ISBN-13: 978-1-59726-435-8 (cloth : alk. paper)
ISBN-10: 1-59726-435-0 (cloth : alk. paper)
1. Environmental management—California—Monterey Bay.
2. Environmental protection—California—Monterey Bay—Citizen participation. 3. Monterey Bay (Calif.)—Environmental conditions—History. I. Sotka, Carolyn. II. Title.
TD171.3.C22M666 2011   333.7209794'7—dc22
2010035374

The paperback edition of this book contains the
ISBN-13: 978-1-61091-190-0 and the ISBN-10: 1-61091-190-3

British Cataloguing-in-Publication data available.

Printed on recycled, acid-free paper ♻

Design by David Bullen Design

Manufactured in the United States of America

10 9 8 7 6 5 4 3

Keywords: Monterey Bay Aquarium; Pacific Grove, California; Cannary Row; Hopkins Marine Station; China Point; Julia Platt; John Steinbeck; Ed Ricketts; marine protected areas; sardine fishery; sea otters; biodiversity

No book is written in a vacuum. For the air in the vacuum, I thank my family: Mary, Lauren, and Tony.

Stephen Palumbi

To Maria and Richard, who instilled a love of being outdoors and of nature; to Erik, who opens my eyes to the ecological wonders of even the smallest marine creatures; and to Kai and Liv, who inspire me to keep looking for ocean treasures.

Carolyn Sotka

Contents

Preface

Walking to work along the shore of Pacific Grove, at the southern end of Monterey Bay, is like a taking a stroll through another century. The walking trail edges the bay, meandering around small coves with fine sand beaches. The tidal rocks are draped with red, green, and brown seaweed, and the water just offshore is peppered with the tops of giant kelp. Sea otters watch your slow amble, and black cormorants shoot through the sky toward their roosts on rock towers. The air is tinged with the tang of iodine and the bark of sea lions.

We began this project in awe of the life of Monterey Bay; it was a celebration of the diversity and plenty that we experience here. We intended to document the progress that had been made in the marine refuge in front of the Hopkins Marine Station, Stanford University's marine lab on the border of Monterey and Pacific Grove. It started out as a project about otters, whales, and fish.

But as stories sometimes do, this one had a mind of its own. An eclectic mix of characters arrived in our narrative and took it over. The people who first hunted otters, whales, and fish off the coast of Monterey lived in an exuberant age of exploration, when the ocean seemed inexhaustible. Then later, when the bay was at its worst, other people fought tooth and nail against its demise. And during the climb from pollution back to plenty, still others displayed astonishing talent and passion to help restore the bay.

So in the end we wrote a book not just about fish but about people, not just about marine ecology but about the ups and downs of economies and about human motivations. We are not historians and do not claim to lay out the whole human history of Monterey Bay. Instead we explore its natural history as it was shaped by people over the last three centuries. We have had to leave much out. And we have chosen to concentrate on a series of people and events that exemplify three stages of any recovering environment: the ruin, the turnaround, and the revival.

These stories draw the path between the death and life of Monterey Bay. They are noteworthy because their trajectory is not all downward. They are noteworthy because no superheroes or omnipotent governments saved the day. They are noteworthy because the same success in Monterey could happen elsewhere. And finally, they are noteworthy because in the end, no act of environmentalism is conceived or acted on by fish. It is people who are inspired to act and whose acts inspire.

THE DEATH AND LIFE
OF MONTEREY BAY

Chapter 1

Julia's Window

Hunkered down in a small rented motorboat, the members of the 1935 City Council of Pacific Grove, California were dismayed to see the weather worsening. They were already nearly out of sight of land, beyond the boundaries of Monterey Bay, and some of them were starting to feel queasy. Cajoled into this particular boat by the mayor of Pacific Grove, doctor of marine zoology Julia Platt, they couldn't muster the nerve to protest very loudly. After all, Mayor Platt had just died and was along only for the boat ride. Yet, even in death, wrapped in canvas and covered in flowers, Julia was still very much in charge.

Twelve miles offshore was the stipulation in Julia's will, 12 miles until her canvas-wrapped body could be cast into the deep. Tradition in 1935 decreed that the Pacific Grove City Council act as pallbearers for a former mayor. No one had ever demanded a burial at sea before, and neither tradition nor small-town pride would allow the City

3

Council to demur with honor. So Julia focused the town's entire attention once more on the dark and rolling ocean and moved the city council just the way she wanted: to protect the sea.

The sea called for help. The ocean that swirled around the jutting rocks of Pacific Grove was no longer healthy. Swirling in the wake of Julia's boat were the typical waifs of the coastal seas: bits of kelp, jellyfish, seafoam churned nearly airborne by the waves. However, the kelp plants lay thin and spare, and the foam spumed an oily yellow that smelled of decay. Even the soaring seabirds gulped fish entrails and fought over discarded fish heads from the nearby canneries. It was the low point in the health of Monterey Bay.

But Julia Platt had left a legacy that could help repair the health of the bay. Few of her pallbearers appreciated fully what she had accomplished in the last years of her life, but her schemes eventually proved to be the kernel of recovery for this wounded shore. As the waves grew higher and the seasick council grew greener and greener, the motorboat hearse passed over Julia's final, clever gift to her town. Below their boat on its way out of the bay lay the undersea lands of two unique realms that Julia had created: two marine parks that protected the life of the coastline with a fervor and a permanence unequaled anywhere else on the California coast. Their invention was as much a political milestone as it was a biological revolution.

In 2012, the view of Monterey Bay from Julia Platt's former living room window shows a scene completely different from the one that greeted Julia in the 1930s. The living room today is filled with a bustling bed-and-breakfast crowd, enjoying the stunning scenery of the Pacific Grove shore during elegant breakfasts or wine-sipping afternoons. Warm days bring families to the beach at Lovers Point across the street. Almost every morning sees a cadre of scuba divers, suiting up in the parking lot and lugging tanks and cameras toward the kelp forest. When the wind picks up and the waves roll around the point, surfers and boogie boarders appear. All this is watched by a constant stream of walkers, bikers, and dog walkers, threading the bike path between Julia's house and the shore. The visitors thoroughly enjoy the environment, its sheer beauty, and its shine of health.

Why is this place so beautiful, so full of wildlife and suffused with the clean tang of the sea? Most of the visitors to Julia's town of Pacific Grove, or to Monterey next door, assume it has always been this way. Little do they know how recently the bay suffered an industrial blight that wrecked the ecology and the economy. Few of them realize how recently the wonderful tourist shores of Lovers Point stood polluted and abandoned—how bad they looked in 1935, the year of Julia's death.

Had it existed when westerners came permanently to Monterey in 1769, Julia's window would have chronicled a steady ruin of Monterey Bay since that time. It would have seen the merchants and hunters turning one wild species after another into a market commodity that was plucked off the shore for profit. French explorer Jean-François de la Pérouse was paying a courtesy call at the Spanish capital Monterey in 1786, when he remarked on the wonderful creatures he saw there: sea otters. He knew the Russians were making a fortune selling otter pelts to the rich Chinese aristocracy. *Odd*, he thought, *that the Spanish do not do the same*. And soon they did.

A whale was worth a pound or two of pure gold in 1854, and J. P. Davenport used exploding lances to deliver them to shore-based vats of boiling oil. In the late 1800s, abalone brought a whole Chinese village to the Pacific Grove shore, complete with lacy incense, smugglers, and the customs of the Celestial Empire. Fourteen million seabird eggs, gathered on coastal islands, went down the gullets of the Gold Rush prospectors, fueling their hunt for treasure but destroying seabird populations. From the 1910s to 1940s, a new canning industry was driven to unheard-of size on the strength of the sardines of Monterey. Every one of these enterprises collapsed in the ashes of its own greed; first the otters, then the whales, birds, abalone, and sardines were exploited until they were largely gone.

As the exploitation of Monterey grew, its natural rugged beauty still called to literary masters and poets. Robert Louis Stevenson crafted *Treasure Island* from the granite bones of the Monterey Peninsula. Robinson Jeffers built an Ezmerelda Tower to his lady love and inspired the poets of the 1900s. In the 1930s, three friends barricaded themselves against a staid church society in Julia's town of Pacific Grove: John Steinbeck, Joseph Campbell, and Ed Ricketts spawned a hundred riotous parties and created a raucous philosophy of friendship that led the literature and philosophy of its day.

Julia's window looked out over this frenzy like a grouchy neighbor eyeing a wild party. And in her last years, the Monterey Bay called for help. Julia couldn't keep herself from striving against the continual onslaught and destruction. She predicted the doom that the canneries would bring and tried to slow their growth. But she was pushed aside by the economic might of the biggest fishery anyone had ever seen. Thwarted in her campaign to save all of Monterey Bay, she conceived a stealthy legacy that would wait quietly until it was needed and until the world was ready for it. She created for her town and her bay two small protected areas, marine gardens for the future. They eventually paid off in a legacy of ecological rebirth, but only after the bay passed through the worst decades of its environmental life.

Good News

Good environmental news is hard to come by these days. Yet when people look out at Monterey Bay today they are seeing an ocean environment that is functioning better than it has been for more than 200 years. It is not perfect, and it faces stunning challenges still, but it has more of the working elements of a healthy ecosystem than it had had in Julia's time, and even for the century before her.

It didn't happen by accident, the recovery of Monterey Bay. And it depended on a few turns of good luck. But it also depended on a set of pioneers with a clear vision of the bay they wanted to leave to future generations. Along the way, the success of Monterey lays out some lessons for possible successes elsewhere. But even if no other bay will ever have exactly this story, the fact that a local shore, the place that generations have called home, has been driven to the depths of ecological ruin and has recovered—this shows that the pathway of recovery from ruin exists, and it is a possibility for places that anyone else calls home.

PART I

The Ruin

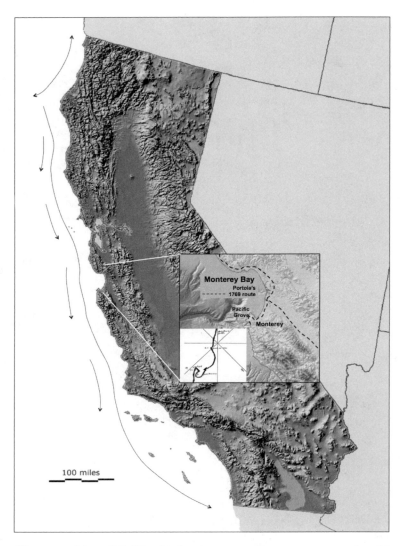

Figure 2.1. Map of California showing summer ocean currents—the cold, south-flowing California Current—and the position of Monterey Bay. The inset shows Monterey Bay, the current towns of Monterey and Pacific Grove, and the 1769 route of the Portolà expedition. The lower left corner of the inset shows a reproduction of the crude map Vizcaíno drew in 1602 to suggest that Monterey was a perfect harbor protected by a spur of land, the Point of Pines, which is grossly exaggerated in this drawing. (Maps based on the National Atlas.)

Chapter 2

The First California Gold Rush: Otters

*E*ARLY FALL is a magical time in Monterey Bay, and French captain Jean-François de la Pérouse, arriving in September 1786, perhaps saw it at its best. The fogs of summer begin to roll back in September, releasing the pent-up sun to warm the hills and quicken the air with the scent of sage and pine. The shoreline gathers raucous seabirds. The beaches are the beds of languid seals. Out in the center of the bay, balls of sardines boil to the surface, driven upward by voracious tuna, often split by coordinated attacks from schools of gray dolphins, and circled by thick clouds of spiraling seabirds. The shallower coast also roils with fish, halibut the size of wagon wheels racing across the sandy seabeds, gulping smaller prey. Fishing lines, dangled for minutes over the ship's sides in 1786, would have brought up a constellation of bottom-dwelling rockfish with such a confusion of colors and patterns that future taxonomists would eventually catalogue more than sixty species of this one type of fish.

To Europeans, the edges of this rocky coast would have seemed strangely coated by a floating layer of thick brown ribbons, the canopy of a kelp forest. Yards thick at the end of the summer, the surface layer of giant kelp fronds would have lined nearly the entire southern shore of Monterey Bay. Elegant herons could walk on this kelp carpet confidently, searching for the bounty of young fish it sheltered. Sea lions might have swum in and out, mixing with smaller harbor seals and the ever-present sea otters. Gray whales gamboling in the surf zone would have been just starting to head south to their Mexican breeding grounds. But probably most of the whales La Pérouse saw were humpbacks that fed off the productive riches of the cold seawater or gigantic blue whales, far too swift for most ships of the day to catch. La Pérouse wrote about their numbers, complaining that whales were so numerous that the very air was tainted by their breath, producing an inelegant, "annoying stench."

La Pérouse entered Monterey Bay as a child might enter a candy store, agape at the bounty, confused by the diversity, eager for a bite. He settled his fleet at the shore and prepared to be received royally. The capital city of Spanish California had expected La Pérouse for months. His arrival as the first foreign dignitary marked a milestone in the history of the tiny encampment and its anxious development into a world capital.

The Three Western Discoveries of Monterey Bay

Monterey represented a long-term investment by the Spanish crown. Nearly two centuries before La Pérouse was welcomed at the Spanish mission, the empire had sent adventurer Sebastián Vizcaíno to scout out the California coast and find a suitable harbor. But Vizcaíno was impatient to be off discovering pearls and gold, not harbors. Perhaps one of the world's first public relations geniuses, he had sent back glowing reports of "the best port that could be desired." He bestowed the name of the expedition's patron, Gaspar de Zúñiga, Conde de

Monterey, the viceroy of New Spain, on the bay and claimed it was "sheltered from all winds." Back in Spain, Vizcaíno's reports elevated Monterey Bay to a legend, and it was designated the future capital of Spain's California.

But Vizcaíno's hyperbole was empty. Monterey Bay is a broad bite taken out of the coastline, but it does not include the perfect harbor Vizcaíno described. When the Spanish colonial administration in the New World eventually got around to sending a land expedition to Monterey, in 1769, the perfect harbor of Monterey was nowhere to be found. The expedition leader, Captain Gaspar de Portolà, walked from San Diego to where Vizcaíno said Monterey Bay should be. He found Vizcaíno's Punta Pinos, the pine-covered peninsula he said defined the southern boundary of the bay. But nowhere was there the perfect harbor Vizcaíno drew and described. Portolà's expedition wandered in confusion and dismay north to discover San Francisco Bay, shrugged off this accomplishment, and walked in failure back to San Diego.

The next time Portolà was sent to Monterey, though, he had a more insistent master. The next expedition to Monterey, only months later, was led by the zealot monk Junípero Serra, who was determined to find the bay and establish the headquarters of his string of Catholic missions. A stern Franciscan priest, barely five feet tall, rapier thin and with sharp features, Serra radiated a relentless desire to expand his church's reach. He did not eat well or sleep peacefully. He believed that mortification of the flesh purified the spirit, and "he would pound his breast with a stone while in the pulpit, scourge himself, or apply a lighted torch to his bare chest." Lame in one leg, he walked, painfully, everywhere—even from Veracruz to Mexico City. In San Diego, Portolà told Serra about his failure to find Monterey, and Serra turned him around and sent him back. Not to be thwarted again, Serra himself took a boat up the coast and landed a few days before Portolà's arrival. Announcing that the current site of the city of Monterey was the right place, Serra sent Portolà home and settled down to the business of building his mission.

Not Alone

The chronicler of the Serra expedition, Ensign Miguel Costansó, wrote late in 1769 that the bay seemed welcoming: "The land which shuts in this immense bay, seen from the sea, forms an agreeable view. Looking to the south can be seen the Sierra of Santa Lucia . . . their summits crowned with pines and covered with pasturage, presenting a magnificent amphitheatre. . . . On the northeast and east shore, the country stretches in beautiful plains."

But the shores of the bay were not empty in the late 1700s, and the Spanish were not alone. Costansó records encounter after encounter with native villages along the Spanish route as they marched north from San Diego. At Monterey Bay, he found a constellation of villages bound by a common language and sustainable culture. Modern-day archeologists would record millennia of life at Monterey and a complex of coastal native cultures that stretched back in time for thousands of years.

At the time, Monterey was home to the Ohlone people, who lived throughout coastal central California, from San Francisco Bay south to Big Sur. The Ohlone showed a strong affinity with the natural products of the coastal environment, harvesting seeds from local grasses and gathering acorns in bulk for processing into flour. The Ohlone formed a loose association of villages, clustered by common dialect within a language group and with at least five permanent villages in the Monterey Bay area. Perhaps 7,000 people lived near Monterey Bay when Serra appeared there. They seemed to the Spanish to have no agriculture, but they carefully tended the oak-covered hillsides using fire to clear the underbrush and produce acorns and grasses. And seasonally they used the bounty of the sea, piling middens high with fish bones, otter skulls, and abalone shells. Whales were for eating but were difficult to kill. The Ohlone waited for them to wash ashore and chased the condors and grizzly bears off.

Because the Ohlone presented little threat, Costansó worried mostly about the reception that the Spanish religion would bring about, whether they could be converted: "The natives of Monterey live in the Sierra.... These Serranos (mountain Indians) are extremely docile and peaceful.... Their good disposition has given to the Reverend Mission Padres well-founded hopes of winning them over." Father Serra wrote in the official record of the Portolà expedition his hopes about the future promise of the missions, "the affability of the Indians, and the promise which they had already made him, to intrust [sic] their children to him to instruct them in the mysteries of our holy Catholic religion."

And so by 1769, the conversion of the native American culture of Monterey Bay commenced.

La Pérouse in Monterey

In 1786, La Pérouse was a famous captain and explorer and was in the middle of a voyage of discovery for his masters in France. Once La Pérouse settled his fleet of two ships at anchor near the Monterey shoreline, the officials at the lonely presidio and mission of Monterey wasted no time in sending a boat to pay their respects to their celebrity guest and invite the illustrious captain to dinner. "No effort will be spared in acquainting you with all the facts and figures of our administration," they promised. La Pérouse seemed an eager student, and he spent the next weeks chronicling Spanish lives in the first Californian mission.

But Serra was not there; the feared and admired head of all the California missions had died in 1784, two years earlier. His reputation was so overwhelming that at his funeral, bits of his undergarments were distributed as sacred tokens. La Pérouse was invited to visit Serra's monument, but the Frenchman cautiously demurred.

La Pérouse's philosophical problem, and the source of his reluctance to approve the Spanish administration, was in the state of the Ohlone natives. La Pérouse found the Ohlone to be sullen, pasty, and depressed. Women were locked up in a dormitory at night. Men were beaten and thrown in the stocks for leaving the mission to visit their old villages. They seemed very different from the vigorous, generous native people Serra had originally described.

La Pérouse became genuinely touched by the good intentions of the priests, but he did not approve of the condition in which he found the Ohlone. Tough love, it might be called in future centuries. Or economic enslavement. No matter what the judgment of history, La Pérouse saw and described a failing colony, a mission system doomed to collapse. It had less than two generations to live.

But La Pérouse also had a keen eye for economic opportunity, which he saw not in the stooped backs of the Ohlone natives planting Spanish crops but rather in the bounty and value of the ocean. The whole of Monterey Bay lay in front of the Spanish presidio, but Colonial Governor Fages and Father Serra had trained their thoughts and hopes inland. As a man of the sea, La Pérouse found a different focus and could see that all around him, the bay erupted with potential. At the very beginning of his journal, he wrote, "No country is more abundant in fish and game of every description."

Noting that the "sea is covered with pelicans," La Pérouse speculated about their foraging habits, wistfully wondering where they found the quantities of fish they needed to survive. He listed the natural capital, the living resources of Monterey Bay, and finally effused, "It is impossible to describe either the number of whales with which we were surrounded or their familiarity."

The Hunt as It Began

Time and again in his journal, La Pérouse hinted about an idea that seemed obvious to him and, he assumed, to his audience. "The reader will soon perceive, however, that a new branch of commerce may procure to the Spanish nation greater advantages than the richest mines in Mexico."

La Pérouse was thinking about sea otters, the small, agile marine mammals possessed of magnificent fur "for which China is a certain market." Abundant all along the central California coast, the otters had long been part of the Ohlone culture. Cloaks of otter fur draped from shoulders to waist were worn in the villages and can be recognized in the earliest drawings of Native American life. The Ohlone hunted otters with snares, or with sticks when the animals ventured far from shore, an ability so at odds with the behavior of today's otters—which seldom stray from the ocean's edge—that some wildlife biologists dispute that this hunting method ever existed. Soon the westerners focused intently on the commerce of sea otter trade and thereby altered the ecology of the entire coast for centuries into the future.

Otter Furs

At 600,000 hairs per square inch, sea otter fur is a protective necessity for a small, warm-blooded mammal trying to make its living in the cold upwelling water of the California coast. It is a typical evolutionary conundrum: The cold water, colder in summer than in winter because of the upwelling currents, produces a bonanza of seafood. But those same currents sap the warmth from a small otter's body. Other marine mammals layer themselves with insulating blubber. Sea otters found a different solution in the fine hairs of their fur. These hairs trap so much air that they keep the frigid water off an otter's skin, cloaking the animal in a thin silver bubble that allows perfect freedom of movement and perfect access to the larder of the kelp forest.

La Pérouse knew of these animals because the Russians had long sought them along the cold, bleak shores of the Aleutian Islands, at the northern reaches of the Pacific. The Russians conducted a highly lucrative trade with China for otter furs and had begun edging south along the Pacific Coast of North America, seeking new coastlines to exploit. It was just this southern expansion that had worried the Spanish Viceroy in Mexico, and it was the possibility that Russia might usurp the rights of Spain along the California coast that finally pushed the Spanish authorities, after leaving Monterey alone for 168 years, to send Junípero Serra to colonize the bay.

"Here sea otter skins are as common as in the Aleutian Island

and those of the other seas frequented by the Russians," La Pérouse announced in his journals. He credited Monterey's Governor Fages as boasting that 20,000 could be collected annually "for the commerce of his nation." But he remained somewhat skeptical of the ability of the Spanish to take full advantage of this trade, lamenting, "It is perfectly unaccountable that the Spanish . . . should have been hitherto ignorant of the value of this precious trade of furs."

Such voracious fascination with otters was driven by high prices for otter fur in China, each pelt being worth $30 to $40 in many years and up to $100 in banner seasons. Compared to the price of a house in San Diego, $96, every otter wore a small fortune.

Greed Nearly Saves Them

The otter market in China was something of a fad: In the late 1700s, otter pelts had become the "royal fur." "Ladies in high social standing wore otter capes," historian Adele Ogden wrote. Otter skin robes were "the style of the day for Chinese Mandarins." European merchants knew how to respond to a fad, and so French and English merchants flooded Canton to try to lock in customers for this lucrative trade. But where were the Spanish?

The Spanish were coming, but slowly. A month before La Pérouse sailed into Monterey, Vicente Vasadre y Vega had arrived at the tattered mission bearing official sanction from the king and the viceroy to begin trade in otters. But he had sought far more, securing the viceroy's agreement that Vasadre would have a virtual monopoly on the otter trade. He had accomplished this by promising to sell otter furs in China, but not for money. His plan was to trade otter fur for quicksilver—Chinese mercury—which was vital in extracting gold and silver ore in Mexico, something the Spanish government needed badly. By promising to turn otter pelts into gold and silver, Vasadre was fulfilling the dream that had driven Vizcaíno to Monterey centuries before and was promising to enrich the royal house of Spain during trying times. Vasadre would gather all the pelts he could from

California natives and ship them on empty supply boats returning from Monterey to Mexico. From there he would travel to the Philippines aboard the Manila galleon sent by Spain to collect riches from its Philippine colony.

The first year of the scheme, 1787, Vasadre took 1,060 skins to Mexico. Once there, he undercut the viceroy's confidence by demanding a treasure trove of expensive gifts for Chinese officials and a vast sum for bribes for the Chinese court. And he needed a higher salary. Vasadre got almost none of these things, but just as he had demanded a monopoly on the otter trade in California, he negotiated an order from the colonial authorities that the Manila governor was not to interfere with Vasadre's mission. Vasadre was answerable only to the Crown, not to the officials in the colonies. He thought.

But intense rivalry over the otter trade was not so easily deflected, and Vasadre seemed an amateur in the politics of trade. Venerable institutions such as the powerful Philippine Company would not be easily sidestepped. "Self interest moved both the Philippine Company and the principal government officials in Manila to oppose his plan," wrote Ogden. The Philippine Company, a well-connected mercantile group, had been granted the right in Spain to trade in Chinese quicksilver, and they refused to share this wealth. At the same time, government officials in Manila had their own interests in the otter trade, and while Vasadre was trying to cut a deal with the Chinese, they brazenly seized his second shipload of otter pelts. These were transferred to the Philippine Company for sale, the proceeds of which were to go to the company, not Vasadre. Exasperated, Vasadre fired off terse letters of complaint that fell on deaf ears. The company's only response was an order for Vasadre to turn over all the quicksilver and the proceeds from his first shipload of pelts. Baffled, boxed in, and outmaneuvered, Vasadre wanted nothing if he could not have a monopoly. He abandoned his mission in 1788 and "with little ceremony left for Spain." Various officials fought over the otter trade for a few years, but royal sanction for the business was soon withdrawn. The Philippine Company dropped plans for pelt shipments, and no other player could secure complete control of the trade. By 1793, Spain's ability to hunt and market otter fur, despite high prices in China and abundant animals in California, collapsed.

Doomed by Yankee Ingenuity

But others cared less for complete control of the trade than they did for annual income, and the coast of California became a destination for a highly profitable, illegal foreign otter hunt. The English merchants had been prevented from trading in California by a treaty signed in 1790, but American ships soon began arriving in Spanish ports, mysteriously in need of urgent repair or supplies. On August 25, 1800 the *Betsy*, out of Boston, sailed into San Diego harbor announcing a dire need for water and wood. Captain James Rowan declared he had been in the North Pacific and Hawaii and was on his way to China. But his letters back to Boston recounted his real itinerary: a trading venture along the California coast, illegally stocking up on otter furs.

Other captains were bold enough to purchase otter pelts right under the nose of Spanish authorities, in Spanish ports. In March 1803 the *Lelia Byrd* arrived in San Diego, pleading the need of supplies, and was given five days to arrange them. The night before their impending departure the Spanish guard on board woke to the sound of a boat being lowered over the side.

"Where is that boat going?" he demanded.

"We are searching for one of our crew who did not return from the hunt today," came the reply from the quickly rowed boat as it disappeared into the night.

Later, another splash roused the guard. The ship's launch had been readied. "Why?"

"To look for the first boat!" The launch vanished.

The first boat returned soon with a load of otter skins, and the crew of the launch was confronted in the act of buying more on the nearby beach. Arrested by Spanish officials, the launch's crew were brazenly rescued by the *Lelia Byrd*'s captain at the point of a pistol and hustled out of San Diego on the dawn wind, pursued by futile Spanish bullets.

Many Yankee ships played this cat and mouse game, cutting year by year into the otter population along the coast. The catch varied by vessel, but often a captain and crew could succeed handsomely. In 1803, a single boat, the *O'Cain*, traded for 1,800 furs. All in all, an estimated 17,000 furs were exported from California to China in 1803, 1804, and 1805. In 1806 and 1807, the *O'Cain* alone exported a total of 4,819 otters. In 1810 two vessels, the *O'Cain* and the *Isabella*, took 3,952 and 2,976, respectively. In 1811, a total of 9,356 otter pelts were taken from California—by four ships and 300 men—the largest number ever recorded in a single year.

This level of exploitation did not prove to be sustainable, and soon ships began reporting bad years when otter pelts could be obtained only in the hundreds, not the thousands. "I do not think we shall get 600 in all on the coast," reported Captain John Rogers Cooper in 1833. The Russians had also arrived, fortifying a promontory north of San Francisco, Fort Ross, in 1812 and populating it with Aleutian otter hunters under Russian command. They took about 2,000 otter pelts a year, but by 1817 otters were becoming scarce north of the Golden Gate.

Revolution's Blind Eye

Father Miguel Hidalgo ignited the Mexican independence movement in 1810, embroiling the Spanish government in a cross-Atlantic conflict at the same time the Spanish monarchs were repelling Napoleon's invasion at home and other conflicts abroad, creating "far more demands on the military and treasury than could be met." California was too far away to be immediately affected, but the missions and military lost support from home. Native populations were especially hard hit; their own culture had been decapitated, and any "effective central government collapsed." The otter trade thrived in this chaos, and by buying pelts from the missions that were obtained from the natives, this illegal trade had the odd effect of bringing California into the international market.

California passed into Mexican hands in 1821, a period of enormous upheaval and social change that led to the Republic of Mexico in 1824. During that period, resources flowing into California from Spain collapsed, and the missions lost their political and economic power. Governors continued to be appointed from the Mexican capital, and they were either in tune with the local population or in conflict. The economy turned away from the sea and concentrated on ranching. Yet otters continued to be a significant industry that brought ships and cash to California shores.

The End of the Otter Hunt

Alarm about dropping numbers of otters produced the first known fishery conservation regulation on the West Coast of North America. In Monterey, Governor José Mariá Echeandía issued instructions that otter pups were no longer to be killed by hunters. Occasional pockets of successful otter hunting persisted into the 1830s: Hunter José Fernandez remarked in 1831 that in San Francisco Bay, "the ground appeared covered with black sheets due to the great quantity of otters which were there." But in general otters were in such steep decline by the 1830s that laws were passed (though widely ignored) restricting otter hunting to Mexican nationals.

Ships from Hawaii occasionally appeared in the decade after 1830, crewed by *contrabandistas* who secured neither permission nor licenses to hunt. These boats, studded with cannon and crammed with guns, were happy with catches that the previous generation of ship captains would have scoffed at. One such vessel, the *Griffon*, considered itself to be unusually lucky when it "after two months obtained 300 sea otter skins!" This success too was fleeting, and hunts of only 100 skins a season soon became more common, so little that "the owners will not lose or gain anything by the voyage." Eventually, in 1841, even the Russians abandoned their outpost at Fort Ross, north of San Francisco. Although otter hunting continued until the California Gold Rush eclipsed other forms of extractive wealth, the decade from 1840 to 1850 saw the end of the commercial otter enterprise.

Much had changed politically in California as well. The old mission system was largely gone, decayed into adobe ruin when the Spanish Empire fell and Mexico won its 1821 independence. But war between the former colonies of the United States and Mexico was coming and would shift the ownership of land out of Mexican hands. By 1848, California left the Mexican republic and was incorporated into the United States. Such a period of upheaval left many land tenure records shattered and lost, with disastrous consequences to the Ohlone and to the former Spanish citizens who had settled in California. It was a time of transformation from the old to the new.

Far-Reaching Effects

The hunters went off to other trades, and the Chinese lost their taste for otter fur. The ships no longer came to California to trade for furs, and the native culture was slipping away. Up in the Sierra the first hints of gold galvanized the attention of the whole frontier. Hope turned inland.

But along the coast the extraction of otters from kelp forests created an unexpected and unobserved cascade of ecological effects. No longer roiling with rafts of otters, the quiet coves and inlets of the coast might have seemed quiet on the surface. But beneath the long ocean swell, a revolution was taking shape that changed the coast for more than a century to come.

Red sea urchins, some the size of basketballs, began to thrive in the absence of their major predator: sea otters. Smaller purple sea urchins that could fill a large man's hand also bloomed. Beside them crawled a new generation of cold water snail, the abalone, that until the disappearance of the otter lived out their lives crammed into protected rock crevices. Freed of rocky confines, these plate-shaped snails grew to extraordinary size and soon began crowding one another off the rocks.

Urchins and abalone eat seaweed, especially the long, luxuriant giant kelp plants that normally grow in abundance along the California coast. Without otters to keep them in check, the sea urchin and abalone populations skyrocketed, and these herbivores, in turn, chewed into the kelp forests. Where once stood thick stems of kelp reaching a hundred feet from ocean bottom to the surface, now there persisted mere wisps of kelp, growing quickly toward the light until the horde of herbivores crawled over and chewed them down.

No one recorded this transformation; it fell to later generations to discover the domino effect caused by the otter hunt. And the otter hunters themselves turned their view toward other targets: gold in the mountains and other prey in the sea. Other marine mammals frequented the coast of California, and the captains who profited from the otter trade also consorted with the whaling fleets that wintered in Hawaii. Otters no longer brought in enough money to make a captain happy or a boat owner wealthy. But there were whales in Monterey Bay.

Chapter 3

Whale Bones
in Treasure Bay

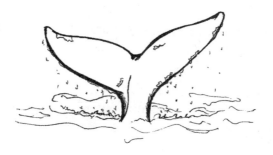

TWO FAST EXHALATIONS interrupted the quiet of a morning seascape. The whales appeared briefly before diving again, a shallow glide to nowhere in particular. Long pectoral fins could be seen when they rolled; these springtime humpback whales had arrived early in Monterey Bay. Offshore, a few gray whales lumbered north, businesslike travelers churning toward the Bering Sea. They were late stragglers on a long migration from Mexico.

A small sailing ship on the waters of Monterey Bay headed toward the quiet town in 1850, sliding through a wealth of marine mammal species found few places on Earth. The trading ship *Alfred*, just in from Hawaii, had long plied these waters, moving goods across the

Pacific Ocean. Today, the ship looked to drop anchor at Monterey, sailing through wildlife so abundant that it was unremarkable.

Pacific white-sided dolphins broke the surface in a school of one hundred, veering suddenly toward a ball of sardines off the port bow. Risso's dolphins joined them, their 13-foot torpedo bodies jetting through the blue-green water. Even sea lions, far from shore but comfortable in their rapid foraging, cut through the waves toward their breakfast. Three orcas, the sharp-toothed predators that ship captains called killer whales, appeared, and the circus parted briefly to let them pass.

Twin Currents

The living bounty of Monterey Bay is a collaboration of two currents, one above the sea and one below. The one above the sea, the wind blowing from the north along the coast, had plagued California travelers forever. The early Spanish explorers Vizcaíno and Portolà suffered it near Point Conception, about halfway between San Diego and Monterey, where they "began to experience cold and violent North winds."

This pestering wind blew winter and summer, sometimes strong, sometimes weak. It even reversed for a few days occasionally. But the steady push of the wind from north to south helped create a faithful friend, the southern-flowing, cold water California Current. Meandering onshore and offshore, this river in the ocean acts as a vast linear refrigerator, cooling the coastline from Washington State to Baja Mexico.

Together, these flows—the twin currents of air and ocean—rule the climate of central California. The wind feeds a thick layer of fog that often covers the Monterey coast. It chills the air and keeps at bay the hundred-degree temperatures that dominate the inland valleys in summer. The ocean current in turn chills the coastal water as it moves from north to south. But the spin of the earth creates another current that pushes the water west, moving the surface waters slightly offshore. As a consequence, deeper water moves up toward the surface. This deep water is even colder than the surface water, and it is also richer in the nutrients and minerals that marine life needs to thrive.

An entire ecosystem has evolved in the North Pacific to take advantage of these cool, nutrient-rich conditions. Giant kelp forests line the coast from Alaska to Mexico, making up the world's greatest concentration of kelp species. One of these kelp, the California giant kelp, is the world's largest alga, which can stretch to hundreds of feet. And the charming sea palm, a foot-high algal version of coconut trees, is found nowhere else on Earth. Along with the algae, a host of herbivores have evolved that feast on kelp, including the delicious abalone. Some species of sea urchins, rock crabs, and their major predator, the sea otter, exist only in the North Pacific. From seaweeds to fish to otters to whales, coastal upwelling greatly enhances the life of the sea. For the maritime traders of the nineteenth century, upwelling turned sunlight into gold.

Swimming Gold

Captain John Pope Davenport, master of the *Alfred*, was no stranger to Monterey. He had made profitable trading runs back and forth from Hawaii to California since 1845, and along the way, like all other captains from La Pérouse onward, Davenport encountered an enticing concentration of marine mammals in Monterey Bay. The sea otters were gone, but the waters of Monterey Bay churned with life. And whales were on Captain Davenport's mind.

Whales were good money in the 1850s. Even with the California Gold Rush in full swing they were worth a businessman's time. At about $0.50 a gallon, 31 gallons to the barrel, and maybe thirty to sixty barrels per whale, oil from a single humpback or large gray whale might bring $500–$1,000. This kind of money was about the same as two to three pounds of refined gold (selling at $20 an ounce at the time), a haul that even goldminers would smile about. Around the world, a century of frantic whaling had scoured the seas practically clean of sperm and right whales. Now other whales were in the crosshairs, and down south in Mexico, Davenport had heard of Yankee whalers making good money hunting gray whales.

In fact, a whale bonanza was going on in Mexico. Ships from Hawaii began to crowd into the protected waters of Magdalena Bay, a broad, shallow estuary on the Pacific Ocean side of the Baja Peninsula. They hunted during the winter, when gray whale mothers and calves appeared. Other ships patrolled the Baja coast to the north, lying in wait as the whales migrated south from Alaskan waters. Captain Charles Scammon counted fifty ships in one year, forming a curtain of death between the whales and their breeding lagoons, although later records could place only half that number there with certainty.

The whales that were hunted in Mexico did not live there year-round. They migrated along the coast between Baja and the cold, productive waters between Alaska and Russia. Each year they passed through Monterey Bay twice: south on their way to Baja and north on the return journey. Davenport knew the hunt was on in Mexico, and Davenport saw the whales of Monterey as swimming gold.

Learning to Hunt

In 1854, with a new wife on board from the eastern United States, Davenport settled in Monterey. The Stars and Stripes had flown over the Monterey Customs house ever since Commodore John Sloat led a detachment onshore and on July 7, 1846 declared California no longer part of Mexico but part of the United States. The unorganized farms of the Spanish missions had given way to huge ranches (50,000 acres or more) in the Mexican period, and cattle seemed to be the future of Monterey. About 1,200 people lived around the Monterey area by then, vastly outnumbered by cows, in a quiet cul-de-sac where the sea still thrived with fish and whales.

With his eye on Monterey's swimming gold, Davenport proceeded to equip California's first shore-based whaling station. He put together a crew of twelve men and launched them into Monterey Bay with two boats, the first ever to go whaling from shore in California. Competing with the gold fields of the Sierra, Davenport could find only three or four experienced whalers. He'd brought some of the modern bomb lances from New England—devices that exploded in the flesh of a whale—but they proved defective. So the inexperienced crew used hand harpoons and hand-thrown lances. "The whales were plentiful and easy to approach," so the boats took eighteen whales— fourteen humpbacks and four grays—between them. But Davenport's crew killed many more whales than they kept while the hunters learned their trade. And their oil production was meager.

Spurred by Davenport's example, a second Monterey whaling company formed in 1855. These experienced Portuguese whalers took about 800 barrels of oil per season—five times what Davenport's novice crew managed. By 1861, their success had drawn three more whaling companies to Monterey Bay.

Davenport managed to import working bomb lances, and he started using hard-hitting harpoon guns instead of hand-thrown lances. Like any innovation, this one prompted predictions of doom for the fishery. The Monterey *Sentinel* frothed, "It should be stated also that the whales are every year getting more shy from the use of the bomb lance. It is said that they hear the bomb explode in the water, even though ten or twenty miles off." C.H. Townsend (1886) was told by whalers that inexperienced hands were to blame, driving whales away from the coast.

Three Days until the Whale Rises

Whaling in the 1850s was a bloody, exhausting, violent, profitable business. Swift boats leapt after the whales, rocketed along by a brace of oarsmen. The harpoon itself was flung into the curved back of a diving whale, going deep enough so that its wide arrowhead would jam irretrievably into the flesh and blubber. One harpoon usually was not enough to kill a whale as big as a gray, and the boat waited quietly until the stressed animal, which dove deep and long after the wounding, returned to the surface. Then they chased it again, throwing harpoon after harpoon until the whale was bleeding and helpless. Then the men tied a float to a firmly placed lance in the mountainous carcass and backed away.

The dead whale might easily sink into the cold sea. Many whales sink after death; right whales, so named for this very reason, usually have enough fat and blubber to float after death. Most shore-based whaling boats of the 1850s did not have the power or size to hoist a heavy whale out of the water. They could lash it to the side of the boat once it was floating on the surface, but a sunken whale was hard to retrieve. So in many cases, the whalers had to wait until the carcass putrefied enough to become bloated with gases and rise back to the surface. This usually took three days or so, and the lance and the float, if still attached, marked ownership of the carcass by a particular crew. Then the crew could tie the whale to the ship, where it was ready to be stripped of blubber and boiled down.

A Dying Industry

Whale by whale, the shore boats captured and rendered their prey. But their success in any one place did not last long. In Monterey, whale catches peaked between 1859 and 1863. Fewer than forty whales were recorded as taken in Monterey between 1870 and 1900, and after that shore-based whaling in California was dead. Although around 1920 steam-driven ships took more than 2,000 whales between Monterey and Trinidad, California, the gray whales that were numerous enough in Monterey that they "rolled around in the surf" had been killed.

The total taken in Monterey during this period is difficult to calculate from incomplete records, but oil from perhaps 900 whales was sold. About a third of these—300 animals—were probably gray whales, the rest mostly humpback whales. But the hunting of 300 gray whales should not have exhausted the Monterey population. Gray whales were not residents; they migrated from Alaska to

Baja, and thousands of whales passed by Monterey every year. With a steady flow of migrating whales, why did the Monterey hunt die off so quickly?

Exploding bomb lances may have made the whales leery of coastlines, shifting their migration offshore, out of the clutches of whalers. Other shore-based whaling stations also sprang into existence, cutting into the population. But the main reason why Monterey whaling—and whaling for gray whales in general—was so short lived was the intense hunt of gray whales in Mexico, on the breeding and calving grounds in Baja. The frantic hunt there pulled the plug on the whole gray whale population, and it drained quickly into the oil barrels of the Pacific whaling fleet.

Just as J. P. Davenport began teaching his novice whalers to throw lances in Monterey Bay, the whaling revolution in Mexico was reaching a crescendo. The decade before 1854 had seen a steady hunt for small numbers of gray whales in the shallow lagoons on the Pacific shores of the Baja Peninsula. But in the decade after 1854, whale ships wintering in Hawaii descended on the lagoons, and in the shallow waters they attacked the mothers and calves they found there. For 10 years, an average of 300 whales a year were killed for oil in the three main breeding lagoons: Magdalena Bay, Scammon's Lagoon (now Ojo de Liebre), and San Ignacio Lagoon. Scammon's Lagoon was virtually scoured clean by Charles Scammon, who, based on his hunter's knowledge, went on to publish the single most authoritative treatise on marine mammal biology in the late nineteenth century. San Ignacio was similarly emptied. Only Magdalena, with its many pools and treacherous channels, held onto a few live whales.

The lagoon whalers had help. Late to the feast, other whalers took up position outside the lagoons and snared whales along the migration route. Some anchored their ships in quiet harbors, such as in San Diego, and sent smaller whaleboats out beyond shore to chase the southerly moving whales. And shore-based whaling, mostly in California but also in Baja in later years, ramped up tremendously.

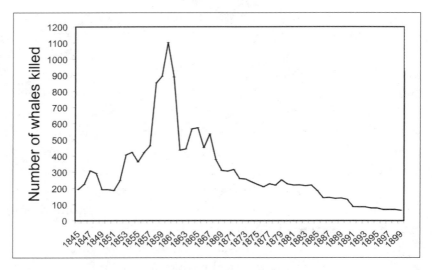

Figure 3.1. An estimate of gray whales taken in California, redrawn from Reeves and Smith (2010) and Reeves et al (2010), including aboriginal species. The heyday of gray whaling lasted only about 15 years. Current estimates suggest that a hunt of 417 whales a year or less should have been sustainable, but few years saw a larger hunt.

In 1854, Davenport's Monterey efforts were matched only in a short-lived whaling station in Crescent City. But by 1861 there were eight whaling stations in California.

Mysterious Disappearances

By 1868, the bonanza of gray whales described by renowned whaling historian D. A. Henderson was over. Another decade passed with ship-based whalers taking declining numbers from the emptied lagoons and with shore-based whalers chasing fewer and fewer migrating remnants. But in the mid-1870s, whalers walked away from the Baja hunt.

Henderson's accounting suggests that all whaling in the "bonanza" decade from 1854 to 1864 took an average of about 490 whales a year. In Henderson's words, this number "must have far exceeded a sustainable kill" because the gray whale population crashed during that decade. The decade after 1863 saw 338 whales killed per year, in Henderson's estimate "still well in excess of that sustainable by a rapidly declining population." Recently, Henderson's accounting has been carefully redone and largely confirmed by Tim Smith and Randy Reeves; their number for the 1854–1864 average annual whale kill, 630, is higher because of a sharp peak in 1860. As in Henderson's data, the hunt tapers off quickly after that (see Figure 3.1).

But there is a deep mystery surrounding these numbers and the history of the gray whale population. Conventional wisdom pegs the original gray whale population at about 20,000 whales before whaling. Henderson thought the number probably was less: about 15,000. Today gray whale numbers are said to hover around the former value, although recent declines have alarmed whale biologists. The U.S. National Marine Fisheries Service, under the Marine Mammal Protection Act, estimates that at this population size, about 417 gray whales per year can be killed by humans without threatening the continued growth of the population. A hunt much larger than this would be needed to drive the population toward extinction.

A hunt much larger than 417 whales surfaces in the historical record, but only for a short period. Barely sixty gray whales a year—across the entire species range—were reported killed by western ships during the decade from 1845 to 1854. Even including aboriginal hunting, the gray whale population hardly would have been dented during this time. The large hunts of the next decade, from 1854 to 1865, were still only a few hundred or so a year higher than would be considered sustainable today. For only four years, 1858–1861, did the gray whale hunt clearly exceed what is currently guessed to be a sustainable hunt: up to 1,100 gray whales were taken across the species range in those years. Yet one largely agreed-upon fact is that gray whale numbers fell sharply in the nineteenth century: "It was such a period of declining rewards that at its end masters of whaleships had abandoned most of the gray whaling grounds."

This is the current conundrum of the gray whale: They were hunted to near extinction by whaling efforts that in today's conservation algebra should be sustainable. In the entire world, only 7,000–8,000 gray whales were ever known to be killed by hunting. How could this number wipe out a population of 20,000 animals? Where is the error in these calculations? One possibility is that there were not 20,000 gray whales when the hunting bonanza began. So how do we know the number of gray whales in Mexico before the whale hunt?

Theories of Loss

One eyewitness to the original population size of gray whales is widely disbelieved by the people who came after. Whaler Charles Scammon, who entered the Baja whaling scene in 1856, recorded a gray whale population size of about 47,000 in the early 1850s, but scholars have long discounted his estimates as "undoubtedly high." Scammon has a historical reputation of exaggerating: For example, he also suggested that fifty boats were lying in wait for the whales outside the lagoons, but whale historians can confirm only half that number during that time. And he estimated that 10,800 whales were killed in the major hunting years and that 8,000–10,000 gray whales survived the hunt. If true, Scammon's estimate of the size of the gray whale herd makes the discrepancy between the modest, accepted whaling records and the rapid demise of gray whales even worse.

So which estimates are true? Henderson's original estimate of 15,000 animals? Scammon's 47,000? Or more recent estimates based on models of twentieth-century population growth that seem to split the difference and suggest 25,000–30,000? Although there are no human eyewitnesses of the past population of gray whales left, there is one other source of past information, a chemical witness buried in each living cell of every gray whale: its DNA.

A Little Digression into DNA

DNA is a long sequence of chemical bases that holds the instructions for cells to make and control their proteins. A change in the sequence is a mutation, which is usually detrimental to the unlucky, mutated cell. Some mutations change the DNA sequence in a way that does not matter to cell function. These are called neutral mutations, and when they happen, they are passed willy-nilly down the generations from cell to cell. Some individuals have the mutation, others don't, and this variation is what makes the DNA different from individual to individual. Among individuals in a population, DNA variation can be measured by how many DNA bases differ.

A mutation, then, is like a legacy, and an individual may inherit one that first occurred long ago. Today's whales carry mutations that occurred long before whaling began, and in this sense, these mutations have been witness to the kinds of changes in population size that whaling caused.

All else equal, a population that has always been big will have a higher level of DNA variation than a population that has been small. All this means is that the amount of variation in the DNA of a population contains information about the past size of that population. So measuring the amount of DNA variation can provide a window into the history of whales.

What DNA Says about Gray Whales

Surprisingly, DNA variation is much higher than expected if Henderson's estimate of 15,000 gray whales is correct. DNA variation among gray whales throughout the North Pacific is more than six times too high, suggesting a population of about 100,000 animals. This counts whales on both sides of the ocean, so we do not know exactly how many were likely to reside along the coast of North America. But if half were North American whales, then 50,000 gray whales might have been the population size before hunting, many more than the 20,000 typically assumed.

Although this number is higher than Henderson's estimate, DNA and Scammon give very similar figures. Yet DNA hasn't helped us solve the conundrum; if anything, it has made the problem worse, making it difficult to understand the demise of the gray whales. We still do not know where the extra whales went. Hidden or undiscovered whaling efforts, hunting by Native Americans, and some previously unknown decline in whale numbers have all been suggested. Yet the end result is beyond dispute. By the end of the nineteenth century, gray whales were no longer a commercial product, and the whalers went off to find gold in other parts of the ocean.

And Then There Were None

The years of gray whaling in Monterey Bay came and went quickly. At the beginning, with sperm whale numbers plummeting everywhere, gray whales were an alternative source of the oil that fueled the world. Captain Davenport and his crew could look out on the bay and see wealth spouting in every direction. By the end, with the lagoons of Baja empty and the coast of California strewn with gigantic ribs, gray whales were gone.

Gray whales remained at the center of the whaling bull's-eye in Monterey only from 1854 to 1865. Another burst of whaling occurred when better, faster ships arrived in the early twentieth century. But the hunting that occurred across those decades sufficed to strip gray and humpback whales from the tally of common Monterey Bay visitors. La Pérouse listed many of the abundant animals of Monterey Bay: otters, whales, and the like. The decades after his visit saw the entries on his list crossed off one at a time as entrepreneurs targeted them for profit. And after the otters and whales were gone, attention turned to a different kind of marine life: the shellfish.

Chapter 4

Abalone Shells and China Point

MONG THE COVES and tiny coastal farms of central California in the late 1800s, Spanish Mary ran a well-known country store, but her name wasn't Mary and she wasn't Spanish. She was Jone Yow Yee, the first child born to Chinese parents in California. Yee's birth, in 1851, was not heralded in the newspapers, and she wasn't included in a U.S. census until 1900. But she was the first living root of a new culture trying to establish itself in an unfamiliar land. Yee's family traveled to America in a flotilla of seven small boats that set off from Kwangtung (Guangdong) Province, fleeing the commercial hub of southern China that the otter traders called Canton. The boats were small, maybe 30 feet long, and the legend is that only two survived the ocean voyage, washing up onto the California coast. One landed in Monterey, and the families aboard started a fishing and merchant culture that endured and thrived for decades. They established a beachhead for a foreign culture on the American coast, made a fortune as fishermen and smugglers, and in the end lost it all.

Refuge from Guangdong

The families of the Guangdong fleet landed in about 1851 at Point Lobos, a spit of rocky land thrust out into the wild Pacific Ocean, about 10 miles south of Point of Pines and Monterey Bay. In April 1853, a half dozen Chinese set up a small fishing camp on the Monterey shore. They chose the protective shelter of a crescent beach between Point Alones (Abalone Point), where the Monterey Bay Aquarium now stands, and Point Almejas (Mussel Point), now home to the Hopkins Marine Station. This was the beach nearest to the rough surge that rolled into Monterey Bay from the Pacific, and it looked out closely on the anchoring site used by Vizcaíno, Serra, La Pérouse, and all the original western explorers of the bay. By 1857, the site was occupied permanently, and by 1860 four Chinese families lived there. They built small, raw wood shacks teetering above the beach, supported on redwood posts. Their house fronts, facing away from the water, made a ramshackle line that defined a short but neat street. Below and behind the houses, on the beach, elegantly curved wooden boats were hauled up on shore. Wooden racks for drying shellfish covered a knoll on the promontory of Mussel Point. The air smelled of wood smoke, incense, and the sharp iodine of drying algae and shellfish. The village bustled with activity.

The small community had sprung up around a new discovery, an amazing source of natural wealth that everyone along the coast of Monterey Bay had so far ignored. Across the rocks and coves of the Pacific coast, large, flat snails the shape and size of oblong saucers blanketed the shoreline. These abalone lived in unprecedented numbers because Yankee hunters had stripped the coast of sea otters, the abalone's main predator. Released from the otter's voracious appetite, abalone flourished like never before. The Guangdong families recognized it as a lucrative product on the Chinese market, especially in their old home province, where a dense human population had long since depleted the coast of spiral delicacies such as abalone.

In Monterey, the Chinese villagers wrenched the muscular mollusks off their rocks and popped them out of their shells. Dried in the cool sun, the Monterey abalone served as a profitable export to China. The first few Chinese families who had survived the perilous trip from Guangdong called their new home China Point, and they fell to harvesting the abalone with huge energy.

The Celestial Empire of China Point

Robert Louis Stevenson visited the Monterey Peninsula, some say, patterning the coastal scenery of his adventure story *Treasure Island* after its coves and jutting rocky headlands. His tour of China Point in 1879 captured its flavor: "You will come upon a space of open down, a hamlet, a haven among rocks a world of surge and screaming seagulls. . . . And yet the boats that ride in the haven are of a strange outlandish design; and, if you walk into the hamlet you will behold costumes and faces, and hear a tongue, that are unfamiliar to the memory. The joss-stick burns, the opium-pipe is smoked, and the floors are strewn with slips of colored paper . . . and a man guiding his upright pencil from right to left across the sheet writes home the news of Monterey to the Celestial Empire."

In large part, the freedom to create a cultural outpost of the Celestial Empire and the ability of the China Point fishermen to fish most species in most places was due to the sleepy, undeveloped nature of Monterey before the 1870s. Yet the Chinese community followed the same path blazed by the hunters of otter and the boilers of whales: They found an ocean commodity and took it.

The wealth of abalone in Monterey did not remain a secret for long. Soon, boat after boat left San Francisco for Monterey, packed with Chinese men anxious to cash in on the trade. By mid-1853, 500 to 600 Chinese had come from San Francisco to divide the abalone spoils and set up shop along the Monterey coast. The Chinese fishers collected and shucked the large, flat abalone around Point Pinos and then headed down the coast for more.

A Snail's Life

Picture a small dinner plate that grows in a spiral. The inner surface looks as though it is coated with liquid pearls; in the sunlight it is translucent with pastel colors and reflects a rainbow of pinks and purples. The outer surface is the palest chalky pink and is punctuated with a series of pea-sized holes in a line that gently curves. The holes are breathing holes, because this plate is the shell of an abalone, one of the largest snails in the world.

Abalone are built like other snails, with a foot to hold them on the bottom, a shell to protect them on top, and the head, mouth, guts, and everything else in between. Abalone grow on a diet of thick brown algae, eating kelp forest fronds that break off in waves. The abalone sit with half a foot raised off the bottom, waiting for a kelp fragment, like a mouse trap waiting to pounce on marine salad. The thick foot lets them perform these gymnastics, but also resists the pull of predators. And this foot is also the gastronomical prize that predators—human and nonhuman alike—relish.

A frightened abalone clamps down and can withstand so much force that often the shell will break before the animal goes loose. Abalone hunters use stealth to avoid this problem. Humans divers quickly slip a knife or pry-bar under a snail and pop it off the rock. Otters are just as fast with their claws and are so good at hunting abalone that where there are otters, abalone must live a life of stealth and evasion.

The abalone shell is flat enough so that these snails can inhabit inches-wide cracks in the rocks, where they wait for kelp and grow up to the limit of their crevice. Several abalone can jam themselves into a crack, so many that it is hard to see how they move or eat. Where otters hunt, only hidden abalone survive.

The California shore in 1850, after the wholesale hunt for sea otters, was a new ecological experiment. As far as we know, otters had never been so rare before. And out of the crevices came the abalone, to cover the rocks on the shore and live even in the intertidal zone where the surf batters them and their kelp dinner is delivered on the waves.

Even with plenty of food and lots of room, an abalone needs five to ten years to grow to the size of a saucer. And so when the new Chinese residents of Monterey began pulling the abalone from the shallow rocks, they were not replaced quickly. Taking the largest snails, the abalone hunters built tall pillars of shell all along the Monterey coast. At first, the snails were probably replaced by younger ones, or from the hoards of animals that lived too deep for the pry-rods to reach. But the younger ones themselves had to be replaced by new baby snails. And some of the quirks of abalone reproduction conspired to drive the population down even more rapidly.

Abalone produce microscopic larvae: tiny swimming forms with a protective baby shell like a wizard's hat. These larvae can transform into tiny, crawling juvenile snails, but they can do it only once, and they need to choose the right habitat. They do this by testing the rock surfaces, waiting for the taste of the right kind of algae. They recognize the chemical signature of a plant that grows like a pink plaster on the rocks, so-called coralline algae, and within minutes transform from swimming larvae into dot-sized abalone. Corallines are abundant where adults are found because the adults eat everything else. By cuing in on the corallines, the larvae in effect land in places that are good habitat for their species. But removing all the adults, like avid hunters do, results in the growth of algae other than corallines, and larvae can no longer find the right cues to transform.

The biological world is full of situations like this, where natural protocols begin to fail as a species becomes rare. Called Allee effects, after W. C. Allee, the biologist who studied them, these consequences of rarity usually mean that a population struggles to survive when adults are sparse. And when hunters reduce a previously abundant population, Allee effects make the population slower and slower to replenish itself.

After Abalone

Abalone hunters worked the shores of Pacific Grove and moved south to Carmel and the Big Sur Coast. By 1856 they had "cleaned nearly all the [abalone] from the waters around Point Pinos." To extend their reach, they took their homemade sampans out of Monterey Bay into the open Pacific, pulled into the deserted coves along the coast, and set up temporary camp. By 1866, the Monterey County assessor declared the abalone supply exhausted all the way to San Diego.

It was easy for industrious hunters to reduce and then extinguish the abalone populations all along the shore near Monterey and then to move on. With few adults left in the intertidal, the coralline algae dwindled and the supply of juvenile abalone waned. Deeper waters retained abalone still, but as a commercial venture they were out of reach. As the hunters worked their way down the coast, they left empty shores behind, scattered with pearl mountains of broken abalone shell.

In essence, abalone were no different from whales. They were valuable and abundant. Enterprising hunters found a profitable market for them. So many people joined the hunt that the prey population could not recover fast enough to replace itself. The prey dwindled and was eventually gone. This path of profitable unsustainability was followed by the hunters of otters and whales, and now abalone in Monterey. And each time, the hunters turned from their old business and looked toward a new one.

By the 1860s, continued life on China Point demanded new export businesses and new sources of living wealth that could be mined. Dried seaweed was valuable in China too. A new market, pearl buttons, was found for the old abalone shells piled up from years of hunting. Sea urchins were eaten directly out of the shell with a spoon. And there were fish.

By the mid-1860s, abalone collecting had diversified into fishing of all kinds, "from sharks to shiners." Processing was very similar to the way abalone were treated: "Smaller fish were dried on the ground or spread flat on racks while larger fish were split, salted, and hung by the tail from poles." The catch included rockfish, cod, halibut, flounders, yellow tail, mackerel, sardines, and of course shellfish, most of which were exported to China by steamer. By 1867, the population of China Point shipped 300 tons of dried fish a year this way. Dried algae were shipped to San Francisco and to China as well. Fresh fish were shipped to the voracious markets in San Francisco.

Though culturally separate, the Chinese had integrated into the Monterey economy. They began paying an annual $200 rent to the owner of the China Point site, local rancher David Jacks, who had purchased a huge land holding in coastal Monterey and Carmel. The census of 1870, counting forty-seven Chinese at China Point, describes that "the village grows all the while and the business this people is engaged in seems to thrive."

By then the village had several rows of houses and a cluster of bachelor huts set off from the family homes. Wong Wah Foo, born in 1853 in California, called himself Tim Wong after his parents moved to Monterey from Sacramento. He had no formal education, but by the age of 17 he was fluent in Chinese, English, Spanish, and Portuguese and was frequently tapped as a go-between by the Monterey business community when it needed to deal with China Point. Tim Wong prospered as China Point grew, acting as rent collector for the village. As a citizen, he also possessed a rare right among the Chinese community: to vote in U.S. elections. Exercising this right, he developed his belief in economic and civic equality. He campaigned against the restrictions imposed on the Chinese as "an American citizen claiming equal rights vouchsafed by our Constitution." Some wanted to see China Point make the transition to an American town, but cultural tensions persisted, and there was trouble brewing about who had rights to the fish in the bay.

The Church and the Railroad

All across the United States, railroads transformed the economy and the land. California boasted a small clutch of competing railroad companies, and one of them, the Monterey and Salinas Valley Railroad, finished the first rail link between Monterey and the inland farming town of Salinas in 1874. The regional giant Southern Pacific Railroad, led by university founder Leland Stanford and Mark Hopkins, along with Charles Crocker and Collis Huntington, also laid plans for the area: In 1880, they bought some of the large ranches in Monterey and on the peninsula of Point Pinos. These changes created a widespread economic boom but also complicated the lives of Chinese fishermen by bringing in competition from other fishing communities.

Within a decade, the ground had shifted strongly under the community at China Point. Their livelihood was squeezed by development on all sides. Toward Monterey, a large community of fishermen of Italian and Portuguese descent was operating fresh fish markets, aggressively pushing the Chinese fishing boats farther and farther outside the bay. On the other side, the Southern Pacific Railroad began turning its large acreage on the Point Pinos peninsula into a new set of tourist ventures.

Summertime heat in the farming valleys of California drove elegant families—ladies in elaborate Victorian dress, along with their children and husbands—to seek the cool temperatures of the coastal hills. The Methodist Church had built a summer camp on Point Pinos in 1875 and had named the new area Pacific Grove. One goal was to emulate the success of the Chautauqua Lake Sunday School Assembly in southern New York, set up by the Methodist Church in 1874 to provide Sunday School teachers and others a place for out-of-school, vacation learning. In Pacific Grove, the Methodists built their own version of Chautauqua Hall—it still serves as the town's civic and cultural center—and ministered to a growing summer community of families escaping the brutal inland heat. In 1875, a three-week summer retreat launched the venture, with large tents so filled with people that many of the church services had to be held outside on the adjacent rocky point. This jut of land faced China Point and was dubbed Lovers of Jesus Point, although today's visitors stroll the grassy lawn thinking that the shortened name "Lovers Point" has another meaning.

In Pacific Grove, the annual success of the summer retreats gave life to a growing community. Tiny tent lots gave way slowly to Victorian cottages, and by 1884 a small town of 100 residents was taking shape, the nearest neighbor to China Point.

Outside Pacific Grove, the Pacific Improvement Company, the land development arm of the Southern Pacific Railroad, bought the land that held the village at China Point from David Jacks, as well as the land under a second Chinese fishing community on Carmel Bay. The company's overall plan included a resort community and the queen of West Coast luxury hotels, built to take advantage of the growing wealth of nearby San Francisco. As part of this grand plan, the Del Monte Hotel rose along the shore of Monterey Bay, palatially built behind the dunes of Del Monte Beach. Elegant roads pushed out from there to carry horse-drawn carriages to the stunning scenery of the Monterey coast. 17 Mile Drive snaked into the woods and around the coves of Carmel, where the Chinese set up roadside curio stands to provide tourist attractions.

The Pacific Improvement Company succeeded in vaulting the Monterey Peninsula into the modern era. Robert Louis Stevenson's description in 1879, "a sleepy city, wholly Spanish in flavor, that time has left behind," did not apply a decade later, after the railroads, a church town, and tourism had stormed the beaches.

The War for Monterey Bay

One morning in China Point in 1880, the Chinese boats came back empty, their nets slashed and useless. For months, the nets placed by Chinese fishermen had been attacked by boats from Monterey. Now it was some of the Portuguese boats that were slicing through the Chinese livelihood. It was another skirmish in the war for Monterey Bay.

Monterey, a Spanish town becoming an American city, had budded two smaller communities that lived side by side. The smaller one, Pacific Grove, shifted slowly from a summer camp to a permanent town. The bigger community, China Point, overshadowed the population of Pacific Grove by two to three times during the winter, but the Chinese village was on the decline. The 400 residents fished and traded and raised the first U.S.-born citizens of Chinese origin. But they also fought territorial battles with the increasingly aggressive fishermen in Monterey.

Fishing grounds were the prize, and the freedom of the Chinese to fish in the bay was being whittled away by the newcomers. U.S. citizens, something a China-born person could not become, had the courts on their side, making civic injustice an easy pastime. Chinese were not allowed to give evidence in court against whites, so when Portuguese fishermen regularly cut away the nets of the Chinese fleet, spilling its fish back into the bay, the Chinese villagers had no recourse.

Still seeking a way to place their grievances before the courts, the leaders of China Point crafted an unexpected plan. One night in March, the boats again went out from China Point to lay their mended nets. But this time, hiding in the bottom of one of the boats would be a friend, a sympathizer from the European side of town—someone who as a U.S. citizen could give evidence in court.

The plan went off exactly as conceived. The Chinese boats retired after placing their nets and setting their fishing floats. They waited. Soon a local boat appeared in the fog, slipping through the mist to rend apart the mended fishing nets. Leaving them again in tatters, the boat glided back toward the Monterey shore, a peal of harsh laughter drifting over the quiet water. Laughter or not, now the Chinese had their witness—and their case.

But the testimony in court, witnessed and sworn to legally, was deemed to be from a biased source. No matter that the witness was a citizen, the local judge threw out the case. The Chinese community was left without legal recourse, and the unstoppable destruction of the Chinese nets drove the China Point fishing fleet and the whole town toward destitution. And then the village remembered squid.

The Ten-Armed Solution

The war for Monterey Bay pushed the Chinese out to the outer coast, where the rough water and persistent surf scuttled the chance for a good living. Displaced in space, the Chinese community turned back to its roots and discovered a way to coexist with the territoriality of Monterey fishing. The villagers' new strategy was to displace themselves in time, by fishing at night instead of by day. And fishing for something that other fishermen did not want.

Squid jet into Monterey in huge numbers during the spring. Solitary while at sea, these sausage-sized animals join together in huge mobs at mating time. Shallow sand patches 60 to 200 feet deep could be choked with squid. Males dart frantically about, finding and identifying females with the touch of their ten long tentacles. An agile male courts a female briefly and then hangs onto her, all tentacles entwined around, buffeted by the waves and the currents. When correctly positioned, one of his specially elongated tentacles slips a gleaming spermatophore—a small, slim package of stored sperm—into a waiting receptacle under the female's mantle. This gallantry marks the male of some species: He loses one of his two specialized spermatophore-handling tentacles.

Once mated, a female squid parcels out these sperm to fertilize her clutches of yolky eggs. Then she lays them in carrot-shaped bundles, attaching the bundles one by one to the seafloor. Female squid prefer to put their eggs in places that other females also find attractive. So the bundles end up laid in large patches of egg masses, thousands all clumped together on the sand, waving simultaneously in the rippling currents like the petals of a gigantic seafloor flower.

The squid of Monterey Bay remained an untapped resource in the

1880s. This resource had a vast market in China, where dried, salted squid could fetch a good price. So the fishermen of China Point carved out this niche in the fishing community. They used bright torches or pitch fires hanging and swinging from the prows of their boats. The lights lured the squid off the bottom, attracting them close to the surface so that they could be netted. Satisfied to be pulling in good catches again, the Chinese left the daytime fishing to the other families of Monterey and concentrated on squidding at night.

The Smuggling of Salt and the Smell of Success

Pictures from the 1890s of acres of drying squid on China Point proved that the Chinese had found another good fishing tactic. They divided the squid into two types: larger animals that would be split and cleaned and dried on racks for food, and smaller ones to be dried whole on the ground and packed in salt barrels.

Second-class squid had an important but unexpected market in China, and the people of China Point fell into a new role as salt smugglers. Emperors of China had long exerted control of inland areas by controlling the salt trade via a high transport tax. As a clever evasion, China Point's small squid were packed in barrels between layers of salt. The China Point families shipped these to inland areas. The small squid were plucked out of the barrels and thrown on fields for farm fertilizer. The salt was the real prize, and it was extracted and used, free of the emperor's tax.

The success of the squid fishery had local impacts as well. Joined by a common view of stern Methodist propriety, Pacific Grove had grown quickly as a frontier town of simple shops and Victorian houses but came into conflict with the operations at China Point. Squid have always been a high-volume, low-price fishery. Chinese fishermen draped thousands of drying squid over the rocks and racks of the fishing village, especially out on the promontory of China Point itself. Pacific Grove sat largely upwind of this smelly business, but on calm, warm days the smell of drying seafood could become choking—at least to the methodical noses of Pacific Grove. Complaints rose up along with the smell, some mere cover-up for prejudice against the foreign, non-Christian culture of China Point, some legitimate reaction to a carpet of dead mollusks and their pungent odor.

The squid smell began to impinge on a new Pacific Grove industry: tourism. The Pacific Improvement Company had made major investments in Monterey, buying the large land tracts that Pacific Grove sat on and building the elegant Del Monte Hotel in neighboring Monterey. And it had brought the railroad to Pacific Grove, carving a path along the Monterey shoreline and ending it at Lovers of Jesus Point. On bright summer days, the railroad brought flocks of people from San Francisco, and they joined throngs from the overheated inland farm towns. A clean, sheltered beach led to a calm cove tucked behind Lovers of Jesus Point, perfect for swimming. A glass-bottomed boat took people out to see the wonders of the shallow seafloor covered in sea urchins. A bathhouse, a Japanese teahouse, and a restaurant made the day pleasurable. Even on sunny days, the Pacific Ocean cooled the air, providing relief from the oven of the inland summer valleys. From a church summer camp, Pacific Grove had transformed into a small tourist hamlet, and it was eager to maintain its reputation as a place of natural beauty.

Dead squid did not help the tourist trade. The towns of Monterey and Pacific Grove complained about the pungent smell that wafted off of acres of drying squid. "Unless we wish to court diphtheria, typhoid and scarlet fever, this thing must cease," commanded the *Pacific Grove Review*. In May 1902, a sudden rainstorm soaked and ruined the drying catch, and it was discarded into the bay. Contrary waves tossed the moldering mass back up onto shore, choking the Pacific Grove residents with the stench. As the complaints rose around them like angry flies on the rotting squid, the landlords of China Point decreed no more drying racks. The China Point fishermen began transporting their catch inland to dry, trying to balance their fishing business and the neighbors' tourism.

Lanterns

Despite the smell, even Methodist Pacific Grove grew to appreciate some aspects of its sister village at China Point. The Chinese opened China Point every year to the outside community, when their neighbors in Monterey and Pacific Grove were welcomed in. Curious adults peeked into Chinese homes and peered worriedly at the central village shrine. Children ran over the rocks at China Point, stealing the brightly colored paper lanterns that lay everywhere. Author John Steinbeck, born in the farming town of Salinas a dozen miles inland of Monterey, described exactly this scene in letters written about his early years visiting China Point, running through the rocks with his sister, Mary.

Even the squid fishing fleet found some admirers. Prime squid fishing was always done in April and May, when the boats could be seen "dotting the bay off Pacific Grove on moonless spring nights." The quiet sparkling of the boat lanterns just offshore charmed the Pacific Grove residents and reminded them of the lantern boats that the Methodist church camps in New York had launched on quiet lakes there. But the charm of both kinds of lantern boats, enshrined today in Pacific Grove's annual Feast of the Lanterns, was not enough to ensure the village's survival.

The End of Chinatown

April 18, 1906 shook itself awake early, at 5:12 a.m. and again 20 seconds later. Sixty seconds after that, the Great San Francisco Earthquake was over. Masonry lay like giant jumbled bones, trapping people and burying streets. Within twelve hours, "half the heart of the city" had burned to the ground. And the disaster was in full swing.

San Francisco's Chinatown disappeared in the flames, forcing thousands of residents to flee. Some came to China Point in Monterey, briefly swelling the population there. But already the small village was suffering under tremendous strains, and the refugees from the disaster in San Francisco were due for a second one.

The village at China Point collapsed in a tragic triple play. Transporting squid inland, several miles away, to dry them demanded too much effort and too much extra land. A new site had been found in the hills behind Monterey, but the operation needed a coastal site to survive. The move spelled the economic doom of the squid fishery. By 1905, squid fishing was no more, taking with it the major income source for China Point.

At the same time, the landlord at China Point, the Pacific Improvement Company, strongly pushed in court proceedings to evict the village. The village had a 50-year history of occupation but no formal lease with previous owner David Jacks and no written guarantees from the new railway landlord. Court battles pivoted on the long occupancy versus private property rights. But by 1906, the lease was revoked. The courts said that the village must move. Villagers were stubborn and refused, but they could hardly expect to resist for long.

In May 1906, the final disaster stuck, turning the village to ashes. It has never been clear how the fire started, but a wall of flame consumed China Point on May 16. The village had survived fire before; the tinder-dry collection of crowded houses had burnt twice in the past. Both times, residents demolished houses in advance of the flames to create desperate firebreaks, saving part of the village, and the economic vitality of the community allowed it to rebuild itself rapidly. The fire of 1906 was different. Contrary winds fanned the flames. Firebreaks failed. And as the ashes cooled, picked over by well-dressed Pacific Grove residents, mindless of the tragedy they sifted, the life of the village expired.

Although rumors of arson blew about, China Point had accepted refugees from the San Francisco earthquake, and an accidental fire might have erupted in the newly crowded village. But the fate of the burned-down village was not an accident. Pacific Improvement Company's general manager responded immediately: "Do whatever it takes to prevent rebuilding," he cabled his subordinates on the scene in Monterey. They responded by erecting a fence around the property to try to keep previous tenants out. Although some families lived there for a few months more, and an alternative beach to the east was provided, the fishing livelihood for China Point had blown away like the ash from the fire. The town never reconstituted, and the land stood vacant.

An Empty Fishery or an Empty Village

China Point stood empty in 1910, its Chinese inhabitants living in other communities and the ash of its shacks, huts, and shrines still blowing in the wind off the bay. Gone too were the squid boats, no longer to be seen floating on the night surface of the springtime bay.

But on the sand beds 60 feet deep, the squid were not gone. All previous fisheries in Monterey had collapsed when the fished animals were gone. This was true for otters, whales, and abalone. It would be true for seals, salmon, and sardines in the coming years. In none of these cases, since the western cultural annexation of Monterey Bay, had it been possible for a fished species and the human population to coexist for more than a few decades. In the case of China Point, the fishery was stopped not by the collapse of the fished stock but instead by political opposition, economic pressure, and cultural antagonism from the surrounding communities. It resulted in the destruction of a way of life and a village that had lived for two generations.

This was not the last conflict between fishing and tourism in Monterey. The railroad had given birth to tourism and brought new life to fishing. In the late 1800s, Lovers Point tourism and squid drying clashed. But these two fighters, fishing and tourism, had entered the ring and were warily circling each other. There were other rounds before the final bell rang.

Ohlone Native American in Monterey, wearing an otter pelt cape, snail shell *(Olivella)* beads, and a marsh grass *(tule)* skirt, 1791. *(Image credit: Sketch by José Cardero, Monterey Public Library, California History Room Archives)*

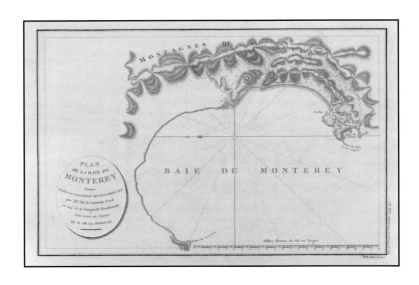

Top: "Plan de la Baie de Monterey," drawn by La Pérouse during his 1786 expedition, oriented with the north bay at left. *(Image credit: La Pérouse, Jean-François de Galaup, David Rumsey Historical Map Collection)*
Bottom: U.S. Navy ships in Monterey's growing harbor, 1842. *(Image credit: Commissioned by Thomas Oliver Larkin, Monterey Public Library, California History Room Archives)*

Top: Shore whaling boat in Monterey Bay, circa 1874. *(Image credit: Plate XXVI, Charles M. Scammon,* The Marine Mammals of the Northwestern Coast of North America, Together with an Account of the American Whale Fishery, *Dover Publications, 1968)* **Bottom:** Harpooned humpback whales waiting to be hauled onshore for flensing and rendering, likely at the Moss Landing whaling station, 1920. *(Photo credit: J.E. Law, Stanford University, Hopkins Marine Station, Miller Library Archives)*

Top: Chinese fishing village between Point Alones (Abalone Point) and China Point (also known as Point Almejas or Mussel Point), 1897. The village burned down in 1906. *(Photo credit: Stanford University, Hopkins Marine Station, Miller Library Archives)* **Bottom:** Chinese fishers dry their squid catches on China Point for shipment, 1897. *(Photo credit: California Historical Society, FN-24184/CHS2010.228)*

Top: Visitors to the Del Monte Hotel in Monterey, dubbed the "Queen of American Watering Places," hold the day's salmon catch, 1900. *(Photo credit: Monterey Public Library, California History Room Archives)* **Bottom:** Glass bottom boat and Japanese tea house at Lovers of Jesus Point, with Hopkins Seaside Laboratory, 1907. *(Photo credit: Pacific Grove Museum of Natural History's Tuttle Collection # 529)*

Julia Platt attacking the beach gate

Top: Below the municipal bathhouse at Lovers Point, a brass band draws a huge crowd to the beach, 1907. *(Photo credit: Pacific Grove Museum of Natural History's Tuttle Collection # 528)*

Right: Dr. Julia Platt uses a hammer and axe to remove a fence blocking public access to Lovers Point, 1930. *(Photo credit: Photo reproduced in Toni Jackson, "Julia Platt—Lady Watchdog,"* What's Doing, *December 1946, Lee Harbick Collection, Monterey Public Library, California History Room Archives)*

Top: Widely believed to be extinct in California, sea otters were rediscovered near Bixby Creek, Big Sur in 1938. *(Photo credit: Wm. L. Morgan Photo, Monterey Public Library, California History Room Archives)* **Bottom:** Aerial view of China Point, Hopkins Marine Station (far bottom), and Cannery Row to the left along water, 1945. *(Photo credit: Fairchild Aerial Surveys, Inc., Map Room, University of California, Santa Cruz)*

Top left: A sardine haul from Monterey Bay, 1948. *(Image credit: George Robinson, courtesy of Dorothy Robinson, Monterey Public Library, California History Room Archives)* **Top right:** Ed Ricketts' 1947 cover story in the *Monterey Peninsula Herald* on the collapse of the sardine fishery. *(Image credit: Monterey Public Library, California History Room Archives)* **Bottom:** Ed Ricketts on the intertidal rocks in the Hopkins Marine Life Refuge in the last year of his life, 1947. *(Image credit: California Views:The Pat Hathaway Collection Image Collection # 81-021-006)*

PART II

The Bottom

Chapter 5

Dr. Mayor Julia Platt

*T*RAVELING SOUTH by train from San Francisco in 1899, on the way to Monterey, the visitor rode around the great curve of Monterey Bay, mile after mile of broad sand beaches edged by steep hillsides covered with dark pine trees. The bay itself was dark, topped by a rolling fog like gray spun sugar that wisped into the coastal forests. Crossing the Salinas River, her glance inland from the lurching passenger car would have revealed a completely different scene: the stark blue sky of late California summer, heat waves shimmering off hills covered with brittle dried grass, the tan landscape relieved only by the narrow, green belt of the winding river.

So it would have appeared to Julia Platt, coming into the tiny train station at Monterey. But she did not stop there. Instead, she kept traveling south a bit, perhaps in a horse-drawn carriage popular among tourists, past a string of Monterey beaches and rocky outcrops that within decades would sprout a dense clot of canneries. The biggest outcrop of them all, China Point, in 1899 still held a bustling Chinese village, home to hundreds of people tending acres of drying squid. A new arrival such as Julia would never before have seen such a sight. But the marine biologist in her would have recognized the squid: *Loligo opalescens*, a close relative of the squid that Julia knew from her research years in Massachusetts.

Turning a bit uphill, Julia confronted the Point of Pines, the same stubby, tree-covered peninsula that Vizcaíno mapped, Portolà missed, and Serra missioned. She left the meaty, iodine smell of squid and China Point behind and moved toward a tall grove of stately trees and a simple town gate.

Pacific Grove

The gate separated the town of Pacific Grove from the outside world. Perhaps 5 miles from the center of Monterey, Pacific Grove was a separate universe. A little-used ridge outside Monterey city limits, it was a place with cathedral trees, a foggy summer, and a new idea.

Inside the gate, serene people in elaborate Victorian clothing floated through a village church camp, their voluminous dresses and elegant manners belying the spare tents pitched among the misty Monterey pines dripping with lichens. The center of activity was a summer educational series sponsored by the Chautauqua Literary and Scientific Circle and the Methodist Church. Launched in 1875, the series attracted famous names such as orator William Jennings Bryan and writer William James. Thousands of people came to Pacific Grove to pitch tents and immerse themselves in an educational fog.

Society life was crowded, spartan, and strict. No alcohol was allowed (a rule not repealed until 1966). Shades on windows (if you had windows) had to stay up until 10 p.m. to prevent indoor (if you had a door) shenanigans. Mark Twain commented that the tent walls themselves were so thin, "you could hear the women changing their minds." Yet it was such a successful enterprise that it attracted the attention of tourism developers from all around San Francisco, who saw it as an alternative to the larger, adobe clutter of Monterey.

A few businesses, including a pharmacy and a hardware store, started here during the early church camp days. They eventually made room for an explosion of building in the 1890s, including a large hotel and an even larger livery stable ("the largest on the coast"), that catered to the boom in tourism. Fairy-tale cottages with fili-greed Victorian woodwork rose from between the massive trees of the grove and displaced the original tents in the center of town. The conflicts between church and commerce defined Pacific Grove, from its founding as a church retreat to its eventual status of junior sister city to Monterey. But there were other conflicts as well: with the commerce of the sea and the religion of tourism.

Julia's Education

Julia Platt was a tall, 42-year-old woman who favored long purple velvet dresses, often highlighted with a blue sunbonnet and yellow gauntlets. Julia probably knew she would stand out in staid Pacific Grove. "She had come, unchaperoned, to study zoology," sputtered the local journal *What's Doing*. Few of the men, and none of the women, held a university degree, as Julia did. And few PaGrovians (as the townspeople call themselves) could stand up to Julia's incisive intelligence.

Julia had entered the University of Vermont in 1879, a year when established society in New England didn't know what to make of women at a university. They allowed her a Bachelor of Arts equiva-lent in 1882 because they didn't give "real" degrees to women then. Afterward, Harvard welcomed her into the Museum of Comparative Zoology—but not as a graduate student. Still, she pursued her studies with vigor and innovation, organizing the description of how chick embryos proceed through the developmental stages from fertilization to hatching. Taking a system that had been ill-defined and chaotic, she devised a simple list of stages that is still used by farmers, students, and scientists today to follow the progress of chick development. As she did throughout her civic career, Julia showed a gift for taking complex issues and boiling them down to their bare essentials.

Summer research at the Marine Biological Labs in Woods Hole, Massachusetts allowed her to delve into marine biology, a career she was determined to pursue. But throughout her training, Julia's ambitions continued to bump against the glass ceiling of academia. A woman could not pursue a zoology Ph.D. in the United States in the late 1800s. However, the University of Freiburg in Baden, Germany offered her a chance to pursue an advanced degree, and she was one of the first women to obtain a zoological Ph.D. there. Julia researched the developing embryos of a small shark named the spiny dogfish, penning the first description of how the primitive vertebrate spinal cord sprouts a brain. She obtained her Ph.D. on May 28, 1898.

These research accomplishments led in the 1990s to the formation of the Julia Platt Club within the Society of Neuroethology to celebrate the anatomical basis of the vertebrate brain. But accolades such as these were a hundred years in the future, and the nineteenth-century world was not very accepting of women scientists. When Julia returned to the United States from her European research, she was one of only about twenty American women with a Ph.D. in zoological sciences. And although Julia's scientific accomplishments were well known in marine biology and she worked with some of the world's most influential zoologists, the academic market for women was narrowly focused on women's colleges. The strictures she faced and the difficulty of finding a job loomed over her.

Perhaps Julia came to Pacific Grove to visit her native California. She had been born in San Francisco, though she was raised in Vermont. Perhaps her visit to Pacific Grove grew out of the unusual fact that Pacific Grove was trying to emulate two institutions native to Julia's New England. The Grove's Chautauqua summer lectures echoed the elegant summer church retreats in New England. More importantly, Pacific Grove was the site of a new Stanford University venture in marine science that was patterned after places Julia knew well: the marine biological laboratories and teaching institutes of Woods Hole, Massachusetts.

The Next Best Thing

Stanford University's first president, eminent fish biologist David Starr Jordan, established the Hopkins Seaside Station in Pacific Grove in 1892 as the first marine biological laboratory on the West Coast. Jordan had been an East Coast intellectual and had frequented summer marine biology institutes established by his mentor, the famous Alexander Agassiz, in Woods Hole. Once Jordan agreed to be the charter president at Stanford, he sought a marine teaching laboratory patterned after the Woods Hole ventures he knew so well. Timothy Hopkins, adopted son of Southern Pacific Railroad co-owner Mark Hopkins, donated funds for the new venture. By 1892, the first buildings of the Hopkins Seaside Laboratory had gone up, built on land adjacent to the railroad and virtually on top of the gathering place for the first outdoor summer church services. The ragged rocks and dark sand beaches at Lovers of Jesus Point were a perfect teaching laboratory for the bounty and diversity of the Pacific Ocean.

Julia moved permanently to Pacific Grove in 1899, "attracted by the little city's world-wide fame in the field of biological research" (see box on next page). She contacted Dr. Harold Heath, who taught summer classes at Hopkins, about a position there. Not receiving a hopeful reply about a job, Julia attended a Pacific Grove lecture given in 1899 by Jordan himself. She followed with a June 2 letter seeking advice on how to secure a faculty position. She wrote, "I doubt if any member of the class just graduated from the High School would find it as difficult to find a place to teach as I, with a Ph.B., a Ph.D. and nine years of graduate work to my credit." After searching for an

Julia Platt Weilded [sic] Mean Six-Shooter, Story Shows

By Julia B. Platt

Grove above High Tide, December 20, 1930 from the PG Museum archives

In the fall of 1899, I came to Pacific Grove, attracted by the little city's world-wide fame in the field of biological research. Soon thereafter I bought five lots extending from Laurel avenue down Seventeenth street built thereon a small cottage and started a garden and a lawn.

There was at that time a wood yard below Laurel avenue between Sixteenth and Forest, enclosed by a high board fence with a wide opening on Sixteenth street through which chickens strolled on scratching tours by day and horses wandered upon browsing expeditions by night. These creatures appeared to feel that long and unprotected use of the lots which I had purchased gave them rights and privileges thereon which were not listed in my deed. In self defense I built a wire fence six feet high about the property. The chickens simply flew to the top thereof and crowed insult, adding to injury. Thereupon I went to Dr. Trimmer, who was then Mayoor [sic] Pacific Grove, told him my grievances and asked permission to shoot those chickens. "Why certainly, certainly," he replied, looking somewhat amused, probably confident that I would do nothing of the kind.

However, I bought a second-hand pistol, opened the gate of my wire fence and dared the chickens to come in. Two of them accepted the challenge. Bang, bang, and two dead chickens were thrown over the fence.

The whole neighborhood went up in the air. Messages flew hither and yon. "Lives of the passing public have been endangered." "People within their thin-walled cottages were not safe." A listener may have pictured me shooting wildly at the sun and stars and accidentally killing the chickens standing at my feet. Marshall E. B. Rich appeared and solemnly told me that my permission to shoot was withdrawn.

For a day or two I studied trapping devices. Then Constable Lee called to ask if I would circulate a petition asking the city trustees to pass an ordinance prohibiting chickens at large. He said he had received many complaints but could not arrest a chicken and was otherwise powerless to act in default of an ordinance governing the case.

A goodly number of signatures were quickly obtained and I presented the petition at the next board meeting. Now it so happened that some of the city trustees—including the chairman of the ordinance committee—kept chickens that ran at large. But they were all nice chickens that never did any harm which apparently warranted the conclusion that chickens as a whole were grievously maligned. My petition was courteously received and placed on file.

I attended the next board meeting, and the next, awaiting action on that petition. On those days it was unusual for a woman to attend board meetings. As I appeared time after time there was an exchange of smiles and whispered confabs with glances in my direction.

Trustee B. A. Eardley went to Alaska, returned from Alaska, and finding me still in attendance remarked, "Haven't they considered your petition yet, Miss Platt? I move that it be made an order of business at the next meeting of the board." Motion carried and on the 6th day of October 1902, an ordinance was passed prohibiting the running at large of chickens and other domestic fowl in the City of Pacific Grove.

academic position for more than a year, Julia perhaps admitted her only major defeat. And she followed her own advice, given in the final paragraph of her 1899 letter to Jordan: "Without work, life isn't worth living. If I cannot obtain the work I wish, then I must take up with the next best."

Chicken Wars and Civic Activism

Next best? Civic leader, innovative thinker, and rabble rouser in tiny, conservative Pacific Grove. As the town grew and transformed from a summer tent camp to a permanent community, Julia quickly established herself as one of the more flamboyant characters around. As an unmarried scientist who discussed the details of reproduction alongside unchaperoned male colleagues, Julia shook the narrow world of Pacific Grove. The local populace was aghast because Julia was working "among a group of men, many of whom being scientists and therefore presumably unhampered by the fear of God, were doubtless of unhampered morals."

Julia's career was hardly the only controversy. Pictures from that time, taken from a hot air balloon floating above the town, depict a checkerboard of tiny house lots and orderly streets. But photos also show a booming tourist enterprise cradling a bustling bathhouse on the beach, with glass-bottom boats and an oceanfront full of visitors being delivered by a small rail line. Here was a town just entering maturity, but there were many conflicts between the new business of tourism and the staid life of a church camp. Bathing beaches were fairly scandalous, and Pacific Grove quickly demanded a strict beach dress code. People needed to be covered up, with double-crotch swimming costumes "with skirts of ample size to cover the buttocks." And there could be no "corrupting" dance styles such as the "tango, turkey-trot, bunny-hug or shimmie."

In this environment, Julia soon learned how to shake things up. Her love of science's implacable logic and rejection of religious conformity combined to create a natural gift for igniting small-town controversy. Was she actually, perhaps like the other scientists down at Lovers Point, an atheist? Rumors dogged Julia her whole life, causing her to exasperatedly take out an ad in the town newspaper announcing, "I am not an atheist."

Gardening was an acceptable woman's pursuit in a conservative town, and Julia was often seen in "mannish" hat and long skirts, carrying a market basket or pushing a wheelbarrow around the public gardens. She started the Pacific Grove Women's Civic Improvement Club in 1903. But gardening quietly and keeping her opinions under a wide-brimmed hat did not seem to suit Julia's temperament, especially because she suffered a persistent problem with her neighbor's chickens. Livestock of all sorts lived a frontier existence in Pacific Grove, wandering through town unmolested and, from Julia's Vermontish perspective, poorly disciplined. She fumed at the damage done to her precious home garden by chickens from next door, but she found that her penchant for detailed debate and convincing rhetoric, amply displayed at city council meetings, didn't work on these chickens or their owners.

Then out came a handgun, and the chicken problem ascended to a new level. Julia shot every bird that came into her yard. When the smoke cleared, she found that her problem was town uproar rather than chicken wanderings. "Lives of the passing public have been endangered," cried Julia's neighbors. "People within their thin-walled cottages were not safe." The town constable was called in. Julia was thrown on the defensive. Here her academic skills came to the rescue, and in the ensuing confrontation with the town police and the city council, Julia insisted that a modern town simply couldn't let animals run wild. Other residents pointed out that there was no town ordinance that restricted animals from wandering about. Julia quickly seized upon the obvious solution and achieved her first triumph of civic activism in 1902 by writing a city zoning ordinance that limited domestic fowl to particular areas.

Citizen Platt

Julia's first lesson in civic affairs started with a gun and some chickens and ended with a city ordinance. In this exercise she found that there was a huge difference between getting attention and getting her way. In Pacific Grove, the first came very easy for Julia. The second took some experience. From then on, around town Julia became an agent of change. "You could call her an early-day conservationist," mused Helen Spangenberg in a 1968 *Monterey Herald* memoir of Pacific Grove. Julia purchased a new home just at the base of Lovers Point, with a living room adorned by "big windows, commanding a broad expanse of bay." She planted the gardens that now occupy Lovers Point and drew up plans for seaside plantings and walkways along the shore from China Point to Lovers Point (the drawings are housed at the Pacific Grove Museum of Natural History). Her association with the ocean had shifted from that of avid researcher to avid protector, and when commerce around Monterey Bay swung away from tourism and toward the fishing industry, Julia's unease grew.

But she had also found the garden of city government to be fertile territory, and from the time of the chicken incident forward, Julia's level of involvement in the machinations of city management accelerated. She attended city council meetings and spoke with fervor and sharp clarity about anything she regarded as needing improvement. According to a city council member, "There was a packed house every time the council met in those days, everyone would come to hear what Julia Platt would have to say. She never hesitated to disagree and always spoke excitedly what was in her mind, but it certainly made people take an interest."

Finding the management of the city too capricious, Julia argued long and hard for a complete revision in the way the city operated. She drafted a new town charter, establishing for the first time a professional city manager, taking city administration out of the hands of the city council. The charter serves as the city's legal backbone today, and although it has been revised extensively, it still contains phrases and stipulations that sound as if they had come directly out of the mouth of Julia Platt. And it includes some of the tools of city government that Julia used later to help to bring the sea back to life. In particular, Article 5 of the Pacific Grove Charter reads, "The rights of the City in and to its waterfront, *lands under water*, and such public wharves, docks and landings as may be hereafter thereon constructed are hereby declared inalienable." This declaration puts the protection of the sea firmly in the hands of the town of Pacific Grove, a responsibility that Julia pursued single-mindedly throughout the last decade of her life.

An Axe to Grind

Julia's most famous battle erupted in the first weeks of 1931 around the principle that public access to the sea could not be blocked by private landowners. The Bath House at Lovers Point had just been acquired by Mrs. J. E. McDougall. On January 16, 1931, in defiance of the property deed, custom, and decades of public use, she erected a gate that blocked access to the beach. Immediately Julia decried the action: The way to the sea was supposed to be open to everyone. Julia tried to cross the barrier but was "molested" by Mr. McDougall. She pointedly reminded Mrs. McDougall that in California, beaches are public land from the high tide mark down to the sea, going so far as to unearth and brandish the original property deed, which guaranteed public right of way to the beach. McDougall was nonplussed, countering that the level of moral values had deteriorated so severely in Pacific Grove that she considered the original deed, crafted back in the church retreat days when windows were always undraped, null and void. No amount of the famous Platt argument, no elaborate public rhetoric, would move Mrs. McDougall. The fence would stay. The beach was closed.

Julia would not have it so. On January 17, 1931, while the town argument still raged, Julia decided that a hammer and crowbar would have to do what her arguments could not. She destroyed the gate padlock and opened the beach to everyone. But Mrs. McDougall simply replaced it. Once more, Julia smashed open the lock. Once more, Mrs. McDougall put it back. Undeterred, Julia decided to tear down the fence once and for all. Dressed in her trademark hat and wearing a workman-like vest, she brought a ladder and a hammer and an axe and demolished the hated barrier between her and the sea. "Twice in succession she filed off padlocks that barred the entrance and then, when the gate was nailed shut, resorted to the axe." Did she sneak in during the dark of night and act anonymously? No, Julia acted in full light of the town's citizenry. Photographers were even on hand to chronicle Julia atop her ladder dismantling the fence.

And to make sure everyone knew that it was not just Mrs. McDougall who bore blame, Julia had prepared a printed placard that she tacked to the gate's remains (Figure 5.1). "Opened by Julia B. Platt. This entrance to the beach must be left open at all hours when the

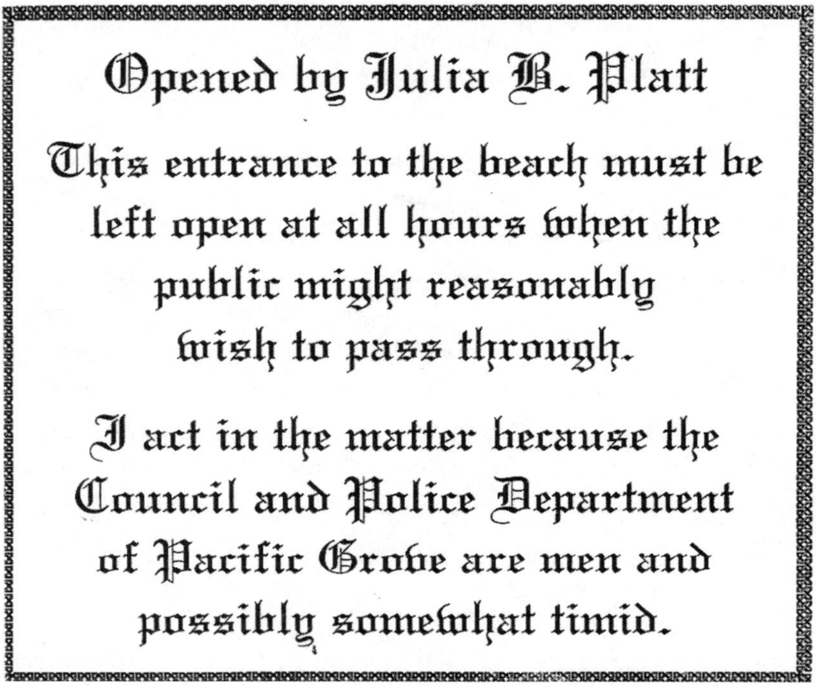

> # Opened by Julia B. Platt
>
> ## This entrance to the beach must be left open at all hours when the public might reasonably wish to pass through.
>
> ## I act in the matter because the Council and Police Department of Pacific Grove are men and possibly somewhat timid.

Figure 5.1. The notice board Julia left behind. (From the Pacific Grove Natural History Museum archives.)

public might reasonably wish to pass through. I act in the matter because the Council and Police Department of Pacific Grove are men and possibly somewhat timid."

The fence stayed down.

Mayor Platt

Town meetings were chaotic during this time. Julia's issues and methods dominated, but the city council continued to think that it, not Julia, was elected to run the place. An exasperated council told her, "If you want to run everything, why don't you become Mayor?" At first, Julia preferred to find someone else to be mayor, but no one stepped up. So she announced her candidacy on March 6, 1931, stating that "neither age nor sex can be considered important in these days of political, social and economic equality." Her election campaign, as biting as her civic opinions, proclaimed, "It will take a good man to beat me." None did, and she was elected by a 2:1 margin on April 11, 1931.

Chapter 6

The Power of One:
Julia Fights the Canneries

ABOUT THE TIME Julia Platt was battling chickens in
Pacific Grove, the town began to undergo a major shift.
The village at China Point went up in flames in 1906,
turning to ash a culture that had thrived for decades. The Chinese
community dispersed and never resettled in the area. But the land did
not sit idle for long. Owned by the Pacific Improvement Company,
it passed into control of railroad magnate Leland Stanford, who in
1912 gifted it to the Hopkins Marine Station. Stanford jumped at the
opportunity to establish new quarters and move from the increasingly
crowded Lovers Point. The choice was fateful. Even as the embers
cooled, the land next door to this new scientific facility was being

eyed for a purpose that would do more damage to the ocean—and bring more wealth to the city—than any previous enterprise.

Next door in Monterey, Norwegian canning expert Knut Hovden had swept into town. The spring salmon run was so huge that the fish could never be used fast enough; as many as 7,000 fish might be caught in one day. Canning was the solution, and several investors were vying to develop the secrets of a successful operation. But the salmon run is short in Monterey Bay, and if canneries are idle for most of the years they make poor businesses. Luckily, other fish were hugely abundant, especially the large sardines that filled the bay each summer.

Unlimited Appetites

Sardines have odd appetites. Most coldwater fish are ferocious carnivores, lunging at other fish or invertebrates with sharp teeth and powerful jaws. Sardines eat differently, steadily driving through the water with their mouths open like a living net. Seawater pours in, bringing with it the nearly microscopic plants and animals that make up the green soup of Monterey Bay. This tiny but abundant food supply is filtered by the sardines' gills and fuels their unending swimming and their fast growth. When the ocean is green, there is always food for sardines.

Beginning as tiny larvae off the coast of southern California, the Pacific sardine swims north against the current, filtering mile by mile. As the summer progresses the sardines get larger and larger, and they begin to spawn as they move north. The sardine populations progress up the coast, arriving at Monterey in mid- to late summer. The supercharged productivity of Monterey brings unbelievable numbers toward shore. In their peak years, there were more Pacific sardines off the West Coast than there were people on Earth.

H. R. Robbins was determined to take advantage of this bounty. He started the first cannery in 1901 between Point Alones (site of the future Hovden cannery and the Monterey Bay Aquarium) and the commercial wharf in Monterey. Pictures from 1902 show fishermen dipping sardines out of the water with hand nets on the Monterey beaches in order to fill the capacity of Robbins's tiny cannery. Frank Booth started the second cannery in 1903, and he bought the Robbins operation soon after. He hired Knut Hovden, who quickly became the key innovator of the industry, inventing solutions to problems as varied as how to move the sardines between the boats and the processors and how to solder the lids onto the cans. At first, the buyers resisted; the world market remained dominated by European sardines. But slowly, canned sardines from Europe gave way to Monterey sardines, and by 1917, five fish plants were steaming away in Monterey.

The canneries were a new business venture, and as their profits increased, they expanded quickly. As they grew, their smell rose up to greet the towns around them. "The juicy rich smell causes everyone to hold his or her nose," reported the *Monterey Herald*. The smell struck at the very heart of the primary engine of the Monterey and Pacific Grove economy: the seaside tourism of the early 1900s. When the canneries came, tourism contracted a long, smelly illness from which it could not recover.

Beyond Food

Canned fish always had a global market. That market grew to supply World War I army rations, giving the new businesses in Monterey a leg up. But once World War I ended, growth subsided. Given the high labor costs associated with canning, the bottom line for Monterey's canning business was a stable but limited income. Left with only a small market for canned fish, perhaps Monterey's canneries would have had a far less dramatic history. But a different customer waited in the wings: the practically unlimited market in California for agricultural supplies.

As early as 1917, Monterey cannery pioneer Hovden had adopted the odiferous but clever Chinese practice of processing the byproducts (offal) of the fishery. The technique, called reduction, processed fish heads, tails, guts, and skin into valuable fishmeal that became fertilizer and livestock feed. A second product, fish oil, turned up in commercial products such as soap, paint, shortening, and salad oil.

Fish reduction faced an implacable obstacle, however. In the early 1900s, food fit for humans was supposed to be used by humans. In the thinking of the time, using perfectly good fish for fertilizer was an immoral waste of food, and a 1919 California state law explicitly demanded that sardines should be destined only for cans. This law limited canners to reducing only fish or fish parts that were otherwise considered waste.

Such restriction did not sit well with the cannery owners for one overarching reason: Reduction was much more profitable than canning. Cannery worker Joe Bragdon, who repaired reduction ovens, explains why: "Canning needed a lot of labor. Cutters, and cleaners and canners, and such. But just a few of us could operate the reduction ovens for the whole cannery, and produce just as much as a whole building of cannery workers."

Dancing to the Whistle

Joe Bragdon's day started with waiting. Like everyone else, he waited for the sardine boats to come back into the bay. And when they did, dawn or dusk, he listened for the whistle. Like many industrial towns, Monterey had a steam whistle. But in Monterey, the whistle knew many tunes, a code for each cannery. And when a boat that worked for Joe's cannery returned full of fish, the town whistle blasted out his code, and he knew it was time for him to head to work.

The cutters went first, the assembly lines of women in hairnets and long aprons who cut the fish into can-sized pieces. Then 30 minutes later, the canners arrived to slap fish into tin coffins. They were followed in another half hour by the cookers, who turned the fish leftovers and guts to fishmeal and fish oil. Joe would be there already, tending the vast, hot drying machines until the fish that had been a sardine school in the afternoon were turned into farm fertilizer that night.

For a decade, cannery workers throughout Monterey and Pacific Grove tuned their lives to the whistle. They worked the lines and filled the cans and stoked the furnaces whenever there were fish to be processed. And for that decade, the whistle was a constant companion as the boats chugged into port, laden with sardines and employment for everybody.

Too Much of a Good Thing?

The booming sardine business was not without its price, and in 1919 the state of California established its first Department of Commercial Fisheries to evaluate the fishery's effects on sardine abundance. Housed in the newly completed buildings of the Hopkins Marine Station, scientists at the new agency worried about the future: "Fisheries are subject to depletion because of too intense exploitation, as has been proved in Europe and in our own country." But they had little knowledge on which to act: "There is almost no adequate knowledge concerning the methods of conservation, or prevention of depletion. We . . . must be sure that we begin an era of scientific investigation of our fisheries in time to adequately guide and control the exploitation." This may have been the first public warning about the potential demise of the sardine fishery. What ensued was a bitter battle, pitting fledgling fishery scientists against the fishing and canning interests in the state.

The scientists had logic on their side, but the fishing industry seemed to have the numbers. From 1920 to the end of the decade, sardines arrived in greater tonnage every year, growing more than tenfold in landings. The sardines were also close at hand: A 1921 map of sardine catch areas shows most of them within a few miles of the Monterey harbor (Figure 6.1).

Bolstered by teeming success, the fishery continued. Eventually cracks began to show in the exuberant fish landings, but they

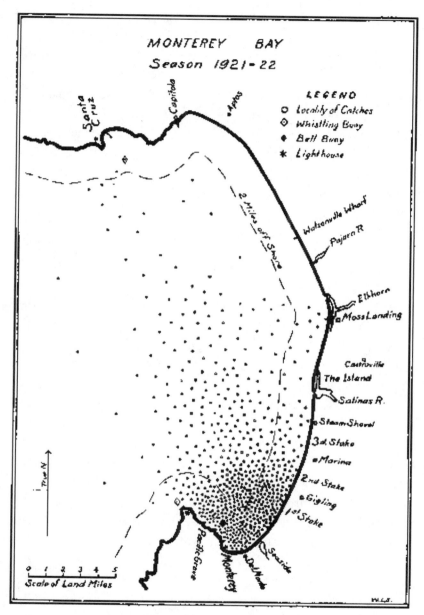

Figure 6.1. Map showing where sardines were caught in the 1921–1922 fishing season. Most were from very close to home; the boats did not have to go far to fill their holds. (Reproduced from Scofield 1929.)

were cracks that only careful science could detect. Sardine scientist N. B. Scofield rejected the use of landing data alone as a sign of fishery health. The important thing, he thought, was how much effort it took to catch those fish. Late in the 1920s, he was convinced the fishery was in trouble, writing, "Although the amount of sardines caught has been increasing each season, the catch has not increased in proportion to the fishing effort expended." But the fishermen and canners thought the scientists were crying wolf, and the industry went about its business of unbridled growth. And they were about to hit the jackpot.

Growing Reduction

The profits from fish reduction made the canneries steady money makers, but more profit could be had if the state legislature would relent about limits on how many sardines could be processed into oil and fertilizers. And relent they did: A series of statutes gradually raised the allowable amount of reduction. By 1929, the Murphy–Youngman bill allowed 32.5 percent of the sardine catch to be shunted into the profitable fish reduction business.

But then a new player dramatically upped the stakes. Several clever canners realized that state regulations were impotent just offshore. Three miles from the coast, state authority gave way to federal authority, where limits placed on sardine reduction by the state meant nothing. In 1930, a reconverted barge, the *Lake Miraflores*, became the first of the "floaters" to operate offshore, and in its first season it converted nearly 11,000 tons of sardines, about half the reduction of the entire Monterey canning industry. Within four years, this unfettered business ballooned more than tenfold, sending the shore-based cannery owners howling to the state regulators for relief. Here started a political chess game that resulted in a complete cannery victory, with the lucrative offshore floater industry dead in the water by 1938 and the canneries in possession of the offshore business. The victory depended on the tragedy of scrupulously fair regulation and the unexpected gamesmanship of the canners.

As he watched the first of the floater boats suck off 11,000 tons of sardines that his own canneries could have had, you'd think Monterey Canning Company founder George Harper would have been spitting mad. But in 1931 he talked the California legislature *out* of revoking the licenses of the fishermen who made deliveries to the offshore factories. "You can't keep those people from reducing sardines on the open seas," he declared. But then the real reason behind his position slipped out when he added, "Why attempt to keep our own people from making money in the same way?"

The rest of the Monterey canners fell into line, and instead of agitating to shut the floaters down, they agitated to increase their own share of the reduction business. The next year, the Fish and Game Commission granted every cannery a 5,000-ton reduction permit and then quickly doled out permission for another 2,500 tons to "give more employment to cannery workers." By the 1934 season each plant could reduce 12,000 tons. Now, it was the floaters who demanded, and got, a liberal quota, just to ensure they got their fair share. And then again the shore-based canners complained and were accorded the same.

This two-step regulation dance unshackled the fishery. As a result, the fishing fleet ballooned, and the business of canning became the sideline of an increasingly lucrative reduction industry. And the fishery scientists ramped up dire predictions of the consequences: "The great expansion of the fishery has been accompanied by unmistakable signs of depletion in the sardine population," insisted N. B. Scofield in 1938. No one paid attention to these warnings, not even Scofield's own Fish and Game Department.

By 1938, shore-based canneries had such a high quota allocated to them that there was no effective limit to the sardines they could process as meal or oil. The Fish and Game Commission had scrupulously leveled the playing field, allowing equal access of shore and offshore plants to sardine reduction. But they did not do this by establishing equal limits; they did it by establishing equal unlimits. The shore-based canners had successfully used the offshore reduction ships as a goad to increase their own access to fish, and they reaped handsome rewards as a result. By 1938, with their own nearly unfettered access to sardines enshrined in state regulations, the shore-based canners finally turned on the offshore canners and destroyed them. On November 8, 1938, after intense legal pressure from the canners, the Fish and Game Commission voted to prohibit all fish deliveries to floaters by California fishermen. Choked off from their supply, the idled floaters were junked in San Francisco Bay by the end of the year, leaving Monterey canneries in complete control of the sardine catch.

Dating and Sardines

On the front porch of a little house in Pacific Grove, Joe Bragdon fretted almost daily. The house seemed like most of the others, a small and unassuming wooden structure packed in tightly by its neighbors. But as far as Joe was concerned, it had one key difference: Doris lived inside.

It was 1935, and Joe was there as he was on many days, hoping to see Doris and ask for a date. Doris worked at the cannery day care center. But Joe worked at the canneries themselves, maintaining the huge ovens that fueled the fish meal dryers, rebuilding them when they became too enthusiastic and burned down the buildings. Arriving at Doris's house from work, Joe never was allowed inside. It wasn't any social stigma about his job; everybody worked the canneries.

No, Joe's real problem was that his job stank. Actually stank. It made him stink too, and Doris wouldn't let him in the house because of it. This left Joe on the front porch, trying to be convincing enough from this distance to get a date for later in the day. And when he did, he would rush home and scrub off the smell.

Joe solved his romantic dilemma through porch-based social skills, and as of 2010 he and Doris had been married more than 60 years. But everybody in town was affected by the smell of the cannery's success, and some didn't do as well.

The Smell of Money

The canneries produced more than canned fish, fish meal, and fish oil. They also produced a stink in the air and a gush of fish parts that was dumped back into the water. When the Hopkins Marine Station first opened its new science labs on China Point in 1917, the next-door canneries dumped all their waste and guts (officially known as offal) in the nearby waters, and China Point floated with "globs of fat and oil," making it extremely difficult to work among the rocks. A 1925 report to the Pacific Improvement Company, which owned the railroad in Monterey, lambasted the "foul condition of the water caused by the canneries discharge of sewage and waste." Cannery operators exacerbated the problem when they cleaned their machines, flushing the offal-laden cleaning water into the bay.

No one has ever accused fish processing of being a tidy, clean business, and the millions of pounds processed daily took a serious toll on the local environment. Few statistics of the pollution impact of the Monterey canneries exist, but Hopkins Marine Station professor Dr. Rolf Bolin complained that "the fumes from the scum floating on the waters of the inlets of the bay were so bad that they turned lead-based paints black." Occasionally other regulations arose that actually made things worse: During the peak of the fishery a minimum size limit was put into place. Instead of saving the lives of smaller fish, it led to huge amounts of small, dead fish dumped into local waters.

In modern fish meal factories, about 10 percent of the catch is lost in this wastewater, and if this were true in Monterey, then waste from processing a million pounds of fish would have dumped 100,000 pounds of fish organics back into the bay every day, more than the sewage produced by the whole city.

The polluting canneries damaged not only Monterey's ecology but also its other businesses. Although canning employed many people, it also reduced Monterey to a one-industry town. Tourism was particularly hard hit. Struggling to stay alive, the hotels in Pacific Grove and Monterey fought vainly against the increasing might of the canneries. In 1934, Del Monte Properties, owner of the landmark Del Monte Hotel, filed an injunction against all Monterey canneries for their odors and for the "large quantities of decayed and putrefied fish" in and around the plants.

The Monterey City Council passed statute after statute to rein in the smell, requiring licensing and regulation. But George Harper, head of the Monterey Canning Company, brazenly fought back. "Nobody has died of fish odors yet," he cried, "it's one of the healthiest things we have." Harper counted on support from his workers, who were unlikely to complain about a smell that represented their livelihood, and they did not let him down.

"You know what you smell? You smell money!" Women working in the canneries widely broadcast this attitude, and many could be found who echoed this feeling. The Great Depression created grateful employees, and the workers who labored on the canning lines valued their paychecks over what they regarded as a merely inconvenient smell.

Ghosts in the Water

A teenage girl looked out at the blissful strand that linked the Hopkins Marine Station to the industrial ranks of the Monterey canneries. A curving white beach with a gentle slope and fine powdery sand lay between the placid academic center and the laboring engines of the busy canneries. Fisher Beach caught the few waves that snuck this far into Monterey Bay from the Pacific Ocean, and each time the water rushed out, the sand beneath shone like white gold. On this bright day, sunshine warming the air, the shore caught the light just like in the tropics, and the shallow water was the brilliant turquoise of a coral sea.

Merilyn Derby gazed in wonder and excitement. Born and raised in Hawaii, Merilyn had spent childhood days in the surf of Haleiwa on Oahu's north shore. She was a Stanford University undergraduate, newly arrived at the Hopkins Marine Station to learn the ins and outs of marine research. Knowing well the turquoise glow of the reefs of Hawaii and faced with her first view of Fisher Beach, Merilyn acted the way every Hawaii girl would. She threw on a swimsuit and threw herself into the water.

Cold. Very cold was that water. But Merilyn expected this. What she didn't expect came next as she opened her eyes.

Fish heads. With gray eyes bulging in death. And tails. Guts. The canneries' discards floated in every direction, long threads of fish intestines wriggling through the water like worms. Even the sea birds couldn't eat everything dumped by the canneries, and the remains were starting to decay. Merilyn bolted from the water, afraid to open her mouth to scream, hoping none of the gobs had caught in her long hair. She raced to the beach, leaving the liquid cemetery behind.

She never swam again at Fisher Beach. Like everyone else, she stayed on shore.

Julia Platt Fights Back

The horrible reek that fumed from the cannery smokestacks blanketed the coastline in a sardine fog. The odor inspired a children's doggerel known to generations of Monterey peninsula residents: "Carmel-By-the-Sea, Pacific Grove by God, and Monterey by the smell." It wasn't just a silly children's song: The odors were killing tourism in Monterey and Pacific Grove.

Civic leaders in Monterey and Pacific Grove welcomed the canning business but not the pollution or the smell. Faced with the fouling of the air and water, Julia Platt saw yet another danger to the coastline and to her town. It may have been especially poignant for the marine biologist in Julia to confront the erosion of the ocean environment right in front of her house. And this may explain the peculiar language in the original Pacific Grove town charter—probably inserted by Julia—that claims "the lands underwater" of Pacific Grove for the town.

In her concern about the health of the ocean, Julia was a pioneer.

But she had powerful company when it came to protecting the health of tourism. Monterey hotel owner and Pacific Improvement Company head Samuel Morse, trying to keep the palatial Del Monte Hotel open for business, watched in frustration as the industrial stench gradually drove away his clientele. The 1929 *Monterey Peninsula Herald* tells of exasperated tourists faced with such "beautiful surroundings made uninhabitable by such a terrible stench." Using desperate machinations, Morse cut a deal with the canneries in October 1926 to temporarily curtail their odiferous production when Monterey hosted the California State Real Estate Convention. The deal worked to hide the town's fishy cloud from real estate noses, but it was only a stopgap, and the sardine smell quickly returned. Julia Platt joined forces with Morse to lodge complaints to the Fish and Game Commission over the cannery stench. Morse followed with a series of lawsuits and injunctions.

But year by year, tourism failed and fishing prevailed. Although the hotels won their early lawsuits and early city councils sided with the populace of Monterey and Pacific Grove, the sheer economic power of the canneries turned the tide in their favor. The magnificent Del Monte Hotel closed for good, selling out to the Navy, and it now stands as the center of the Naval Post Graduate School. By 1939, few battles were being fought because the canneries were too powerful. As historian Connie Chiang sums up, "Though the conflict diminished, the smells . . . probably worsened."

Morse bemoaned his business losses. Julia bemoaned the destruction of Pacific Grove's natural beauty. But Julia, perhaps frustrated with what would be a losing legal attack, also found other, more direct action to take.

Julia's Solution

Julia's house at 557 Ocean View Boulevard commanded a view of the battle zone from China Point to Lovers Point, and from this vantage, she carefully crafted a scheme that would consume all her political capital and demand all her argumentative skill. Julia settled her focus on the five-mile swatch of coastline surrounding Pacific Grove. Extending from the wild Pacific coast and stretching into the quieter waters of Monterey Bay, the string of beach-lined coves and rocky headlands cradled the best of the Pacific's shorelife. Julia anchored her plans at the China Point headlands and intertidal beaches of the Hopkins Marine Station. Next door to the biggest of all the canneries, the shoreline at Hopkins was awash in fish entrails, so many that an army of pallid sea anemones had grown up along the rocks to partake of this oily feast. This part of the shoreline cried most loudly for help, and Julia planned to protect it.

The basic problem had a clear solution: Cannery operations had to be cleaned up. But Julia knew that no single person, not even a mayor, could stop the cannery stench or reclaim the coastal waters that had become a soup of fish guts. She faced the simple fact that ocean problems are usually bigger than something a single person can solve. The vast ocean could usually absorb a lot of hurt, but when it complained, the true solution usually transcended the help a single person could provide.

But were there ways to help besides completely solving the pollution problem? Julia never said when the solution occurred to her or how long she sat at her window looking out over the bay, pondering the problem. Julia's solution recognized that pollution was not the only threat that Pacific Grove's ocean life faced. Fishing pressure was another one, and destructive collecting of tide pool life, and the development of the shoreline. And if Julia could not solve the pollution problem on her own, perhaps she could help by reducing the other problems. Perhaps healthy shores in Pacific Grove could reseed other shorelines if the problems in Monterey were ever fully solved. These two goals—reducing local threats and banking areas of healthy marine life for the future—became Julia's core plan. Of course, this plan presented a formidable challenge too. Just the type of challenge a bold mayor could face.

Stealing the Shore from Sacramento

Julia was fully aware that the Pacific Grove coast, just like all of California's shores, was owned by the state rather than the city. Although protecting the shoreline was technically outside her jurisdiction, she believed that through force of will and some political capital, she could defend the shoreline from stresses besides industrial pollution.

Julia sought powerful help in her quest to save the shore. Stanford University's Hopkins Marine Station had transformed from a simple summer classroom into a world-class research facility, and it sat as the uncomfortable neighbor of all the canneries in Monterey (Figure 6.2). The Hopkins Marine Station housed many of the fishery biologists who were the most vocal critics of the fishing and canning industries, and Julia reasoned that this respected group of scientists could be powerful allies. Support for ocean protection was not long in coming from the researchers at the Marine Station.

Unfortunately, still standing between Julia and her vision of shoreline protection, like the steep rock of a walled fortress, was the state law declaring that underwater lands belonged to the state, not the local towns. But Julia had already test flown a solution in the 1926 town charter. She merely needed to alter state law to parallel her local ordinance and give the right of shoreline management to the town. So Julia drafted a new state law titled "An Act granting to the city of Pacific Grove the title to the waterfront of said city, together with certain submerged lands in the Bay of Monterey contiguous thereto."

From her position as mayor, Julia easily persuaded the Pacific Grove City Council to petition the state legislature for passage of this new law. Then Julia turned her persuasion toward the state capital in Sacramento, convincing the state legislature to pass the act. Governor James Rolf signed the law into effect on June 19, 1931, for the first (and last) time granting a city the right to manage its own coastline. On April 21, 1932 a local version of the act was passed by a unanimous city council vote and became City Ordinance No. 284.

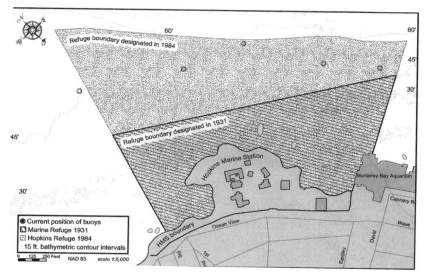

Figure 6.2. Boundaries of the Hopkins Marine Life Refuge as designed by Julia Platt in 1931 and as amended in 1984. In 2007, the refuge was joined to the new Lovers Point Marine Reserve, which extends about one mile to the northwest. (Image credit: Paulo Serpa)

Julia was free to manage the Pacific Grove shoreline and police its access. This was Julia's ultimate goal all along, and she had gained the legal authority to do it.

A Refuge for the Future

Anchoring the protection of the shoreline was the Hopkins Marine Life Refuge. Its designated boundaries encompassed the shore from the boundary of the Hovden Cannery (currently the Monterey Bay Aquarium) to the waters surrounding China Point. The rocky outcrops and coves that had sheltered a treasure of abalone would now be protected against all collecting of shore life. The exceptions were researchers who collected for scientific purposes.

In her plan, Julia reasoned that the refuge would be the center for scientific research and also would serve as a nursery for invertebrates "from where the tiny larvae may swim or be carried by currents to all points along the shore and become attached, grow up and replace those taken for food or curio." This rationale is stunningly similar to modern reasons for protecting marine areas: the replenishment of sets of marine species that interact together. In today's scientific world such sets of species are called ecosystems, a term that wasn't popularized in the academic world until 40 years later. It seems that Julia's subtle appreciation for the biology of the sea and her scientific acuity had not diminished during her three decades of intense devotion to civic affairs.

Julia knew that she could repair the damage being done to Monterey Bay most effectively by setting aside something intact and bountiful, something that would be there when needed to naturally seed other areas. Basically, she set up a trust fund for future residents of Monterey Bay, one that was invested not in stocks and bonds but in rocks and kelps and in the prodigious life of the sea. It would be held in reserve until the ocean's bounty could be realized.

The Hopkins Refuge was tiny, barely bigger than the 11-acre land area of the station. So Julia did more. Further along the shore, she crafted the Pacific Grove Marine Gardens. This area encompassed the wild shoreline of the Pacific coast outside Monterey Bay. Along its rocks and beaches, Julia's law would allow only small quantities of marine life to be taken for noncommercial purposes by hand.

Julia's specific mention of noncommercial collecting suggests that part of her effort was to thwart one particular Pacific Grove businessman. Marine biologist Ed Ricketts ran his Pacific Biological Supply house from a small building just up the street from Julia's house. Ricketts fed himself and his family by collecting and selling marine specimens for classroom use. Perhaps Julia tried specifically to stop him, or perhaps her targets were the collectors of mussels and sea urchins and abalone who sold their catch. The answer has never been clear. What is clear is that the industrialization of the shoreline in Monterey would not be permitted in Pacific Grove. Sea life would be protected and would remain to help repopulate the industrialized shores next door.

The Legacy of Foresight

Dr. Julia Barlow Platt died on May 28, 1935, just two years after the end of her single term as mayor. She died of heart attack in her home and had explicitly outlined in her will exactly how she was to be buried. Eccentric to the end, Julia had requested a burial at sea, sailor fashion. Such burials had to be outside U.S. territorial waters, 12 miles from shore in those days. So a line of cars drove slowly through the town of Pacific Grove to Monterey's Municipal Wharf, with Julia encased in canvas, laid in a wicker basket covered with flowers.

"Civic dignitaries traditionally accompany the body of a Mayor to its last resting place." So on a bright spring day, in the chartered motor boat *The Two Brothers*, council members and friends accompanied the body and set out for the 12-mile limit. The weather started getting rough, and "a few were seasick." The body shifted from side to side in the boat as it crested each wave. The pallbearers were not holding up well, complaining that "there were times they wished they could trade places with her!" Finally, they tied a 50-pound metal wheel to the canvas-covered body to sink it to the ocean floor and splashed the body feet first into the waves. Accounts say that her body bobbed to the surface once, with her head above water, as if she were taking one last look at her beloved coastline. A shaken city council sailed home.

Julia's legacy is engraved in bronze within a natural granite rock cradle at Lovers Point: "Julia B. Platt in recognition of her unfailing loyalty to the right in interest of humanity." Reverend Lee Sadler, pastor of the First Christian Church, mirrored these thoughts: "We place this tablet, that future generations may recall the splendid stand for conviction, the interest in civic welfare, the honor and the respect in which we, of this generation, hold Julia B. Platt."

Julia passed away in a decade when the health of Monterey Bay was in steep decline. She left a town where the air was foul, the water oily, and the future uncertain. It took 32 years for Julia's foresight to pay off and help restore the health of the bay. Julia's house, now a bed and breakfast, stood sentinel during these years, her front window facing out onto the bay as its ocean life declined and as it came slowly back to life. The worst years were coming, and Julia would not be there to help. But her Refuge and Marine Garden would serve the needs of the bay and would be there when, at last, they could help.

Chapter 7

Ed Ricketts, Ecology, and the Philosophy of Tide Pools

E D RICKETTS WANDERED happily home to his little Pacific Grove cottage late on a spring night in 1932, and as usual a huge commotion greeted him there. Joseph Campbell lived just next door, and John Steinbeck was making a racket inside. And since they were all buddies, Ed burst into Joe's house to demand an explanation for the uproar and maybe add to it a little.

It was a séance, and it was going badly. Joe, John, and a third conspirator, artist Ritchie Lovejoy, were summoning the spirit of Rick's grandfather, working very hard at this unfamiliar task. Steinbeck had already grown incensed that the only spirit to actually appear all evening wouldn't talk to him, and in a corner of the kitchen, the three amateur occultists held onto the séance table with increasing alarm as it rattled and banged like a door in a storm. Ed entered this scene, immediately surveyed the situation, and threw himself at the table to hold it down for his friends. But Ricketts slipped, fell under the table legs, and brought the table, and everyone else, down on top of him in a heap on the floor.

The Writer, the Philosopher, and the Scientist

Such was the outlandish world of these outcast friends in otherwise staid Pacific Grove. In 1932, John Steinbeck had written one failed novel but was incubating the narrative skills that eventually let him pen classics such as *The Grapes of Wrath* and *East of Eden* and win the Nobel Prize for Literature. Joe Campbell, known to the world as Joseph, was exploring the philosophy of heroes and mythology, a lifelong career that netted him the Medal of Honor in Art in 1985, produced the plot line of the *Star Wars* movies, and secured his reputation as perhaps the foremost authority on the literature of heroes. Ed Ricketts was writing the book that would be Stanford University Press's bestseller, and he was the planet around which both Joe and John orbited.

But in 1932 none of this fame had materialized yet, and the three friends formed their own fan club. Ed's house in Pacific Grove was perched above town, a tiny cottage beyond the stink of the canneries. Long a misfit celebrity in town, Ed was used to explaining himself to the local police and letting them sample whatever new drinks he concocted from lab alcohol. He ran a little business of collecting and selling sealife specimens to university classes around the country. The business variously thrived and foundered, but it kept Ed's small family fed. His business schedule was ruled by the tides and the class calendars of far-away colleges, and it wasn't odd for Ed to rouse friends from a party, or family from their beds, to go out to the great tide pools of the Pacific coast in order to hunt starfish, collect sea urchins, and discover sea slugs by the fog-dimmed headlights of his beat-up car.

Ed had been in Pacific Grove for seven years, an old timer with a wife and three children, when Steinbeck arrived in 1930. Campbell showed up a year later, at the end of a West Coast trek after two years of academic fellowships in Europe. Ed adopted these two new friends wholeheartedly and included them in the cold business of tide pooling and in the hot business of understanding the philosophy of the universe. After Ed died an early death in 1948, both Campbell and Steinbeck looked back at this short time, when they were all together, as one of the most important parts of their lives.

Although Steinbeck and Campbell soon migrated, Ed remained rooted in Monterey. He was close enough to the pulse of marine life to know, as Julia Platt had known, that the bay was in trouble. And in the final throes of the worst industrial pollution the bay would ever see, when it was at its absolute worst environmentally but was thriving economically, Ed was among the first to clearly see the coming economic doom.

Marine Life in Miniature

The years after Ed Ricketts moved to Pacific Grove, when his friendships with Steinbeck and Campbell were forged, saw an eightfold rise in Monterey sardine landings (Figure 7.1). From the 1930s until the death of the sardine era in 1947, an average of about a million pounds of fish a day were hauled out of Monterey Bay and into the canneries. Even during the Great Depression, the canneries churned out products that kept people employed. Pumped from floating fish hoppers onto the cannery floors, silver sardines shone the color of money.

Yet this economic boom passed unnoticed by the three friends, who had their heads in the tide pools, not the fishing nets. Ed's business made him into something of an ecological generalist. And he

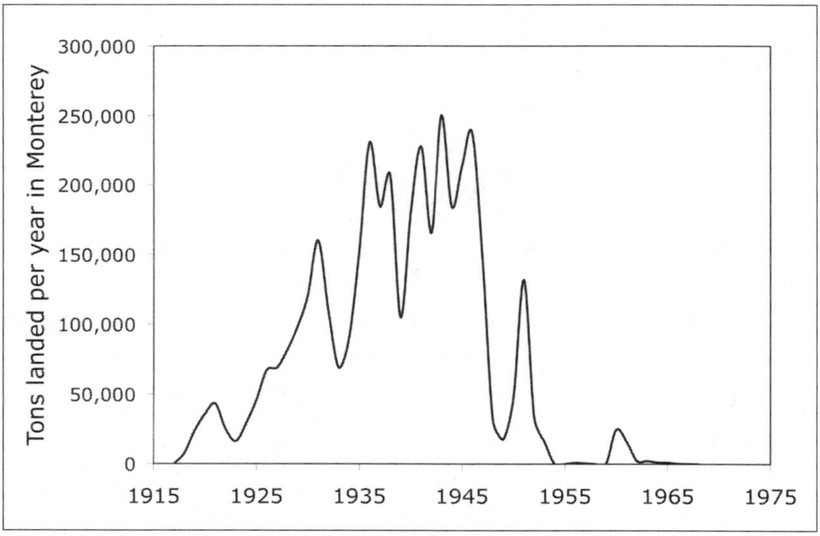

Figure 7.1. The rise and fall of the sardine industry in Monterey. Annual landings of sardines rose dramatically and hovered around 200,000 tons for the decade between 1935 and 1945. This represents 400 million pounds of fish, about a million pounds a day. (Data from the National Marine Fisheries Service.)

sampled widely: shark embryos for dissection to show vertebrate development, sea urchin larvae growing stage by stage and placed on microscope slides, picked starfish, and much more.

Pacific Grove was the perfect spot for his endeavors. Here lay a wealth of marine life that could easily supply Ed's modest needs. The rocky shores crowded close to the road around the tip of the Monterey Peninsula where Pacific Grove lay, surreal stone castles with moats of churning water at their bases. The shore itself was often covered in fog, which muffled the sounds of the waves and dulled the sunlight. The waves slipped away at low tide, uncovering a short forest of rockweed and leaving tide pools brimming with the life of the sea.

The Great Tide Pool became one of Ed's favorite sites. On the Pacific side of the peninsula, facing away from the quieter waters of

Monterey Bay, the pool was sometimes a tempest of churning foam that Ed would stride through in hip-high waders. Other times it was a quiet bowl, isolated from the waves by low tide and a rocky rim.

Wide algal blades hide the surface of the pools. Scooped away, they reveal the animal cities underneath. Starfish that often miscount their own arms and grow six instead of five glide on hundreds of tiny tube feet. Spiral-shelled snails act as Lilliputian cows, grazing among the tiny fronds of turf-like algae for the tastier threads. The large green sea anemones hold their saucer-sized disks up to the sunlight, waving their ring of tentacles for a taste of stumbling crab. Sea slugs the color and size of lemons move effortlessly among the patches of brightly colored sponges, smelling and tasting for the right one to eat. Dense crowds of hermit crabs bustle around the pools, cleaning up debris and attacking unwary animals tinier than they. They also keep an eye out for a better shell and are not above trying to steal one from its current owner. In the pools on some coasts they smell a snail in trouble, in the clutches of a crab or the stomach of a starfish, and wait around like anxious morticians to squabble with one another over the empty shell when the predator moves on.

These tiny ecological dramas give structure and stability to a tide pool's riot of life. Ed looked into these pools and discovered the complex interactions that ruled the little lives there. And the rules were intricate. Species did not form a simple food chain where snail eats algae, fish eats snail, and heron eats fish. Instead they told a thousand stories of the way animals and plants live and die. Life was affected by the environment: when and where the waves rolled in. It was affected by the other species present. And it was affected by chance events and unlikely contingencies. Ed's peculiar gift was to be able to see these connections. His mission was to try to chart and understand them and to explain them to others.

The diversity of the tide pools allowed Ed to make a living selling specimens. But the complex interactions between species also fertilized his philosophical roots and anchored him forever to the two friends who saw the world of human affairs in the same way: not as a simple food chain of ideas but as a skein of interacting desires, ambitions, and circumstances. Steinbeck and Campbell were aware of this complexity but could not at first put a name on it. But even they could see it clearly when Ed showed them the churning tide pools of Pacific Grove.

Ed's Philosophy of Ecology

Ed appears in photographs as well built, slim, and dark, sometimes with a Clark Gable *Gone with the Wind* mustache. Steinbeck scholar Susan Shillinglaw points out that Ed usually looks down in photographs, as if he were always looking into a tide pool—like a heron contemplating lunch. A smile rarely graces his pictures, but Ed was known for being intensely social and surrounded himself with friends.

Collecting specimens primarily with family and friends from 1923, when he moved to Pacific Grove, Ed seems to have decided that there was a grand mystery to solve among the seaweeds and invertebrates. In today's world of science, he might have become a community ecologist, learning the quantitative skills and statistical language that describe species interactions. But although he had been initiated into science at the University of Chicago, Ed did not have the university degree that would give him entry into academic life, and he had not developed a quantitative approach to ecology. Instead, he crafted his analysis as a blacksmith crafts iron and built a nonquantitative, working-man's philosophy of ecological interactions. What was the mystery that needed solving? What were the mysteries of the tide pools? How did the interactions between species produce the kaleidoscope of tide pool life?

Seeking Answers in the Company of Friends

Ed's steady scientific study was raucously enlivened by Steinbeck and Campbell. Suddenly, Ricketts had a club, a Parisian-style intellectual's salon in which to thrash out his ideas. And here Ed's simplest personal philosophy, "from the tide pools to the stars, and then back again," found traction.

It was a philosophy that engaged them all: exploring life to the fullest. Ed's ecologist mentor at the University of Chicago, Professor W. C. Allee, wrote extensively in 1931 about the role of cooperation in animal ecology. Another of Ed's influences, marine scientist W. E. Ritter in San Diego, also espoused a view of groups of organisms coming together into "superorganisms." As a result, Ed was fascinated by how organisms acted in groups. Does an individual creature behave differently when in the close company of others of the same species? Does it change what it eats? How it defends itself? If organisms change their patterns of behavior this way, then ecological interactions between species are not fixed or immutable but might vary depending on context. The complex interactions that Ed saw in tide pools—which species eats which other species, where and how the algae grow—might be even more complex if the rules of engagement changed all the time. How could this be understood?

The friends must have discussed this at length because John Steinbeck used the notion in his 1936 novel *In Dubious Battle*. In this book, Steinbeck assumes that a person's behavior changes dramatically in a group. Naming this effect the philosophy of the phalanx, Steinbeck took Ed's ecological musings and injected them into human society, using the canvas of his novel to paint the implications of such a change. And like the effect of changed interactions on ecological complexity, human society also becomes more complex when the rules of human interaction change in groups.

Joe Campbell, too, absorbed a wealth of new ideas. Although his academic writing career didn't begin for a decade, he wrote later that this period was when "everything that has happened since was taking shape."

It would be a mistake to think of these three as bookish scholars, however. They did not follow a monkish lifestyle of quiet contemplation but instead usually engaged in loud personal debate and social experimentation. Campbell describes a mutual face-slapping contest he and their friend Rick Lovejoy tried on the floor of Ed's house one night. Parties that went on for days seemed common enough for the police to have gotten used to them, even in stolid Pacific Grove. Another episode saw Campbell, on the floor again, and Rick's wife, Tam Lovejoy, trying to "gaze each other's hearts out."

Finding a way to amplify experience, to intensify life's events and bring the inner meaning of happenstance into sharp focus—these were the tasks that occupied Ed and his friends. Mystic revelations might help, and so discussions of the pursuit of "quietism" from the Tao or Jungian psychology commenced. And perhaps here lay the answer to the mystery of the tide pools, some way of connecting the ecology of the tumultuous shoreline and philosophy of tumultuous life.

Then one day they found what Ed later called the key to the whole problem. John Steinbeck's wife, Carol, discovered it while innocuously reading a poem by Robinson Jeffers called *Roan Stallion*. Poem in hand, she stormed into the Pacific Grove house and interrupted the three friends' discussion, commanding, "Listen to this."

> Humanity is the start of the race
> Humanity is the mold to break away from
> . . .
> Humanity is . . . the crust to break through

For Ed, John, and Joe, this passage had momentous implications. It told them that what they were seeking was a way to break through the crust of humanity and experience life's intensity beyond its normal boundaries. From this night on, they called it the philosophy of breaking through.

Breaking through meant different things and occupied pages of Ed's writing for the next 16 years. And for the small crowd that orbited around Ed, it meant they finally had a focus that would let them push their thoughts ever higher, out of the tide pool and closer to the stars.

Trouble in the Tide Pools

If Ed and his confidants had their feet in the tide pools and their heads in the stars, it was the organs in between that were beginning to cause trouble. Ed was rumored to be having affairs, including with teenage women, and his relationship with his family became strained. Never present at the philosophy sessions, Ed's wife, Nan, drifted away from the intellectual center Ed created. It was worse for Steinbeck and Campbell: Joe had fallen in love with John's wife, Carol, and this poisoned the men's friendship. The new philosophy demanded that they use the experience to break out of old molds, however, and so they had a tense confrontation at Campbell's cottage.

"I'd like to talk a little, John," Campbell told him.

John sat heavily in a usual chair, the same one he'd been sitting in the previous Friday night. He looked shot and at a loss.

"It's positively ridiculous even to think of my marrying Carol," Campbell declared. "How am I to withdraw from this mess with the least pain for her?"

"And what about yourself?" John asked.

"To hell with myself," Campbell replied.

Campbell writes that "it pleased me to see after that John was able to look me in the eye again. . . . The sense of rivalry had been broken into the warmer sense of conspiracy against Venus."

But Campbell's personal recollection may not have captured all of Steinbeck's feelings. Carol and John left Pacific Grove for Montrose, California right after this confrontation and did not return for seven months—only after Campbell left for good.

In Ricketts's house next door to Campbell's, things were also not going well. Nan decided to move out, shifting the family to Carmel and beginning a period of four years in which Ed and Nan were intermittently separated. Both Ed and Joe faced these losses with a retreat: Ed decided to go collecting in Alaska with his friend and cowriter Jack Calvin, and Joe decided he might as well come along too.

Ed and his friends immersed themselves in this new expedition.

Their salon of philosophical ecology had them peering deeply into the tide pool kaleidoscope and into their own heads. And they were very happy to keep the concerns of the world at bay.

The rest of Monterey was busily cashing in on the inexhaustible sardine crop. By 1932, the fishing fleet was expanded, the canneries ready to process almost any amount. The sardine business seemed completely different from the arcane complexity of ecological interactions that Ed conjured up in the tide pools. The fleet took the sardines, and the next year the sardines came back. They all eventually discovered that Ed's philosophy of complexity applied to the sardine as well, but this lesson was decades away.

The Breakup

Ed, John, and Joe all fled Pacific Grove at about the same time, pondering their philosophies and troubles and bent on turning the tumult of the Campbell–Steinbeck love triangle into positive product. Although Ed was committed to thinking all the way from tide pool to the stars, he had missed out somewhat on the middle bit: the part of his life where actions and consequences played out at a local level. From notes that Ed wrote later on, he did not pay a great deal of attention to his children during this time. When his son Ed Jr. moved in with him in 1938, at the age of 15, Ed wrote himself a short note in his journal: "Thoughts on my first (substantial) taking over the responsibilities of a parent" (these notes must have worked, because Ed Jr. stayed with his father for five years).

And there was a lot of other action around Ed at the time that he might have noticed. Julia Platt was mayor, after all, and had just completed her successful drive to have the Hopkins shoreline fully protected for science. And she had placed the entire Pacific Grove shoreline off limits to commercial collectors, a designation that presumably included Ed. A fire in 1936 burned most of Ed's correspondence and his notes and journals, and there is no record of his being involved in the civic life of Pacific Grove or of any confrontation with Julia Platt.

Despite Julia's efforts, the Monterey Peninsula had almost completely morphed from a tourist destination into a full-blown cannery town in the 1920s and 1930s. As Ed's children grew, and he was enmeshed in picking marine creatures out of tide pools and picking the brains of his friends, Ed saw the sardine fishery exploding around him. Cannery after cannery shoved its way onto the Monterey shore next to China Point, creating a line of wooden factories that formed a new human-made coastline. Soon, terrible smells reeking from the plants rose over the peninsula, and the waters along the shores carried the globs of fat and oil that the canneries spewed into the bay.

Ed's Ecological Philosophy and Steinbeck's Novels

When Ed and Joe returned to Monterey after their Alaska trip of 1932, some problems solved themselves and some didn't. Joe had never really put down roots in Pacific Grove, and he finally got a teaching job on the East Coast. After a few memorable parties and a brief revival of the old carousing, Joe left Pacific Grove forever. This cleared the way for John and Carol Steinbeck to return, so that Ed and John—the philosopher and the writer—could settle into a new bohemian routine of thinking, drinking, writing, and tide pooling. But Ed never permanently reunited with his wife and children, and he eventually moved his belongings to his tiny lab building on Monterey's Cannery Row, jammed between the Del Vista and Del Mar canneries. A new era had arrived in Ed's life and in the life of Monterey Bay.

Based at the Cannery Row lab, with the canneries erupting in activity all around him, Ed collected animals at the Great Tide Pool, along the clean shoreline of the coast outside Monterey Bay, and steadily typed revisions of a major book project, *Between Pacific Tides*. This work was Ed's major legacy and described the life of the shores of California, from the upper wave-splashed rocks to the pools that were uncovered only at the deepest low tides. It was at once an encyclopedia of ecological description and a personal memoir of Ed's years of collecting and observing. Other marine biologists tried to prevent its publication because Ed was an academic nobody, without a university degree of any kind. But the book was Ed's stunning achievement and sold more than any other science book printed by Stanford University Press.

Ed also diligently produced version after version of several philosophical essays. Chief among these, Ed's essay on what he called nonteleological thinking attempted to describe his mental model of the way the world worked. The essay tried to show how Ed used the lessons of the tide pools to forge his philosophy of life.

Simplifying Ed's stance on nonteleological thinking would be to (ironically) say that oversimplification should be avoided. Although he allowed that is it possible to identify some individual causes of a complex pattern, Ed insisted that any one cause was but a part of the picture. The life of the rocky shores, chronicled in *Between Pacific Tides*, provided Ed a constant road map for this view. Proximity to the sea largely controls which species of marine alga or animal can live on the intertidal rocks. But there are other factors important to rock life besides tidal height. Ed could name many—wave action, sand or mud in the water, exposure to the sun, the presence of predators or herbivores—and included them as elements in *Between Pacific Tides*. But Ed felt it was important to "remember the big picture" and recognize the constellation of other effects that operated at the same time at the same places. Ed's life philosophy was structured in exactly this way. Yet Ed struggled to explain his stand. And his philosophy, though a boon to Steinbeck's writing, never did much for him personally. Writing projects besides *Between Pacific Tides* foundered, and he never really broke through the limits of his small collecting business and his gritty life on Cannery Row.

But while Ed was focusing on the big picture of ecology and life, Steinbeck figured out that complex ecological relationships could create a wonderful plot line. His novel *Tortilla Flat* again used as an engine of its plot the idea that people's behavior changes when they are in larger groups, and it brought him national attention. His 1937 novel *Of Mice and Men* won the Pulitzer Prize by bringing to life a complex web of human relationships, with sometimes unusual consequences. But a more direct link between ecology and the human condition simmered in Steinbeck's mind: the simple yet devastating ecological causes of the Dust Bowl.

Huge wind storms ravaged the U.S. Midwest in the 1930s. The peak year of 1935 saw storms measuring 400 by 600 miles stripping soil from 50 million acres. Although the wind was to blame, a more fundamental cause was overfarming, the tendency of poorer farmers during the Depression years to work the soil to exhaustion and leave it bare for the wind to scour clean. Steinbeck's ecological literacy, a gift from Ed, allowed him to see the irony and tragedy in this human-caused disaster. He wrapped this theme into the explosive plot of *The Grapes of Wrath*.

In an irony that played out for the next decade, a similar disaster was beginning to occur in Monterey, where the voracious cannery industry was overstripping the sardine populations, fouling the sea, and creating the conditions for an economic collapse.

The Philosophy No One Wanted

Fishing as a philosophical enterprise tends to be a man-against-fish conflict that pits stubborn determinism against, say, a white whale. Ed's triumph was that he saw the consequences of fishing as the ripple effects of one kind of activity—the taking of fish—throughout the ecology of the whole ocean world. Ricketts wrote to Joe Campbell in 1946, "I'd rather be an ecologist and have for stock in trade that sense of integration with a whole picture."

Nobody had thought this way before except philosophers. And fishermen, cannery owners, and the working population of Monterey didn't want to start, because Ed's complex thinking about ecological causes and consequences might mean that the sardine industry couldn't live forever. And it could mean that the canneries might create a dust bowl of the ocean that would ruin everything.

Chapter 8

Dust Bowl of the Sea: The Canneries Collapse

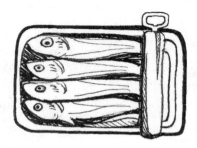

IT HAD BEEN a tough decade, but at last things were going well for Ed Ricketts. True, his best friend John Steinbeck had been gone for years, and Ed's marine science supply business was basically dead. But Steinbeck's novel *Cannery Row* had made something of a folk hero out of Ed. And more importantly, the booming canneries in Monterey wanted to buy his little waterfront lab.

Crowded and dark, and smelly from the business of pickling dead sea creatures, the lab sat shoehorned between two of the most active canneries on Earth. They needed the room. Ed needed the money. Even the stuffy academics at the Hopkins Marine Station had relented, and they agreed Ed could build a little lab in their scientific enclave next door. The war was over. Ed was writing. For Ed Ricketts, 1946 would be a good year.

And then the sardines disappeared.

Counting Sardines

As early as 1919, when state legislation gave the Department of Fish and Game legal authority to regulate the sardine industry and establish a scientific monitoring program, concerns surfaced that fishing intensity was unsustainable. Fishery scientist Will Thompson tried to make the connection between sardine overfishing and the rest of the ocean ecosystem: "The sardine is a source of food for almost all our other great fisheries, such as the albacore, barracuda, sea bass and tuna. Tampering with its abundance may result disastrously to many interests." "Nonsense," the canners replied. Hovden expressed a sentiment widely shared on Cannery Row: "The sardine supply could not be exterminated."

Frances Clark, one of the only women fishery biologists in the state at that time, also recognized the ecosystem-wide implications of what had become the world's largest commercial fishery. She set up a tagging program designed to see where the sardines in Monterey came from and what percentage of them ended up in the cans. She recognized that oceanographic conditions and natural causes might be influencing the abundance of sardines in Monterey Bay. But she still insisted that the populations could not withstand the intense exploitation by the Monterey fleets and adamantly argued for a reduction in the catch. As her predecessors had found, such warnings fell on deaf ears. Regardless of the numerous Department of Fish and Game scientists who wrote alarmingly about the fish supply, no catch limits were imposed.

An Era of Change

Seeing his long-held philosophy of ecological complexity becoming suddenly useful, Ed Ricketts was awakening to the ecological impact and collapse of sardine fishing in Monterey. In a 1938 letter to zoologist Torsten Gislen, he wrote, "The canneries are going strong—they will extract every single sardine out of the ocean."

Of course, Ricketts had a front row seat at the cannery show, his lab sandwiched between two of the most active factories, listening to engines of prosperity so loud that they "shake the building." But Ed was more and more on his own. Steinbeck's career was in ascendancy, as he wrote movies and cashed royalty checks, and John and Carol moved to New York to manage his fame. Left to handle a marine specimen business that was slowly failing, Ed seldom left Monterey after that, and he presided over a loyal but shrinking circle of friends, playing his phonograph records at terrific volume, blasting Gregorian chants into the noisome air between the canneries. All around him the cannery business netted prosperity. But the canneries were the only industry in town, and everyone's livelihood depended on the stream of fish.

World War II: Sardines Over There

If there was a small spark of interest in regulating the sardine industry, it was extinguished during World War II. Any worry about ecology took a back seat as the canneries geared up to supply the troops abroad with canned fish. Landings of sardines climbed yet again, and with the canneries in full swing—now producing canned fish rather than mostly fish meal—a new economic surge filled the pocketbooks of Monterey. In 1941, the canneries tinned nearly 60,000 tons of sardines, about twice the typical production of the 1930s. Ed disdained what he saw as their false patriotism. "The canneries started up as soon as war was declared, the first of the profiteers," he wrote to Xenia Cage, the wife of local composer John Cage. But the fishing fleets had special dispensation from the military, and nothing would stop them from finding and taking the last sardine, if that was what the Army wanted.

Everywhere, life turned to the exigencies of conflict across both oceans, and the sardine became as crucial as any other wartime product. Sicilian fishermen in Monterey were relocated away from the coast in 1941, and although they shared this indignity with Japanese Americans all over the country, in Monterey the Sicilians were needed on the fishing boats. The federal government allowed them to return to their homes within about six months. Ed was drafted into the Army and spent the war in Monterey as a clerk. His son, Ed Jr., was in combat overseas, and like almost all parents of his generation, Ed Sr. went to bed each night with a gnawing dread.

The canneries hummed with an invigorated mission. As the fishing boats combed the waters around Monterey for all the sardines they could find, the numbers of fish began to oscillate wildly from one season to the next. And a new puzzle worried fishermen and scientists alike. Unlike the mid-1930s, when any additional fishing effort returned additional fish in about equal proportion, in the mid-1940s the amount of effort expended bore little relationship to the success achieved. This meant that launching more boats could not increase the catch. It also meant that the whole Monterey fleet, operating at maximum capacity from about 1937 to 1947, might bring home either a bumper crop of fish, such as the 250,000-ton year 1941, or a skinny return, such as the 26,000-ton year of 1946 (see Figure 7.1 in Chapter 7).

The canners and the military greeted poor fishing years with alarm, and efforts to increase the catch ramped up. Spotter planes soon left the Monterey military airstrips and circled the bay looking for sardines. Especially when populations were low, sardines accumulated in balls of fish near the surface, easily visible from slow-moving planes. A simple radio message to the fishing fleet could send each new sardine ball quickly into the hold of a fishing boat, and the bay was steadily scoured of fish. The economics of finding fish from planes often presents a disastrous bottom line. Plane, pilot, fuel— all this could cost more than the fish are worth. But national need erased the economic part of the sardine equation. And so the last of the Monterey sardines were entombed in cans just as the war was ending.

Cannery Row

"It's mostly about me," Ed wrote to Ed Jr. Late 1944 eased into 1945, and Ed had just reviewed a new manuscript by Steinbeck. Sparked by wistful comments of soldiers in Europe, "Write something for us to read—we're sick of the war," Steinbeck created fiction out of fact and forever romanticized the tattered edges of cannery life in his smile-along novel *Cannery Row*. An instant best-seller, the folksy, friendly narrative of the calm, Zen-like inhabitants of Cannery Row struck a national nerve. Critics fumed that the plot went nowhere, the narration stumbled, and the book succeeded only in being a "sentimental glorification of weakness of mind." Steinbeck grumbled that they missed the entire point of his novel.

Superficial? Yes, even Ed called it that. But it was a metaphor for what Steinbeck had absorbed over the years as Ed's partner in ecology and philosophy. Its structure hid a philosophical essay where obscure ideas were turned into characters enmeshed in a charming community. Steinbeck scholar Susan Shillinglaw likens *Cannery Row* to a busy tide pool. She describes its action as the scuttling activity of varied creatures, free to live their lives, every day slightly differently, after the tide goes out. It is a portrait of eccentric people wandering about their wacky world.

Other Steinbeck watchers have called it an ecological satire, based on the principles of nonteleological thinking in which clear avenues of cause and effect are intersected by a tangle of detours. If nothing progressive happens in a tide pool, few biologists are surprised. If the intersecting web of relationships in a down-and-out community of loyal hooligans gets a little complicated, few philosophers are surprised. The most fundamental similarity between pools and hooligan neighborhoods might just be that a change at one end can ripple through to the other end. And although you might be able to follow the stream of interactions from one end to the other, as one player affects another, who affects a third, and so on, a prediction of the ultimate ripple effect would be impossible. Ed and Steinbeck came to believe in the ripple and came to disdain the prediction.

Cannery Row has chapters that sit like a cut-off corner in a tide pool. Looking into a pool, you can usually see a crevice where some new set of species has set up housekeeping, living their complex lives in isolation from the rest. A family of flatworms or a cluster of nervous shrimp might appear only once in the pool. *Cannery Row* created characters that starred in but a single three-page chapter: a quarreling couple or a dead girl in the water. Even the flood of waves that washes over a tide pool has an analogy in *Cannery Row*. The truly interesting characters in the book emerge only after the silver flood of the sardines hits the row like a wave and then leaves. Once it ebbs and the business of the canneries quiets, sending the hourly workers and gainful employees home, the "crevice" characters of the novel emerge like tide pool denizens to scurry the streets and alleys and work the interactions of their lives.

The success of *Cannery Row* had ripple effects in the real world too. Ed became Doc to the entire country and was forced to have his native, humble generosity on 24-hour display to gawking tourists. The novel created a goofy, romantic world in which the canneries had gone to seed, leaving behind a set of misfits and ne'er-do-wells to populate the streets. Although it was not meant to be prophetic, the doom of the canneries began before the ink was dry on *Cannery Row*'s first printing. And the age of the misfits and ne'er-do-wells was about to begin.

The Last Scales Fall

The canneries had one last blast of success in 1944, but the sardines never really returned after that. Barely 14,000 tons came into the whole city on boats in 1946 (see Figure 7.1), less than the total for a single cannery in some previous years. Not for want of effort: Just as many boats went to sea as in 1944. But they came back with empty hulls.

Ed worried about the sardines. By 1946, his collecting business had folded, doomed by the war. Instead, Ed worked for the sardine companies as a chemist. His personal life was in shambles, and book projects since *Sea of Cortez* never materialized. His *Between Pacific Tides* continued to be popular; a second edition grew in his mind and finally on paper. But plans for books about San Francisco Bay, Alaska, and even the South Pacific sputtered like the sardine catch.

Around Ed, Cannery Row was gasping for lack of fish. Writing to Joseph Campbell in 1946, Ed complained, "For years the canners ... and the fishermen have been warned they are taking too much fish. They refused to listen, selected their evidence ... [and] always got their way." And in musing to his old friends, Ed explained the subtleties of the ecology of overfishing. It was not just about taking too much, because some years the sardines were so productive that the fishermen couldn't possibly take all there were. Rather, it was that sardine populations naturally cycle up and down. And the canneries, Ed told Joseph Campbell, eat away at the population at both its peak and its trough. This factor "pulls down the high a little, tho not so much as it pulls down the lows. ... It could conceivably sometime hit them so bad, when they were at a trough anyhow, that the margin by which they survive ... would be wiped out completely, and they'd go down." Ed saw this clearly because he had sensitized himself to the connections between different elements of ecology, including people, and to the fact that ocean life is ruled by cycles like the tides.

Ed also somehow knew that part of the problem was not overfishing but a change in the ocean. This hidden shift affected the very base of the food chain, causing "sudden plankton imbalances" that disturbed everything else. He alerted John Steinbeck in 1946 to "published reports that red water in south Calif. (dinoflagellates, but this time apparently not the poisonous type) was so intense that many shore invertebrates including even lobsters, were killed by suffocation—low O_2 content."

Letters to friends such as Steinbeck could not possibly help the sardines, and so Ed wrote a front-page article for the annual sardine edition of the *Monterey Herald* in 1947. Titled "Science Studies the Sardine," it was a pioneering discussion of marine food chains and the connections between sea temperature, currents, and productivity

of the ocean. Ed also argued passionately that there was a clear connection between Monterey's economic collapse and Steinbeck's powerful novel *The Grapes of Wrath*. Overfarming and disastrous drought
had ruined farmers in the Midwest Dust Bowl: Their own frantic
need to extract yields from exhausted soils doomed them and their
families. Like a nightmarish echo, overfishing and a change in ocean
conditions destroyed the sardine harvest, and the fishermen's frantic
need to extract yields from an exhausted ocean doomed them and
their families. This cruel parallel was clearest to Ed, who (perhaps
alone in the world) possessed a deep understanding of the ecological
underpinnings of Steinbeck's fiction, a ringside seat to the destruction of Monterey Bay, and a philosopher's tragic ability to compare
both.

But this increased understanding did not magically return the sardines to Monterey. The season of 1947 was even worse than 1946. The
catch hadn't been this low since 1917. Ed published a second article in
the *Herald* under the headline "Investigator Blames Industry." The
sardine's fate, he wrote, was not mysterious and not sudden, having
begun to decline as early as 1936. But he characteristically avoided a
simplistic answer to the sardine problem: A section of the article was
titled "Nature Shares Blame." Ed thought that ocean conditions in
the northern Pacific had shifted and that the sardines could no longer
fill their bellies with food as they migrated from southern California
to the colder waters off Oregon and Washington.

Despite the qualification, Ed made clear where the balance of
blame lay. He argued that although humanity probably couldn't
exterminate sardines entirely (after all, rats, bedbugs, and cockroaches
were still around), we could "reduce their numbers to the point of
commercial extinction." And he lampooned the canners' reaction to
warnings about the fishery. "Don't pay attention to these scientists,"
he quipped. "Let's listen to the hard headed down-to-earth businessmen. There is no chance of depletion. There's just as good fish in the
sea as ever's been caught."

Tragedy in Monterey

Ed's article conveys a deep frustration that Monterey's downfall could have been averted: "If conservation had been adopted early enough, a smaller and more streamlined cannery row in all likelihood would be winding up a fairly successful season, instead of dipping . . . deeply into the red ink of failure."

His anger may have been fueled by a more personal heartbreak, this one inexorable. A few months earlier, the daughter of Ed's long-time companion, Toni Jackson, had succumbed to brain cancer after a long, painful illness. Her death had left Ed and Toni drained and estranged. Toni left soon after. Ed's letters about mother and daughter still spoke of hope, even at the end, but they were also colored by the numbed grief of an immutable tragedy.

Another followed. On May 7, 1948, the night train killed Ed Ricketts. He had left the lab in the middle of a party—to get food, he said. On its regular run, the train came around its typical curve near an empty cannery warehouse and blindsided Ed's 1936 Buick on the tracks. "Don't blame the motorman," he gasped upon being pulled from the wreckage. John Steinbeck was informed in New York and rushed to the West Coast but did not get to Monterey before Ed died of serious injuries two days later. Steinbeck stayed a while, holed up in the lab reading and re-reading Ed's correspondence and essays, burning the parts he thought too personal. And then he left.

After Ed

John Steinbeck and all of Ed's friends walked away from the sardine problem in Monterey once Ed had gone. And after a partial return in 1949 and 1950, the sardines vanished. The 1953 landings into Monterey were 49 tons—about the amount that would have been netted in an hour in 1942.

Abandoned by fish and prosperity, Monterey lay wounded by the canneries, strewn with the wreckage of a 30-year party whose spirit had gone out. Where a quiet town had greeted the promise of the twentieth century with exuberance, only a skeleton remained. Gone were the Chinese villagers, drying squid, and abalone. Gone were the glass-bottom boats at Lovers Point and the summer tourists laughing on the train from San Francisco. The grand hotels no longer echoed with activity but loomed dark or had burned to the ground. The shoreline of Monterey, once the launching point for a prosperous fishing fleet, was roofed over by tin and planking, the thick legs of the derelict canneries pounded into the living rocks of the coast. The gulls roosted still on the tin gables of the canning factories, fighting over fish scraps and looking in vain for a living sardine to make a meal. The shore still stank of diesel oil. The rocks still stank of fish.

People remained, some because they had no alternative. Others drifted off when they could. Steinbeck left for New York to brood over his friend, and some critics have said he never found a replacement in his heart or his books for the character of Ed Ricketts. "He was my partner for 18 years," Steinbeck said in an interview a decade later. "He was part of my brain."

Slowly the wounds in Monterey began to heal, but not in the way anyone expected. Ed himself always had confidence that the sardines would collapse, but he also thought they would quickly recover. It was the nature of the fish to rebound. But Ed turned out to be more right than he knew when he published his last piece in the 1948 *Monterey Herald*. Overfishing had been the trigger of sardine ruin. But another factor loomed as well, something no one knew about at the time, and something no one could change. Ed's second sense about the ocean had been right: It *had* changed. And the shift in ocean climate kept sardines on the sidelines for two decades longer than Ed ever thought likely.

But south of Monterey, the catalyst for ecological and economic recovery was growing closer and closer. Former denizens of Monterey Bay worked their way up the coast, unheralded and unexpected. And when they arrived a decade and a half after Ed's death, the sea otters changed everything.

PART III

The Recovery

Chapter 9

The Otter Returns

U N UNUSUAL CALM blanketed the sea, barely rocking the
low, gray rowboat as it slipped quietly into the small cove on
the Big Sur coast. Four friends fished, talking only in quiet
whispers, jostling their lures through the clear water below, thoughts
attuned to the fish they would catch and to the silent partnership
of fishing. At the mouth of a cove the morning mists parted for a
fraction of a moment, and a few rounded bumps appeared. Bull kelp
floating on the slick surface?

"No," John Pfeiffer told his guests. He lived along the rough Big
Sur coast, and he knew the ocean and the hills. "Not kelp. And not
seals."

Twisting around in the boat, Hans Ewoldsen clearly saw three
pairs of eyes and three sets of bristled white whiskers staring back.
"They don't look like seals," he agreed.

"They're sea otters," Pfeiffer told him quietly, "and they're extinct.
Don't tell anyone."

The mania of the Roaring '20s still gripped much of the United

States in 1929, but the brittle intensity of that era did not penetrate the steep grottos and cliff-hung coves of the California coast. The boat with the four friends drifted away from the curious heads of the small sea creatures. Pfeiffer looked back as the fog rose up to shroud them, like a curtain being closed.

"Stay hidden," his gaze said. "It's not your time yet."

Otters in Shangi-La

Glittering in the sun, rough fingers of rock reach out into the cold waters of the Big Sur coast. They catch and channel the waves between them, concentrating the surge into combers that crash onto creamy beaches nestled between dark stone walls. It was a difficult place for a Depression-era workforce to raise bridges across five canyons and extend U.S. Route 1 along the California coast. Earlier builders had given up and sent the highway inland from Big Sur, to emerge back at the ocean miles farther south. The detour had been dictated by old engineering limits: The canyons of the open coast are deep, steep, and wide. Until the 1930s, this stretch of the coast was lonely and isolated. It was a tiny Shangri-La for a surprising survivor.

The new coastal road opened in 1937. In the early spring of 1938, Mr. and Mrs. H. G. Sharp repaired their little telescope and, turning it toward the mouth of Bixby Creek, made a startling discovery. Down below in the ocean canyons, they saw a small group of furry floaters, quieter than sea lions and smaller than seals, rafting in the waves and lolling among the healthy kelp forests. Without realizing the significance of their find, or that others had kept the secret for decades, the Sharps rediscovered the "extinct" southern sea otter.

The last heyday of the sea otter in central California had occurred in the 1800s, when hundreds of thousands of animals gave up their pelts to the voracious fur trade. A treaty in 1911 prohibited the trade of sea otter pelts while allowing Alaskan natives to continue traditional use. For Californians, the treaty closed the barn door long after the horse was gone: Few otters had been seen south of Alaska for 50 years. The southern population, once so large that it had spurred wild speculation by explorers and missionaries, had disappeared by the early twentieth century. Although reports of one or two animals occasionally surfaced, the otter was one more tiny victim of unrelenting commerce.

The Sharps estimated the sea otter population at several hundred, a number that Hopkins marine biology professor Rolf Bolin found "beyond belief." So on March 25, 1938, Bolin hurried south to Big Sur to see for himself. There is a scene in Michael Crichton's *Jurassic Park* when stunned paleontologist Alan Grant first looks up to see a living dinosaur calmly munching its lunch. This same sense of wonder and surprise must have greeted Rolf Bolin when he drove his old car down the highway from Pacific Grove to Big Sur, headed across the new bridge at Bixby Creek, and beheld the sea otters there. Despite the hundred-foot cliffs, he clambered down to the beach and encountered two otter sentinels: "They approached to within about 60 yards and stood upright in the water, eyeing me." In Bolin's understated words, the otter's reappearance "excited much local comment."

Munching on sea urchins and abalone, the sea otters displayed a stunning nonchalance at having narrowly escaped extinction. Local citizens were not so laissez-faire and demanded that Fish and Game officials assign a warden to guard the population from harm. Although they couldn't prevent a reported attack by a pod of killer whales, the otters were soon protected from human hunting, and their population numbers began to grow.

The otters were a genie, now let out of their bottle, and they would revolutionize Monterey Bay.

Endless Appetites

Otters eat a lot. Almost alone among marine mammals in cold water, sea otters are not layered with thick blubber. Without this insulation, they rely on two things to stay warm: their luxuriously thick fur and a voracious appetite. An otter has a metabolic rate about three times higher than that of a similarly sized dog and will consume about one quarter to one third of its body mass each day, or 15 to 20 pounds for a 60-pound animal. Not eating for a day drops their weight about 10 pounds. Losing 25 pounds will kill them. So otters need food—plenty of it—all the time.

A variety of marine shellfish can provide this bounty, from sea urchins and abalone to crabs, octopus, and snails. Long-term otter watchers have found that many individuals specialize on certain kinds of prey, some refusing all but abalone meals, some searching diligently for scarce sea urchins, with others being dedicated to dining on abundant but small turban snails. Whether the force of habit or some advantage to specialization drives these differences has never been determined.

No matter what they eat, otters try to never miss a meal, and a dense population can quickly affect the life of a kelp forest. Rolf Bolin used a healthy part of his published article about the rediscovery of the otters to catalogue their diets and eating habits: "Resting on its back and holding the food with its front paws, it proceeds in leisurely fashion to nibble or gnaw at it." Although later researchers covered this ground in great detail, Bolin's description provides the first account of the way sea otters interact with their environment. Before the twentieth century, otters were a source of fur. They hid out while the science of ecology grew. They reappeared when field biologists were just beginning to document the precise ways in which organisms could dramatically affect the species around them. Otters provided a textbook example.

Foragers and Bandits

Unlike their Alaska cousins, California sea otters regularly use tools. After a dive, they pop back to the surface carrying a tidbit snail or a frantic crab, also bringing along a handy stone. Lying on their backs with the hapless shellfish on their furry chests, they bash the shell with the stone until their meal cracks open. They scoop out the innards, drop the refuse, stone and all, then dive back down to snatch another snack. They also use tools to eat abalone, creatures that are

Coming back from near extinction, California sea otters *(Enhydra lutris)* returned to Monterey Bay in 1963 and helped restore the kelp ecosystem. Today about 2,600 sea otters can be found off California's central coast. *(Photo credit: Jim Capwell, www.divecentral.com)*

Top left: The Bay hosts a diversity of life, including vermilion *(Sebastes miniatus)* and kelp rockfish *(Sebastes atrovirens)* near Del Monte Beach, Monterey. *(Photo credit: Clinton Bauder, www.baue.org)* **Top right:** Blue rock-fish *(Sebastes mystinus)* in the kelp forest of the Point Lobos State Marine Reserve. *(Photo credit: Robert Lee, www.baue.org)* **Bottom:** California market squid *(Loligo opalescens)* arrive at night to lay eggs at Del Monte Beach, Monterey. *(Photo credit: Robert Lee, www.baue.org)*

Top: Once threatened by egg hunting and use of pesticides, brown pelicans *(Pelecanus occidentalis)* and Brandt's cormorants *(Phalacrocorax penicillatus)* are abundant in the Hopkins Marine Life Refuge, now expanded into the Lovers Point State Marine Reserve. *(Photo credit: Chris Patton, Stanford University, Hopkins Marine Station)* **Bottom:** Giant brown kelp *(Macrocystis species)* in the Pacific Grove kelp forest. *(Photo credit: Clinton Bauder, www.baue.org)*

Top: Pacific harbor seals *(Phoca vitulina)* historically avoided the coast because of intensive hunting. Today Hopkins' West Beach in Pacific Grove is one of California's largest colonies, with as many as 400–600 seals. *(Photo credit: Chris Patton, Stanford University, Hopkins Marine Station)* **Bottom:** Harbor seal *(Phoca vitulina)* near the Old Fisherman's Wharf, Monterey. *(Photo credit: Jim Capwell, www.divecentral.com)*

Top: Brown pelican *(Pelecanus occidentalis)* off the coast of Lovers Point, Pacific Grove. *(Photo credit: Jim Capwell, www.divecentral.com)* **Bottom:** Barnacles *(Balanus nubilius)* with strawberry anemones *(Corynactis californica)* off Point Pinos, Pacific Grove. *(Photo credit: James Watanabe, Stanford University, Hopkins Marine Station)*

Top: The Hovden Cannery was the largest sardine factory on Cannery Row and the last to close in 1972. Its derelict rooms gave birth to the idea of a Monterey aquarium. *(Photo credit: Steven K. Webster, Monterey Bay Aquarium)* **Bottom:** Kayakers paddle though the lush kelp forests off Pacific Grove and pause to observe an otter. *(Photo credit: Catherine Munsch)*

Top: The Monterey Bay Aquarium rose from the bones of the old Hovden Cannery and opened its doors in 1984 to nearly 2 million patrons. *(Photo credit: Jonathan Blair, Monterey Bay Aquarium)* **Bottom:** The Outer Bay exhibit at the Monterey Bay Aquarium brings the natural beauty and life of the open sea within reach of millions. *(Photo credit: Randy Wilder, Monterey Bay Aquarium)*

Top: A male orca *(Orcinus orca)* cruises the waters off Point Pinos, Pacific Grove. *(Photo credit: Jim Capwell, www.divecentral.com)* **Bottom:** Once known for whaling, Monterey Bay is now known for whale watching. A humpback whale *(Megaptera novaeangliae)* breaches in the Bay. *(Photo credit: Catherine Munsch, courtesy of Monterey Bay Whale Watch)*

all foot, hanging onto the rocks for dear life. Human divers need a crowbar or a stout diving knife to pull an abalone from its rock home. How does an otter do it? Ernie Porter, a local diver in Monterey, reported seeing the simple answer. Otters first find a grapefruit-sized stone. Then they find an abalone and pound it until the shell fractures, allowing them to easily pull the animal off the rock. Earl Ebert catalogued the condition of the shells of abalone brought to the surface by otters, and 80 percent had been broken.

Foraging takes up about half of an otter's day, usually the early mornings, later afternoons, and night. But during breaks, sea otters loll indolently among the waves and kelp fronds, famously rafting on their backs with their webbed back feet thrust out of the water. They raft in groups, grooming one another, quarreling, or caring for pups. Some serve as nervous sentries, floating vertically with their round heads bobbing up and down, their white whiskers framing a stern, blunt snout, their jet black eyes staring, unblinking, at any possible threat.

With curious, innovative brains, otters often come to explore a new sight in their world. Encountering a discarded glass bottle on the seafloor, an otter might well decide to pick it up to test its value. Using a bottle as an anvil to crack shellfish became a fad among California otters in the 1970s. Sucking octopus out of discarded soda cans also proved popular.

Otter societies are flamboyant and passionate, based on prolonged grooming sessions to tease out kinks in thick fur, and centered on largely same-sex groups of rafting animals. Young males form forag-ing parties to explore the edges of their territories. These gangs can be the vanguard colonists along new stretches of coast and can move into a new kelp neighborhood overnight to start pounding down the local shellfish. The rest of the population fills in behind. Through these forays, sea otters slowly left the strict confines of Big Sur and mile by mile moved up the central California coast.

By 1947, while Ed Ricketts brooded over sardine populations from his cramped lab on the doomed Cannery Row, the recovering otter population had bounded north to Yankee Point, south of Carmel. By then, 500 or so sea otters rolled and dove along the California coast, and the population looked to be expanding rapidly.

Fishermen along the shore regarded otters as marauding bandits bent on wiping out their supplies of abalone. Public meetings erupted with demands that otters be stopped. But where were they? Glimpses from shore teased the biologists but stopped short of delivering a perfect map. Hopkins graduate student Dick Boolootian had landed in Pacific Grove in 1952 from a stint as a fighter pilot, so he pursued a different idea.

Otters from Above and Below

Dick Boolootian was holding court in a little restaurant in Pacific Grove. We were meeting to talk about his days as a graduate student in Monterey Bay in the 1950s. Nearly 80 years old in the summer of 2007 and having retired from his professorship years before, Dick was compact and energetic. He'd brought along an unexpected entourage and was delivering instructions to everyone around him.

"No, you can't get up from the table. What? Drinks? Fine. No, you can't have the adult menu. Yes, go to the bathroom."

His cohort, a group of ten gifted middle school students, called him Dr. B and spent the next two hours testing the limits of their independence. "These kids are great," he said. "I have them for a week of science camp, on-the-road science camp."

Dr. B spends his summer introducing kids to science, hands-on. These ten, between about 10 and 12 years old, were bundles of energy. They occasionally paid attention to what Dr. B was telling me about otters.

"There was a lot of fighting over otters—they are extremely controversial creatures. Fishermen hated them for taking their abalone. Wildlife people were thrilled they were back. So when they were starting to spread up the coast, everyone wanted to know where they were, how many there were and what they were doing."

"Nobody really knew how many otters there were along the coast," he continued. "And I knew the commander of the big Army base at Fort Ord. The Fort Ord commander lent me a helicopter—actually landed at Hopkins to pick me up, and we traveled the coast photographing otters from the air."

Whack-whacking through the air above the rocky coves of the Big Sur coast, Dr. B encountered the otter population filling the coves and populating the kelp beds. He quickly saw that a luxuriant kelp bed usually was a good indication of high otter counts. But he decided that to get a better picture of otters, he needed just the opposite perspective: not from the air but from under the sea. So he shucked the helicopter earphones and grabbed a diving helmet, plunking himself down into the kelp forests off Carmel Point.

"It was one of those old diving suits, with a big old helmet, and me walking around on the bottom twenty feet deep. The bottom was covered by the skeletons of sea urchins and mounds of broken abalone shell. The otters were definitely eating their way through the area. But there were still abalone left."

Drying off and grabbing a camera, Boolootian then spent 10 hours each day during May and June 1956 monitoring the otters at Rocky Point, just a little south of Carmel. One of the first people to record otter behavior in detail, he watched a raft of fifty animals eat 5,280 sea urchins during that time, about ninety a day, cleaning out one sea urchin bed before moving on to the next. Abalone and sea mussels also topped the menu.

A few years later, with scuba diving possible, other students also swept through the area looking for signs of the otters' impact. Jim McLean logged about 20 hours underwater in 1959 and 1960 south of Carmel, noting that "one large invertebrate that might normally be expected was not found in the areas . . . the large sea urchin." The bottom, however, held abundant sea urchin spines and shell fragments. McLean knew why the creatures were missing: Otters had eaten them. Areas without otters were full of them, especially near the shoreline of the Hopkins Marine Station and China Point, which he called Mussel Point. He wrote, "The subtidal rocks in Monterey

Bay at Mussel Point at the depth of 10 to 20 feet are covered with urchins and abalones spaced only a few feet apart," explaining that "the otters do not range into Monterey Bay."

This is why there is such a connection between two such odd creatures, otters and giant kelp, and why the abundance of one parallels the other so strongly. The voracious appetite of the otter chews into the populations of animals that eat kelp—sea urchins especially— and so where otters go, kelp follows.

The next decade saw otters expanding north as far as Pebble Beach. By the early 1960s they reached the southern, exposed shores of Pacific Grove and were dipping into Ed Ricketts's Great Tide Pool. But now they were poised for a major change, a turn from the rough and rugged outer coasts, dominated by the pounding Pacific surf and dangerous winter storms, to the quieter shores and dense-packed larder of Monterey Bay.

Back at the restaurant, Dick Boolootian explained, "There were no otters in Monterey Bay in my time. They were still eating their way north, changing everything. Controversial creatures, otters. Very controversial."

The Oscillation

As the lights went out on Cannery Row in the 1950s, recovery of the bay began slowly. Canneries no longer dumped 100,000 pounds of fish entrails and other parts into the bay every day. No longer did the reduction ovens foul the air with the odor of burnt sardine. But missing too were the cannery jobs. And the question for everyone was, "Now what?"

Ed Ricketts had always thought the sardines would disappear, taking with them the economic lifeline of Monterey and the pollution of the bay. But Ed also thought that the sardines would soon come back. Such is the normal expectation of an ecologist thinking about a little fish with a prodigious reproductive rate and a short life span: Little fish with a large capacity to produce eggs can rocket back in abundance.

However, Ed's fishy calculus also tried to keep track of the bigger picture of the ocean environment and took into account that the ocean seemed to be changing in the late 1940s. Plankton abundances went haywire, and all manner of odd creatures floated ashore in the late 1940s. Something was happening in the ocean, and as the years clicked by after the sardine collapse of 1948, one season after another came and went without a return of the silvery fish that turned to gold.

Ed didn't know—no one did—that the changes occurring in the ocean in the 1940s were not fleeting. The whole Pacific felt a metamorphosis in those years that eventually was named the Pacific Decadal Oscillation. With a period of 20, 30, or sometimes 50 years, the northeastern Pacific Ocean oscillates between a slightly cooler phase when deep cold water upwells easily to the surface and a slightly warmer phase when upwelling is weaker. A reconstruction of the Pacific Decadal Oscillation charts its changes over the past 500 years, showing that these oscillations are not a regular ticking climate clock. Before 1850, the oscillations showed warm phases that lasted 50 years or so and occurred roughly every century (Figure 9.1). Though still uncertain, the cause for this older cycle may have been a slow brightening and dimming of the sun in a series called the Gleissberg Cycle. But after 1850, the warm phases became shorter and came along more frequently. The warm phase that created Cannery Row lasted only a few decades, from about 1920 to 1942—one of the shortest on record. It didn't turn warm again until the mid-1970s.

California sardines mill about in southern California until spring, then move up the coast toward Oregon and Washington. During the Pacific warm phase, the upwelling of cold water off the California coast lessens, creating warmer conditions that allow sardine feeding and spawning ranges to creep northward. Spawning congregations sit off central California during the warm phases, and when they are near the highly productive waters of Monterey Bay, the populations stay longer.

During cool phases, the upwelling currents intensify and colder water along the coasts tends to keep sardines a bit farther south. The Pacific Decadal Oscillation warmed the ocean steadily from about

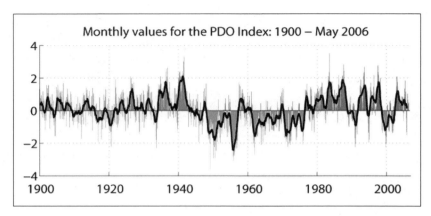

Figure 9.1. The Pacific Decadal Oscillation over the twentieth century, showing the rapid shift from warm to cool phases between 1942 and 1948 and the persistence of the cool phase until the late 1970s. Warm phases are positive in the index, and cool phases are negative. Warm phases are favorable to movement of sardines into north-ern waters near Monterey. (Source: Climate Impacts Group based on N. J. Mantua, S. R. Hare, Y. Zhang, J. M. Wallace, and R. C. Francis. 1997. A Pacific decadal climate oscillation with impacts on salmon. Bulletin of the American Meteorological Society.*)*

1920 to 1942, but after 1942 it took the fastest nosedive of its history, collapsing by 1949 to an index colder than anything that had been seen since the mid-nineteenth century (Figure 9.1). The sardines fled the flip-flop of ocean climate and did not venture north of south-ern California in any great numbers. The cold phase persisted for decades, resisting whatever natural tendency to increase the sardines might have had in the absence of fishing. And in the interim, the city of Monterey held an empty Cannery Row.

From the Ashes

Thanksgiving turkeys were in the oven, and Merilyn Derby Geor-gevich's was cooking away like everyone else's. Surrounded by friends and fellow teachers and artists, Merilyn looked downhill from her little house atop Prescott Street. The view was of a clear day with the tranquil blue waters of Monterey in the hazy distance. Cluttering the shoreline, like an abandoned playroom of building blocks, were the shells of the old canneries.

Suddenly, a siren sounded from down below, and a plume of smoke began to curl up from one of the vacant canning factories. In a flash, the gas mains of Cannery Row collapsed in a gout of flame. The gas supply to the whole hillside cut off as a gigantic valve slammed shut. Every oven died, and every turkey went from cooking to cooling. Thanksgiving was long in coming that year.

Fires in Cannery Row punctuated many days. The canneries had been emptied, first of the fish they thrived upon and then of the very equipment that powered them. The idle machines had been packed up and shipped to South America, where fish still swam and canneries could still make money. The skeletal remains of the buildings provided nothing anymore to the town or the people. Or the owners. A convenient fire or two could bring in serious cash from insurance, money that did not actually have to be spent on refurbishing anything on Cannery Row. If the canneries had insurance, that is. If not, an empty lot might be less troublesome than an abandoned factory.

Of course, fires commonly flared even when the canneries were busy; one burned down Ed Ricketts's lab in 1936. The hot reduction fires cooked fish products until they congealed and then dried, and these fires could get out of hand on a busy night when the boats brought in net after net brimming with fish. But idle factories also proved strangely prone to the contagion of fire, and over the years, as Cannery Row waited for a rebirth, one by one, the canneries burst into flames and then smoldered to ash on the shores of the bay.

Fifties Diving

"We used to have contests," Dave Greenfield said. "After school, we'd go abalone diving. The limit for abalone was five then. The winner was the guy who could get five in one breath. But back then, five in a breath was easy."

The self-contained underwater breathing apparatus had already been used by its inventor, film pioneer Jacques Cousteau, to explore the sea, but Cousteau's invention hadn't made it yet to Monterey. Besides, the local high schoolers wouldn't have had such an expensive item. Of course, they didn't have wet suits either, and they dove into the cold waters off Pacific Grove in their long underwear—three sets at least.

"We came out pretty cold," Dave said, his eyes widening out, head thrusting forward, and shoulders adopting a demonstrative shiver. Dave is a world-renowned fish biologist who left Monterey to pursue coral reef fish in warmer water. But he still remembered his first underwear dives: "All that cloth kind of slowed you down."

But things were changing fast in the late 1950s. "One day these guys who ran a car repair place in Monterey got a roll of neoprene." Dave said. "They were divers too, and we all went up there to see it. We used newspaper and made patterns for wet suits, laid out the newspaper on the roll, and cut out the pieces. Then we used that black goopy glue to seal it all together."

"We had to fight in and out of those suits by slathering up with corn starch," he said. "But it sure was warmer than my old underwear."

They went diving after abalone mostly, straining down through the emerald green waters, popping the big saucer-shaped shells off the rocks 10 to 20 feet deep, and letting them reattach themselves to their chests so that their hands were free for the next one.

"We went once a week I guess," Dave said. "I'd take one or two home, but some of my friends, I think, lived off abalone, taking most of what we caught back to their folks. It was thin times in Monterey for some of them."

An abalone grew large in the 1950s. Dave slid over an envelope that contained a single photographic slide taken of his buddy Nick holding the catch of the day from 1959.

"Nick's a big guy," he said, "so the abalone don't look that impressive. But I'm still in touch with him, and I got him to measure the length of his hand and the width of his head." Assuming Nick's head has remained a stable data point for the past four decades, the abalone clocked in at 10.4 to 11.5 inches.

"Legal size was six inches, I think," Dave said, leaving unsaid that no one would even consider taking such a midget. Today, of course, the only commercial abalone you can get in California are aquacultured— and are harvested at 4 inches.

Not only were they large in the 1950s, but abalone populated the underwater rocks as thickly as cars crammed into a drive-in movie. The deep rocks heaved with the flat snails, from the canneries toward the mouth of the bay, past the Hopkins Marine Station and out to Lovers Point and beyond.

"The area in front of Hopkins and Lovers Point were off limits to abalone divers," Dave said, "being part of the Hopkins Refuge and the Pacific Grove Marine Gardens." Decades after Julia Platt had set up the refuge and the gardens, the bay water of Cannery Row was finally clear of pollution, and abalone carpeted the shore of the Hopkins Refuge. There, the abalone even abandoned their fear of heights and crawled up the intertidal rocks to jostle one another for space out of the direct path of the waves.

The edges of the refuge were marked by the hordes of intertidal abalone. When not chasing otters, Dick Boolootian measured abalone reproductive capacity by sampling ten red and ten black abalone a month. "You just walked out and got some from the tide pools," he remembered. Asked whether anyone ever actually counted them, he looked quizzical for a moment and replied, "Nobody thought to— they were just all over the place."

Other big, bottom-dwelling invertebrates grew abundant too once the water began to regain its health, particularly the spiny purple sea urchin named *Strongylocentrotus purpuratus*. These animals hugged the lower rocks in wave-swept areas but put in their strongest appearance on the shallow seafloor among the holdfasts of kelp plants. A kelp holdfast secures the plant to the seabed and looks like an explosion of hot-melt glue, gone green and stringy, with a riot of kelp stems (called stipes by alga lovers) shooting up from the center. In the 1930s, an intrepid graduate student named Harry Andrews donned a diving helmet and counted the animals that lived among the kelp holdfasts in Monterey Bay. He generally found about 30 or 40 purple sea urchins per square yard, sometimes as few as 6 or as many as 100, along with dozens of other species.

Divers disdained the sea urchin fishery until the 1980s, and even then they concentrated on just one species, so these animals were unaffected by hunting and, unlike the abalone, could live outside the refuge with spiny impunity. They roved, and prospered, and ate. And by eating the kelp, nibbling away at its holdfasts and gnawing through stipes, they trimmed the giant kelp forests back year after year. Now, with the water quality improving, the urchins were thriving, and they ate the kelp forest.

Shells and Spines

If a crazy ceramic artist were to design life, the result might be a sea urchin. An urchin's intricate, globe-shaped shell accretes from a set of curved plates that lock together in a fragile armor of thin panels made out of white calcium carbonate. The tiny plates link up in rows that run from the south pole to the north pole of the shell, giving the structure a radial, Christmas ornament look. Hundreds of pairs of tiny holes penetrate this delicate crust in lacy lines, flanked by flat bumps and cones arrayed in five major, complex arcs from the south to north.

Each pair of holes serves a tube foot, the sea urchin's major appendage. Like a garden hose with a suction cup at the end, a tube foot snakes from each pair of holes to attach to food or rocks. A sea urchin has no brain, and a thin ring of nerves running in a circle around the mouth serves as its closest imitation of a central nervous system. So it is in brainless unison that hundreds of hose-like tube feet attach to rocks and pull and reattach, to haul the whole animal around the seafloor. The thinner, more delicate hoses on the top reach out to snare passing algae or, in some sea urchins, grab onto shells and pebbles to hide from passing enemies.

In live animals, each bump or cone on the shell supports a sharp, conical spine, held firmly at the base by a ring of untiring muscles and tiny tendons that keep the spine erect. Some species use tiny light-sensing cells to aim their spines at passing predators. The purple sea urchin of Monterey Bay holds it spines out erect and stable as a strong defense against simple predators such as snails and starfish.

Otters are undaunted by the spines and can get through them to open an urchin more easily than modern humans can open the packaging of a new DVD. Both hungry otters and frustrated DVD owners rely on brute power and clever pounding. Lying on their backs with an urchin and a rock, otters can pound through the spines and shell, scoop out the goopy innards, and be back on the ocean floor looking for more in less than two minutes. A few weeks after a new raft of otters arrive in a cove, the only urchins left are ones that live very deep or those that cram themselves so far into cracks in the rocks that even the sharp-clawed otters cannot pry them out.

A Bad Century for Kelp

By the end of the 1950s, Monterey Bay had largely cleansed itself of the waste and pollution of the 1930s and 1940s. True, the sardines had not returned, nor had the fishing economy. But the air didn't smell and the water didn't carry fish guts. Asked in the 1960s what might be done with abandoned and economically listless Cannery Row, John Steinbeck wrote sarcastically about what it would take to restore it to its former glory, demanding that "the rocks and beaches be stocked with artificial fish guts and scales" and musing evilly that "reproducing the billions of flies that once added beauty to the scene would be difficult and costly." But by the launch of the Space Race, the Cold War, and the Kennedy presidency, Monterey had shrugged away this polluted past.

But a different sort of race was still playing itself out under the clean waves. Although the life of the bay was improving, the community of sea creatures still bore a wound that had persisted for a century. Carpeted with sea urchins, the bay still resisted the return of luxurious kelp forests, and without them the ecosystem couldn't return to its normal state.

Julia's Refuge Pays Off

Like the pioneers and explorers of human society, otters that explore the edges of their world tend to be the young ones. Small bands of young male otters venture along the coast, seeking greener pastures under the waves. In their case, of course, they seek purpler pastures, or redder ones, stocked with purple or red sea urchins or red abalone. Even the earliest otter watchers realized that these quick and charming animals moved like a plague of locusts across the landscape, depleting resources in an area and then moving on. So it was no surprise that the first otters to round Point Pinos and enter Monterey Bay were a few young males, who turned the corner of California history in 1962.

As these youngsters paddled in from the Pacific, one place in particular must have been hugely attractive. Julia's Refuge at the Hopkins Marine Station was carpeted with an otter's favorite food: abalone. There were also huge mussels on the shoreline rocks, protected from being collected, and a carpet of sea urchins in tide pools. From their perspective it must have been like Jean de la Pérouse first entering the bay, seeing what he thought was the greatest concentration of wildlife in the world. Like La Pérouse, the otters knew what to do with this abundance: They started eating.

It wasn't long before more followed, and when they did, they came in droves. Just off China Point, a raft of seventy-five otters took up residence in April 1963, and they have been there ever since.

This was big, big local news. Isabel Abbott, Hopkins Professor of Phycology and the world's foremost expert on the algae of California, remembers that time. "Everyone wanted to get a look at them," she said. "And it became known that they tended to feed in the evenings between Point Pinos and the Monterey Harbor. Cars would line the road so that people could see them. They'd feed a while, and then wrap themselves up in a kelp blade for the night."

"Like pandas," she said with a wistful look, "sea otters are enchanting creatures."

These enchanting creatures took up residence at the Hopkins Marine Refuge and began transforming Julia's protected area back into the kelp forest it had been before otters were hunted. Where the 1930s and 1940s saw a polluted coast next door to one of the world's biggest canneries, clean water and sea otters re-created the ecological community that the area typically had. It took more than three decades for Julia Platt's stubborn advocacy to lay the foundations of this change, and maybe otters would have found an enticing home at Hopkins even if the shore had been stripped of abalone and mussels. But the shoreline was protected, the abalone were there, and otters made a beeline for it.

The Kingdom's Boundary

The ecological army of otters swept through Monterey Bay from south to north, the vanguard of young pioneers, 50–150 strong, finding abundant food and moving on. Where they found hard rocky bottom, they fed happily on sea urchins, and they left luxuriant kelp forests growing in their wake. But soon the moving line of sea otters found less favorable habitat: Wide sandy beaches stretched across the middle third of the Monterey Bay, bare of algae and shunned by sea urchins and abalone alike. So otters made do with feasting for a time on pismo clams and other sand dwellers. But the phalanx moved quickly northward in order to find rock once more. There the pickings were not as good: A disease of sea urchins dropped their numbers in 1976, and divers had long since cleaned out the abalone.

To the north of Santa Cruz stretched another long rocky coast, replete with otters long ago but now brisling with urchins and heaving with abalone in the coves where divers did not go. A rough stretch of shoreline, it also housed a growing population of a far larger marine mammal, the elephant seal.

Here the otters could not cross in any numbers. Despite a few individual animals leaking north to the very gates of San Francisco Bay, an abundant otter population has never gotten a beachhead far north of the elephant seal island of Año Nuevo. Could the two-ton seals be intimidating their tiny marine cousins? "Probably not," thinks otter expert Jim Estes. He points out, "There is a little colony of otters pretty persistently right next to Año Nuevo. They don't seem to be incompatible."

But otters have been stalled at Año Nuevo for decades. Why? No one knows for sure, but Estes has a theory.

"Hundreds of otters have washed up dead along that coast over the years," he remembered. "And some of them look perfectly fine, perfectly normal. It is only after a detailed necropsy that you see what killed them—a line of puncture wounds, or a bone scraped by something razor sharp."

Sharks. Great white sharks attracted to the bonanza of an elephant seal rookery also nibble on otters in quiet moments. "Of course, they could bite them in two," Estes admits. "They can bite a seal in two. They could bite me in two." But the otters are seldom dismembered.

Few people venture into the water at Año Nuevo to look for otter habitat, but one person who did just that in the 1970s was John Pearse. "It was awfully murky," he recalled, "and you just knew it was not a very good place to be. Bad visibility, dim light, and there goes a decapitated seal carcass floating past you."

"But a little deeper, when you could spare looking around you all the time for what ate the seal's head, there were walls of abalone, and a bottom covered, just covered, with sea urchins."

"I don't know what it's like now. It was a bad place to be, and we never went back."

Jim Estes is a little more clinical about the impact of sharks. "It's like they do with humans. Great whites bite down a little, and then release something they don't like, like a human. The otter is punctured—it dies. But it isn't dinner, or even an appetizer. It's spit out like a moldy grape."

It may well be that white sharks, mostly intent on feeding on big seals, have set the limit on otter expansion, keeping them from moving north past the seal rookeries. But many other aspects of California's kelp forest ecosystem shift near San Francisco Bay too. The abundant perennial giant kelp gives way to beds of stringier, annual bull kelp, changing the dominant "trees" in the forest.

Whatever the reason, the rapid northern expansion of the sea otter slowed after the repopulation of Monterey Bay. The expansion left behind a string of changed shorelines and a restored bay. Where there was once subtidal rock bristling with urchin spines, there now bloomed kelp forest with sea urchins and abalone restricted to crevices in the rock. Where kelp bloomed, there now thrived a bustling community of fish and invertebrates. And where these communities churned, the next layer of sealife began to reappear. The seals and sea lions and seabirds came back.

Chapter 10

Kelp, Seals, and Seabirds Rise Again

IZZIE ABBOTT has always been a small woman of large stature, with laughing, no-nonsense eyes and a matter-of-fact knowledge that's yours for the asking. She was born and raised in Hawaii, and her passion and her fame were wrapped up in the algae that grew profusely along the California coast. Some of these algae grew in the intertidal, and a trip during low tide to the Hopkins shore, always under the protection of Julia Platt's refuge, could provide a bucket of new specimens.

She had arrived as a lecturer at Hopkins in marine algae while Truman was in the White House, sardines were a legend, and the canneries were dying. Izzie had published renowned papers and accumulated an unprecedented storehouse of knowledge, eventually cracking the gender barrier at Stanford University by becoming the Department of Biology's first female full professor. But for collecting new specimens, the west beach at Hopkins was a favorite place of hers.

Facing into the sunrise, the shallow bite of beach lay pristine, like a sand canvas, when the tide left. Izzie placed a line of tiny footprints along it, marking the drift line where the night's waves may have deposited a treasure. "Some days it would be full of kelp tossed up from just offshore. Some days it would have very little." Those footprints marked the beach as the years turned from the 1950s to the 1960s, and the fortunes of the bay turned too. The day in 1963 that the otters came back was a day like any other for Izzie. But the huge kelp—the massive trees of the offshore forest—from that day on grew thicker, and more permanent, and forever different.

Students at the Hopkins Marine Station looked out over China Point in amazement as it was transformed. John Pearse's recollection of his first time underwater echoed the studies of Jim McLean. "The bottom was a sea of purple, covered in urchins, and you couldn't walk in the intertidal without stepping on black abalone, they were stacked on top of one another. The only kelp forest around was over at the Hovden cannery and grew off of old pipes, out of reach of the urchins." At the time, the refuge had no kelp forest because there was no place to attach to; urchins bulldozed every last square inch of the rocks.

The first signs of the change in the refuge were seen a mere six months after the arrival of the otters. In the winter of 1963–1964, Izzie Abbott and colleagues at Hopkins noted massive sprouts of a kelp forest in the refuge. They agreed that it had never been so thick in their years of observing the coastline of the peninsula.

The Forest of Algae

In the spring and summer, giant kelp grows so quickly you can practically hear it expand. The cold deep waters of the abyssal Pacific

Ocean well up to the surface in Monterey Bay, bathing the kelp in chilly water infused with concentrated nutrients. By early spring, the upright fronds, carried toward the sunlight by small football-shaped gas-filled floats, grow to strike the surface and begin to coil and spread out. A thick canopy of photosynthetic cables slips and slides in the waves like a carton of serpents, capturing the light and leaking a cool green glow down into the forest below.

Stipes and fronds of the giant algae form safe chambers for thousands of juvenile fish to live and grow, eventually venturing out to take up adult residence in the forest world. Even filter-feeding mussels and barnacles thrive on the bounty of the kelp, sipping the complex sugars leaked from the algae and gorging on the plankton that grows in the canopy. Deep beneath, an algal understory of short-tufted species carpets the bottom with iridescent reds and crisp greens. Too delicate to live where the light is not softened by the canopy overhead, these types disappear beyond the edges of the kelp forest.

Vast numbers of other species benefit from extensive kelp. Charles Darwin, taking a holiday from inventing evolutionary biology, wrote in his 1845 description of the voyage of the *Beagle*, "The number of living creatures of all Orders, whose existence intimately depends on the kelp is wonderful. . . . Amidst the leaves of this plant numerous species of fish live, which nowhere else could find food or shelter."

The Classroom in the Forest

By 1970, otters had placed their stamp on the kelp forests of southern Monterey Bay, especially the shorelines near the Hopkins Marine Refuge and the old canneries. John Pearse and Lloyd Lowry ventured underwater at Hopkins in 1971 to carefully map both urchin and abalone populations. They found them readily, but the heavily shelled and armored urchins and abalone had jammed themselves in cracks and crevices. Instead of marauding over the seafloor looking for food, they subsisted on the algae that drifted to them on favorable currents.

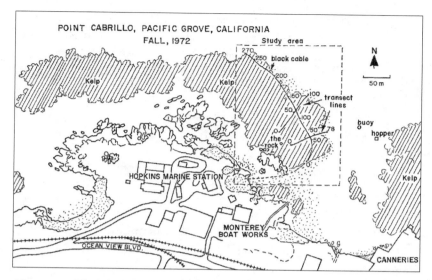

Figure 10.1. The kelp forest returned to Monterey after the sea otters came back. This drawing from John Pearse and Lloyd Lowry shows extensive kelp forest as early as 1971. (Source: L. Lowry and J. Pearse. 1973. Abalones and sea urchins in an area inhabited by sea otters. Marine Biology *23:213–219.)*

But now algae were no longer hard to find: The kelp beds bloomed after the otter invasion, and by 1972 they had spread across the whole of the Hopkins Refuge and beyond (Figure 10.1). By then John Pearse had a new job: one of the early faculty hired at the brand new campus of the University of California at Santa Cruz. What could be better than to bring students to Hopkins, launch them into this new habitat called the kelp forest, and let them see how it functioned?

"I found a cable out there," John said. "The Navy had laid it as part of a listening post during the fifties, before the kelp forest was there." John immediately saw how useful this was, and he treated it as a guide—like the banister of a set of stairs underwater—to measure and map the kelp. So a scant eight years after the otters returned to Monterey Bay, the kelp forests had bloomed to such an extent that they were an obvious classroom.

Some marine species have this special property: They are so profuse and abundant that they create the habitat for many other species. These architecture species, such as corals, sea grasses, kelps, and oysters, play a huge role in marine ecosystems by building the cities that other species depend on. The cities of kelp in Monterey attracted new tenants: large schools of fish. And this created a good environment for seals.

Seals Come Back

In March 1967, for the first time in more than a century, six frightened Pacific harbor seals lumbered onto the rocks of China Point. Their ancestors had been taught to be notoriously shy of the coastline by generations of hunters. By the end of the nineteenth century, sealers had dropped the California population to only a few hundred individuals, and these had learned to distance themselves from human fancies and furies. The 1972 Marine Mammal Protection Act folded harbor seals into its protection of dolphins, whales, and sea lions. As a sign of the law's success, by 1979 more than fifty harbor seals draped the rocks off China Point like a flotilla of sausages left by the tide.

The seals needed quiet—from fierce waves and curious humans. China Point provided both, and because they were protected from hunting and from even casual beachgoers, seal numbers climbed to more than 100 by 1990 and more than 500 by 1997. Many of the new seals were females, turning the beach from a male-only social club to a productive nursery. In spring 1997, at least thirty moms gave birth on the refuge's beach, the first pupping to be witnessed in Monterey since California belonged to Mexico.

The Hopkins Refuge at China Point probably became home to a major seal population for two reasons. The first is that its waters are calm compared with beaches just outside the bay on the outer coast. Yet these quiet refuge beaches are close enough to the rocks and deeper canyons of the bay to provide good forage. Opportunity rules the diet of a harbor seal, and they will crunch through crabs, pursue schooling fish, and take a bite out of hiding halibut and flounders. Although they range widely through the bay for food, the second reason for their return to the beaches of China Point is the return of the kelp forest and all the species that thrive within it.

Ocean Dominoes

No one documented these reasons when the seals showed up; the link between otters and kelp had just been proposed by Jim Estes and colleagues in 1974, and the connection between healthy kelp forests and seals has not been rigorously proven. Yet the hundreds of seals on the Hopkins beach chose this stretch of shore above all others.

Visible here perhaps is another domino effect of Julia Platt's legacy. Her protected shore accumulated abalone; the otters took up residence there, ate the herbivores, and gave the kelp a chance to grow; the fish community diversified and rebounded; and the seals moved in. The scientific literature reports myriad such cascades of ecological effects on land and in the ocean. The removal of sharks by the world's fisheries has let ray populations bloom in some estuaries, and the rays have eaten the scallops there. When herbivorous fish are removed from coral reefs, the resulting bloom of algae smothers the corals. Other links are more surprising. When seabirds were removed by hunting on Alaska islands, the grass populations changed, because it turns out that the grasses relied on fertilizer from the guano from the seabirds.

But all these changes show the ecosystem collapsing one link at a time. The *reconstruction* of an ecosystem, link by ecological link, is seldom seen in the modern environmental narrative. Julia's protected areas may have been one of the catalysts for such a construction cascade in Monterey Bay, although many other elements also had to fall into place.

Scrambling for Advantage

They look like a cross between a penguin and a tiny stork—thin, black, regal birds that fly underwater as easily as they fly above it and pluck fish out of the sea like a pair of tweezers with sharp eyes and paddle feet. On land, cormorants cluster on offshore rocks, making simple shallow nests, overloading them with several eggs and chicks. Even when not in the family way, cormorants loiter on the rocks, drying their wings in the sun because, unlike other seabirds, they do not have oil glands to keep their downy feathers dry. Their real estate stands out along the shorelines, glowing starkly white against a slate-colored sea because of the deep layers of chalky guano left by the birds.

The cormorant population in central California is a big one, with small roosting spots such as Bird Rock at the Hopkins Marine Station but also with a few big centers. If the length of the Big Sur coast is a line of cormorant highrises, then cormorant San Francisco lies about 20 miles offshore among a cluster of gigantic granite monoliths called the Farallon Islands. And cormorant Los Angeles lies to the south, on the Channel Islands offshore of Santa Barbara.

Their tendency to nest in large colonies makes exploitation of seabird eggs a very economical business. Not just cormorants but other abundant seabirds, such as the penguin-like common murre, nest in huge groups on isolated rocky outcrops. The Farallon Islands, though 20 miles offshore in rough seas, attracted a pack of egg collectors in the 1850s, a business that grew exponentially after the California Gold Rush brought an influx of hungry would-be miners to the mainland mountains. Across the 45 years of this business more than 14 million eggs from common murres were taken from the Farallons, a devastation that dropped murre numbers from an estimated 400,000 birds in 1860 to a few thousand in 1920. Other birds, though not used for egg collecting, also suffered from this business. Gull eggs were smashed because gulls were predators of other seabird chicks. Cormorants fled their nests during the destruction; both Brandt's cormorant and the larger double-crested cormorant plummeted in numbers from tens of thousands in the 1800s to less than 3,000 by the turn of the century.

The Farallon Islands were a different place after the egg hunting of the Gold Rush, with bird populations only a thin ghost of their former abundances. Yet other environmental problems arose after the Farallon Egg Company closed its doors in 1881. Four lighthouse keepers and their families occupied the islands after 1855. Oil tankers began visiting San Francisco after 1900, regularly flushing their tanks close to the Farallon Islands. The demise of sardines removed a vital food supply for some birds, especially double-crested cormorants and tufted puffins. And all along the coast, a very different specter stalked seabird populations in the 1950s and 1960s. That problem also damaged other bird populations across the United States and the rest of the world, and required a massive shift in the pesticide industry to solve. That problem was DDT.

Silent on the Sea

In September 1962, when otters had approached Pacific Grove but were still circling for their landing there, an environmental earthquake took place that would ripple across the entire country and help yet another stage of the restoration of Monterey Bay. Rachel Carson published *Silent Spring* that month and launched the western environmental movement.

DDT had silenced the birds, in some cases by destroying their insect prey and in other cases by thinning out their eggshells, causing them to crack and fester. Until then, DDT was to agriculture what penicillin was to medicine. In fields and alongside roads, farmers and public health officials sprayed this wonder drug in vast quantities, to kill insect pests, clear malaria-infested swamps, and increase farm production. It held two other advantages as a commercial pesticide: Companies found it cheap to manufacture, and it was slow to decay.

DDT enters the marine food chain through runoff from agricultural fields and from chemical dumping. Near Los Angeles up until April 1970, so much DDT was sneaked into sewers by chemical companies that the marine sediments in front of the city were choked with the stuff, demanding an EPA Superfund designation. Robin Burnett, a graduate student at Stanford and one of the future designers of the Monterey Bay Aquarium, discovered this DDT plume while researching his Ph.D. thesis on the toxic load found in beach crabs.

The industrial advantage of slow decay created a biological time bomb: The chemical built up year after year inside animals and plants, from plant to herbivore to predator to top predator. Moving up the food chain, from lowly sardine to the highest predators, the metabolic byproducts of DDT build up to the point where they became deadly toxins. For fish-eating birds, this buildup made eggshells so brittle that they cracked. The embryo inside died.

By the late 1960s, southern California seabird colonies looked like the abandoned Cannery Row of Monterey. Almost no baby California brown pelicans took wing in 1969, in once-thriving rookeries of the Channel Islands, part of a national trend that Gress and colleagues write about quite bluntly: "All Brown Pelican colonies in the United States and north-western Mexico produced thin-shelled eggs in 1969 and 1970." Double-crested cormorants suffered the same fate. Populations, deprived of a generation of new chicks, collapsed in the 1960s and early 1970s.

Ticket for a Return Flight

Solutions were slow in coming. The key in the Farallon Islands was to prevent egg hunting and limit access to the islands. The area is now fully protected against all exploitation, and national legislation such as the Migratory Bird Act helps keep it that way. Few visitors are allowed under the management provided by the Point Reyes Bird Observatory, and some of the bird populations have rebounded strongly because they have been left alone. Likewise, legislation halted use of DDT in the United States in 1972, and slowly, eggshell thinning receded as a major environmental problem. Populations of some birds have rebounded. Today, back from near extinction, brown pelicans fly in V-shaped formations again over Monterey Bay, their prehistoric, pteranodon heads belying their grace and poise in the air.

A steady comeback of cormorants is harder to find. They were probably extirpated from near-shore rocks when the Chinese village boomed along the Hopkins shore. Glimpses of offshore boulders such as Bird Rock in the Hopkins Refuge in photos from the late 1800s do not show the stark white coating seen today. But later, the birds may have thrived during the cannery era. In September 1925, the S. S. *Cleone* foundered on the rocks near Hopkins, and a photo of the wrecked ship shows Bird Rock chalked with guano and home to cormorants.

The canneries may have been an ironic boon to some of these seabirds. Seagulls, which delight in dining in garbage dumps, probably feasted on the offal from the canneries. Many accounts record that dense flocks of noisy gulls resided in and among the canneries, roosting on the roofs. Aerial photos from the 1930s and 1940s show huge numbers of seagulls, highly visible as white dots, floating among the pollution tracks in the waters in front of the canneries. But other birds are more finicky and may have been seriously harmed by the massive effort in Monterey. Double-crested cormorants on the Farallons were never burdened by the DDT levels they absorbed in southern California. But nevertheless, their numbers did not recover like those of the smaller Brandt's cormorant.

A diet analysis suggests why: Double-crested cormorants, being bigger birds, ate bigger fish, such as the sardines that formed the heart of the Monterey fishery. Having been decimated by egg hunters in the mid-1800s, their recovery may have been thwarted by the decline in their food supply as the fishing fleets took a larger and larger fraction of the available sardines. Once the fleet crashed and the ocean climate changed, anchovies, not the bigger sardines, took up position as the California coast's most abundant fish, and these did not venture as near to the Farallons. Today, the double-crested cormorant is still at low numbers on the Farallons.

May Day Is Lei Day in Pacific Grove

"You can make flower leis out of almost anything," Izzie Abbott said. In 2008, she sat cocooned by her beautiful Hawaii house, where she had settled after retiring from Stanford and after the death of her zoologist husband, Don Abbott. The house erupted with flowers and plants of all kinds.

In the warm breeze of the late morning, amid the cooing of the doves, Izzie was thinking hard about Pacific Grove, thousands of miles of open ocean, four and a half decades, and another career away. "In the '60s, I'd collect algae at Hopkins, but at all the other beaches too," she said, because other beaches caught the algal waifs from deeper in the bay. "Some mornings I'd pop up, about 7:30, after collecting near the Monterey wharf, and go see what the fishermen had for our dinner that night."

She laughed. "There weren't too many fishermen, and we all knew one another. Me, the little crazy lady out in the dawn with a bucket of seaweed.

"They'd complain to me if there weren't enough seaweed to wrap their fish in, but they'd slide a fish into my bucket anyway. A rockfish or a cabezon."

The fishermen saw this one value in algae, as a wrapper, but Izzie saw many others. Born of deep Hawaiian traditions, Izzie looked at plants the way a master carpenter looked at well-used tools: as irreplaceably useful and beautiful things, fabulous in their own right but possessed of a utility that careful husbanding could unleash.

"My mother taught me that," she remembered. "It's part of my nature. My mother told me you must love the plants around us because they take care of us and feed us." Making flower leis in childhood, she transplanted this skill to Pacific Grove, making leis of *Digi-*

talis, *Geranium*, and *Fremontia*. "Those only last an hour or so," she admitted. But from their construction, a world of knowledge about their shape and color and architecture would flow. By stringing together the strands of tiny, delicate flowers, you can look closely at each element, understanding and appreciating it. And you can see how they all fit together into something that is more than the individual parts. Not just a collection of reds or blues, but a flower tapestry that has a delicate beauty, and, like a complex jigsaw puzzle, it gifts you with joy in its completion.

So, too, the story of the ecological tapestry of Monterey Bay became clearer and clearer as the elements were reassembled, they began to work together, and the whole picture, as opposed to its simple parts, emerged. Researchers finally could see a major piece of the puzzle, long absent: Otters were back, bringing with them a kelp forest that hadn't been seen for centuries. Previously, the bay had functioned as an ecosystem, but it had been a wounded one, limping along for decade after decade.

Many elements had been there, except otters, but many of the elements were tipped out of balance because of the thin kelp forests or because of the industrious depletion of whales, seals, abalone, squid, sardines, and anything else that yielded to the commerce of the sea. It was like a lei without the full strand of plump flowers or without the ends tied together in a loop that would fit comfortably around a neck or cradle a head. The bay had been damaged for centuries. It was now healing again.

Chapter 11

The Aquarium

T HE CITY FATHERS of Monterey puzzled over what to do with their rusting neighborhoods and dead canning business. By the 1970s, the fire of a possible rebirth had been started several times, always to sputter and smolder like wet coals on a rainy Fourth of July. In large part, the city was going through the classic five stages of grief over the death of its past: denial, anger, bargaining, depression, and finally acceptance.

Denial was common at the end of the sardine era, of course. Fishermen and canners alike declared, "The sardine is inexhaustible," while the fishery scientists logged statistic after statistic that painted the fishery's doom.

Anger flowed as the canneries closed, and thousands of people lost their jobs. "What would Monterey be like without a fishing industry?" demanded Hovden Cannery manager W. O. Lunde.

The bargaining phase began with the first Monterey tourism

development plan, in 1963, when the idea emerged to turn Cannery Row into a sort of nostalgic tourist attraction, full of the warm glow that Steinbeck's *Cannery Row* had bequeathed to the region. Hovden Cannery's W. O. Lunde reasoned that the canneries should not be continued for their own value, but they "need to stay open because visitors wanted to see a working waterfront." In *Travels with Charley* Steinbeck observes, "They fish for tourists now, not pilchards." The idea faltered when tourists showed up wanting to see the places in Steinbeck's fictional world, not the real Monterey. They were looking "for Lee Ching's grocery, for Doc's Western Biological Laboratory, ... and the girls of the Bear Flag Restaurant." But those places never existed, and the reality was a mess of moldering wood and steel, plagued by fires and stripped of human activity.

Depression settled in and paralyzed Cannery Row for a decade. In the mid-1970s, conflicting plans and half-spun dreams never really achieved traction, and the Row decayed even more.

But Steinbeck had had the right idea all along, having prophesied in his remarks during the christening ceremonies for the street Cannery Row that a reborn Cannery Row could not grow from the bones of the old but only from a real transformation. Bold new architects and visionaries were at large in the world, he said; "I suggest that these creators be allowed to look at the lovely coastline, and to design something new in the world."

The fifth stage, acceptance, did not come until the "something new" was born. Ironically, that "something new" was first proposed by cannery entrepreneur Frank Booth, who petitioned the city of Monterey to build the "largest and best equipped aquarium in the world" in 1914. But it took a collapse and rebirth of the bay to breathe new life into this vision.

Four Friends in Monterey

The sunset was always behind them, casting the long afternoon shadow of a ruined cannery in front of four close friends on the

Monterey waterfront. But they didn't see the cannery's shadow; instead, their eyes sought the undulating top of the kelp forest, the seabirds that patrolled it, and the occasional sea otter. With the lights of the small city of Monterey in the near distance, Chuck Baxter, Steve Webster, and Nancy and Robin Burnett held court in the derelict Hovden cannery building. Just another Friday night party.

They were teachers and students of ecology and conservation, and they were the first generation at the Hopkins Marine Station to think that the recovery of the life of the bay was normal. Throughout the United States, the environment and the science of ecology were becoming an important part of the social culture, spawning national laws in the 1970s such as the Clean Water Act and national events such as Earth Day. Ecology as a research topic overtook the Hopkins station too, and there were suddenly more students diving in the new kelp forests than there were laboring in the old biochemistry labs. For the first time in a century, the ocean environment in front of the marine station was beginning to thrive, and the students of marine biology who worked there were in a golden moment of nature discovery. They relished this discovery, didn't worry about why the bay had recovered, and wanted everyone—*everyone*—to share their enthusiasm.

The giant Hovden cannery, ruined and vacant next door to the Hopkins Marine Station, crumbled bit by bit into the sea. "We knew it pretty well," Steve Webster remembers. "It was abandoned, and Hopkins owned it by then. For Friday night parties we'd break in."

Steve Webster and Robin Burnett were recent Stanford Ph.D. graduates. Nancy Burnett, married to Robin, was a daughter of Palo Alto industrial giant David Packard and had just finished graduate work at the California State University marine lab in Moss Landing, 20 miles away. Chuck Baxter taught the kelp forest ecology class at the Marine Station, a course made possible only by the return of the sea otters. The four had a deep love of Monterey Bay and the creatures in it, and they had the evangelical drive of the truly committed.

Nancy recounted a second connection to the cannery, as viewed from her office at Hopkins in Agassiz Hall. "Robin and I shared an office in the middle of the top floor of Agassiz and we looked at Hovden cannery all the time, worrying about what was to become of it."

Built long before building codes, Hovden's cannery had been added to, burnt down, built back, and let rot from 1911 onward. The building had been built so haphazardly that the pilings meant to prop it up over the rocky shore were nothing but old railroad rails cemented into the granite outcrops and intertidal channels.

"They were rusted out so much," Steve recalls, "that I remember one that had corroded in the middle, down to about an inch thickness, barely holding up that building. Some had rusted all the way through and the stalactites and stalagmites of the iron rail met with a foot of air in between."

Graduate student parties wheeled around on top of an old sardine tank, situated at the back of the building, with a good view through the wrecked walls to the bay beyond. "It was about where the Portola Cafe is now at the Aquarium," Steve recounted. "We knew the whole ghost cannery. The old cutting rooms, the fish meal reduction ovens—all wrecked, all falling into the ocean."

One night, Robin Burnett proposed building a restaurant there, with an aquarium in it, like the one they all knew on Monterey's Fisherman's Wharf. Nobody liked that idea. But these four friends tried on the clothes of other dreams and spent so much time imagining the future that exactly when it was born is no longer clear.

"There was a weekend we had at Robin and Nancy's house in Carmel Valley—and many pitchers of Margaritas," claimed Steve Webster. "The Monterey Bay Aquarium swam out of those pitchers."

Loose in the Candy Shop of Marine Life

"The real idea of an Aquarium, I don't really remember who said it first."

Steve Webster is a teacher. When we met to talk, it was after a long session he had just run for the volunteers at the Monterey Bay Aquarium, something he did weekly, for fun, after retiring from the post of education director there.

"It's what I like, what I really am," he said. "I could've been perfectly happy in my standard college job at San Jose State University. But I got tenure and almost immediately quit to help build the aquarium idea." That was in the late 1970s, a decision that launched him on a lifelong relationship with the aquarium and with marine education in Monterey.

"There is just so much here in Monterey. The underwater habitats, and the animals, and plants in them. We thought we should share it with those poor people who didn't dive." Steve said.

In the mid-1970s, Steve and friends were diving in an ecologically different bay than previous generations of students. Merilyn Derby had fled the beach after one swim with the fish heads and roiling guts of the 1940s. Jim McClean had described acres of sea urchins and abalone milling around thin stands of chewed-up kelp in the 1960s. John Pearse and his students had found the kelp forests restored in the early 1970s after otter populations revived. The next generation of students and teachers knew about all those changes, but they were the first to experience, the first to expect, the bay's new abundance. The wonder and beauty of the life of Monterey Bay had come back, and Steve and his friends were let loose in this candy shop.

"Almost immediately after we started thinking about an Aquarium, we knew it had to be about the habitats of Monterey Bay," Steve recalls. "And the life in them. What was there? Why was it there? What did these species do?" These were the questions they loved finding answers to, and the group launched into a process that could build a space where everyone else could share their enthusiasm.

The idea was both traditional and revolutionary. The tradition grew from Ed Ricketts's single strongest legacy: his book *Between Pacific Tides*. Ed had written it in the 1930s about the different habitats of Monterey Bay and of the Pacific coast. *Between Pacific Tides* was standard issue for marine ecologists of the time. The new aquarium would not be an overt monument to Ed or his book, but his thinking would be built into the very walls and pipes.

At the same time, this was also a revolutionary idea because the only two existing grand aquaria in the country at the time, the New England Aquarium in Boston and the National Aquarium in Baltimore, included few displays of local marine life, concentrating instead on magnificent coral reef exhibits or big sharks. The Baltimore Aquarium even sprouted a rainforest on its glass-covered roof.

The Monterey venture would be different. It was local. But would it attract? Steve and friends felt in their bones that it would. Others were not so sure.

The Marketing Study

Steve Webster describes the beginnings of the Monterey Bay Aquarium as a project for one of the West Coast's most influential foundations. About 1977, David and Lucile Packard were looking for a foundation project, and their daughters Nancy and Julie were both training in marine biology. It took a while for the right plan to develop, and when it did, it was in Monterey, not Palo Alto. And it was something a little more than they expected.

Nancy and her husband, Robin, conspired with Steve and Chuck to propose a Monterey aquarium as a special Packard Foundation project. They drafted a description and pored over different versions of it through the early part of 1977. Finally Nancy and Robin brought it to the foundation for a look. It seemed to hit a nerve, not only for the foundation but also for the family. It was sufficiently new and visionary to be interesting, and it seemed feasible. But the key questions about this project were the same as for any other that Hewlett-Packard might have launched: Was it practical? Would it thrive?

The first checks were written—not to buy anything but to hire a consultant at the Stanford Research Institute to study the idea of an aquarium in Monterey and gauge whether it would attract enough interest.

"Nobody could tell what would happen," insisted Steve Webster.

"It could go either way," agreed Chuck Baxter.

So Wrong and So Right

In late 2008, Julie Packard peered out her office window at the busy scene below, Cannery Row at the bustling center of a warm winter afternoon. Families towing small children hurried across the street, heading for shopping, snacks, or home. Clusters of tourists stood about, talking idly and planning their next moves. Halfway down the street, the way was blocked by a huge construction project: the next big hotel going in.

"I helped Nancy and Robin and Chuck and Steve put together the first proposal, the one to fund the feasibility study," Julie said, studying the scene below. "The study that was so wrong, and so right."

The Monterey Bay Aquarium has had only one executive director: Julie Packard has held those reins since before the aquarium opened. A graduate of the University of California's Santa Cruz campus, she had just wrapped up a degree in phycology, the study of marine algae, when sister Nancy and brother-in-law Robin broached the idea of an aquarium.

"But I wasn't, like, some incredible marine biologist," she insisted. "I was a botanist, that's what I studied, but just happened to work on algae."

"None of us particularly spent a lot of time at the ocean, until Nancy and I moved to Monterey Bay," she continued. "Our vacation place was in the Sierras. We didn't have a lot of coastal land, except for Rancho Grande. My father liked hunting and ranches."

"But my parents raised us to give back to our community in various ways. I was an environmentalist, and still am. Nancy too, even more intensely. And it was the huge Santa Barbara oil spill that galvanized my attention."

This spill caused a major shift in how millions of Californians viewed the ocean environment, Julie Packard among them.

The oil spill was more of an oil volcano. On January 29, 1969 one of the oil platforms six miles off the coast of Santa Barbara erupted. Having just drilled 3,500 feet below the ocean floor, workers were retrieving the pipe when a natural gas explosion ripped through the rig. Quickly capping the well, the workers stemmed the blowout but created so much pressure underground that five massive breaks in an east–west running fault cracked open deep under the sea. More than 200,000 gallons of crude oil leaked to the surface, spreading over an area of 800 square miles. Even Richard Nixon thought this was deplorable.

Julie took this event to heart. But the public reaction to even a major oil volcano didn't focus enough attention on the life of the sea: "It's taken the last quarter century or so to realize that the ocean deserves as much environmental attention as the land," Julie said, with a complex mixture of resignation, indignation, and hope.

"Letting people fall in love with nature, so that they come to care about it" was her mission for the aquarium, and it guides the way she directs the institution now. The Gulf of Mexico oil spill of 2010 dwarfs the Santa Barbara disaster and emphasizes the global scope of this goal.

The preliminary study by the Stanford Research Institute, funded in 1977 by the Packard family to gauge the viability of an aquarium project, came back positive. The gurus at the Stanford Research Institute thought that a major aquarium in Monterey might bring in as many as 300,000 people a year—enough for a viable project—and maybe grow to 500,000 visitors eventually. The cost would be $7 million.

It turns out that the institute was wrong. By the time the Monterey Bay Aquarium opened its doors in 1984, the Packard family had spent nearly $50 million on it. But more than two million patrons visited its stunning galleries in the first year alone, and it overturned everyone's assumptions about the ability of marine life to entertain, educate, and promote a city.

The Philanthropist

David Packard deftly avoids pigeonholing. Co-owner of a Fortune 500 company by age 50, he nevertheless sat on his local town school board when his children were young and played an active role at his alma mater, Stanford University, for four decades. He was an unusual tycoon with a strong social agenda. He wrote poignantly about a high-flying business meeting in the late 1940s at which the subject of corporate responsibility came up: "I was surprised and disappointed that most of the others . . . felt their only responsibility was to generate profits." David Packard felt a company had a duty to give back to its community.

But in addition, David Packard remained a highly conservative Republican. He relished his role as chairman of Richard Nixon's re-election campaign in California, and he served as a guiding member of groups such as the Hoover Institution at Stanford and the American Enterprise Institute. Week-long vacations with Herbert Hoover in Florida forged deep bonds between these personalities, cemented by fishing and talk.

After his acumen as a manager and administrator became widely known, David Packard took on a different role, in government, serving from 1969 to 1971 as deputy secretary of defense under Melvin Laird in Richard Nixon's cabinet. But David Packard showed a level of personal financial integrity that is hard to envision today. The many defense contracts held by Hewlett-Packard were well known. So he agreed to give up all income from his HP stock while he was in Washington, and he also gave away all the increase in stock value that accrued while he was in government service. This arrangement cost David and Lucile Packard about $20 million during his three years in public service. He dismisses this as being all too easy: "There were some charities I wanted to help." It is hard to imagine other government figures with major corporate wealth doing this today.

The Packard Family Foundation had been another way to give back to the community. Launched in 1964 with $100,000 in personal cash, the Packard Foundation grew to nearly $5 billion in the 1990s. It allowed the family to play a larger and larger role in the community of arts and science and in environmental conservation.

They believed that owning land, and how you used it, could reflect a person's philosophy about the future, a way of approaching life. Early on, David Packard, along with Bill Hewlett, bought ranches in California and preserved them as wild areas for hunting. These ranches served as a place to think things through in a different setting than a boardroom or an engineering lab. And they became emblems of David Packard's style. Soon after taking up his Washington post, David Packard brought a brace of generals from the Joint Chiefs of Staff out to one of his ranches so they could go hunting, so he could get to know them, and so they could get to know him. It was a no-frills place where everyone pitched in to cook or clean up. Packard's management style soon had the generals of the Joint Chiefs leaping up from dinner to do the dishes. And the all-inclusive style took hold as the new aquarium was being planned.

Making Waves

"Our notion was that everyone on the project should be able to see exactly what we were trying to achieve. That meant teaching the architects a lot of marine biology."

From a local bar stool, across the street from the Hopkins Station, Chuck Baxter launched himself into the past, trying to remember the early days of the Monterey Aquarium. A gentle bear of a man, Chuck tried mightily to keep a rein on exuberantly large eyebrows and a deeply genuine smile. Recruited to Stanford University in the early sixties to teach basic biology in Palo Alto, he ended up being an anchor at the Hopkins Marine Station for the group of four who, as a result of the positive Stanford Research Institute study and Packard family backing, had invented the Monterey Bay Aquarium and new careers.

"I had started teaching invertebrate zoology," he said, those eyebrows bobbing up and down with memory. "In the sixties or so. And one day Don Abbott at the marine station asked me to come down to Hopkins and teach a class there. It must have gone well, because then he asked me if I would move my whole teaching load down to Hopkins. After four or five milliseconds, I said YES."

That was in the early 1970s, when Steve Webster and Robin Burnett were still Ph.D. students at Stanford, working down at Hopkins occasionally.

"Robin got his Ph.D., and he and Nancy moved to the Carmel Valley house. We would go there a lot—or down to Rancho Grande to make the first aquarium plans." Rancho Grande was a 120-acre property on the Big Sur coast south of Monterey. A small house set back from formidable cliffs led down to the rough waves pounding the beach and gave access to the cold, wide expanse of the Pacific Ocean.

"We set up shop in the old Marine-o-stat building at Hopkins," Chuck said. "Nancy and Robin and I were there—and Steve was up in Palo Alto, at first hiring people and still teaching half time at San Jose State."

Of course there had to be a major central tank, but it would have a live kelp forest in it, not a plastic coral reef. "Sharing the beauty of the kelp forest was always a centerpiece of the vision," according to Nancy Burnett.

And that was a serious problem: "No one had been able to grow kelp before. Wheeler North tried it in pens, and they just grew stringy and weak," Chuck said.

But these friends knew the kelp forest from within its cathedral groves, from beneath its green-brown fronds, and they knew that it never stood still. Instead, it rocked back and forth with the passing of each wave, each individual plant stretching and contracting as the moving water passed by. Papers were being published on this idea—that the kelp was tuned all the way down to the very structure of its stems and blades to live with the waves. Maybe the kelp relied on the waves to grow correctly?

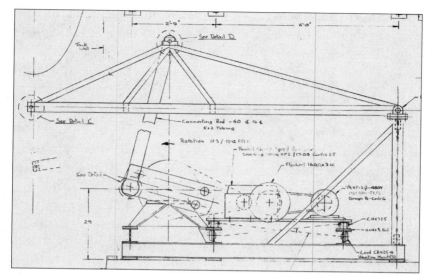

Figure 11.1. The original drawing of the Monterey Bay Aquarium's wave machine, co-designed for the kelp tank by David Packard, Derek Baylis, and Randy Hamilton. (With permission from the Monterey Bay Aquarium.)

We needed a wave machine, we decided," Chuck remembered. "Something to move the water in the kelp tank so that the kelp would grow thick and healthy. I think the architects at first thought we were crazy—crash waves into the tank to keep the seaweed happy?"

Crazy. And impractical too. No wave machine existed. Chuck remembers their consternation at trying to figure out how to get one designed and built. Then at one of the weekly meetings, David Packard spoke up, "Oh, I can do that. What kind of water motion does it have to deliver?"

A wave gizmo appealed to the engineer in Packard's past and was a new challenge to someone who built factories, offices, military planes, handheld calculators and ran a private forge for a hobby. Packard took the challenge to aquarium staffers, including Derek Baylis and Randy Hamilton, who built a series of ingenious prototypes and created the wave machine (Figure 11.1). The gears and levers power a plunging piston to create a periodic surge in the kelp tank. They fiddled with the strength and timing, and eventually got the kelp and the fish swaying slightly. The wave machine remains there today, sending surges into every corner of the tank. And the kelp love it.

Supervised

Dave Packard was not always simple to work with. "You sort of quaked in your boots sometimes," Steve Webster admitted. He met with David and Lucile and the rest of the initial aquarium team every week "for four years. No, six years." First they met in Palo Alto, and then when the design phase was in full swing they met in the first aquarium offices at Hopkins.

"I never really figured out what would satisfy him and what wouldn't," Steve said. "But there were signs. A really reliable sign was that he would spin his eyeglasses around if there was a problem."

We were talking one cloudy, chilly afternoon in November, in the same little bar where we'd talked to Chuck Baxter. The subject? Not the birth of the aquarium. Instead, what we really kept talking about was the embryology of the aquarium—how it grew from an idea in Robin and Nancy Burnett's Carmel Valley home, through various stages of development, and ultimately became the queen of public aquaria in the world.

"Every week, we had a meeting, and would lay out our progress. Every week there needed to be something new. He and Lucile might like it a lot—or not."

"One week we were presenting plans about the rock we would need in the exhibits, and how to create it," Steve paused a bit. "Fake rocks."

"So we were presenting the tally of how much fake rock we needed, some along the tide pools, some in the deep reefs. We could see something was not resonating with David."

"And those glasses started spinning. He'd hold them in his hand by one of the earpieces and spin and spin them. The faster it was, the worse it meant."

"Finally David burst out, 'That's enough fake rock. No more fake rock!'"

Steve's expression repeated what he must have felt at the time, a combination of alarm, chagrin, and an instinctive desire to please. He took a drink of the beer we'd ordered. "So that was that," he said in a resigned tone. But then Steve got agitated again, reliving the day. "The huge problem we had was, we hadn't even described the big kelp forest tank yet! And the whole back and sides of that were made of massive amounts of fake fake fake rock!"

"The four of us figured we had better regroup a bit. We settled on a six-week cooling off phase. We didn't bring it up again for six whole weeks and six whole meetings. But on the seventh, we presented the kelp forest tank designs, complete with fake rock, and it sailed through with flying colors."

"And no spinning glasses."

Monterey Reinvents Itself

The year the aquarium was born in the minds of Nancy, Robin, Steve, and Chuck, the same year they regularly snuck into the old Hovden Cannery for Friday night parties, the State of California reported a total income from sardine fishing of $580. During the seven-year period between the conception of the aquarium, in 1977, and the day its doors opened, in 1984, the state recorded landing about 50 tons of sardines, a catch that would have taken approximately an hour at the rates seen in the heyday of Cannery Row.

Clearly, the ocean was a different place than in the past.

By 1977, the city of Monterey had finally accepted the loss of its sardine industry. The air smelled sweet without the canneries belching burnt sardine, the water did not harbor swirls of fish heads and guts, the rocks were not covered by the fish scales and flies that Steinbeck complained about. Sardines were nowhere to be found, but fishermen had learned to live a leaner life on other species. The United States started to declare its exclusive right to the fish resources all the way

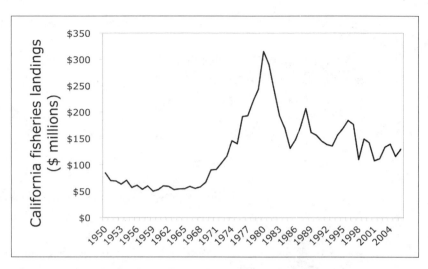

Figure 11.2. Commercial fishery income in the State of California from 1950 to 2006. (Data from the National Marine Fisheries Service.)

out to 200 miles off the coast. Kicked out of the area from 12 to 200 miles offshore, international fleets sailed away. Local fishing incomes were high again as the local boats mined the offshore seas for fish.

In 1977, tuna were the hot fishing commodity. The State of California brought in nearly $200 million in fishing revenue that year, half in tuna, more than any year since 1950. And fishing climbed in value almost every year until 1980 (Figure 11.2). Some of that climb included fish of the kelp forests and invertebrates of the coast, species that began to thrive in Monterey with the return of its native ecosystems. Even the kelp itself served as a resource, bringing in almost as much value each year of the late 1970s as fishing for the rockfish that inhabited its groves.

But success lined the pockets of fishermen for only a short time. By 1984, the statewide take had collapsed by 50 percent, mostly because offshore tuna fishing slid disastrously. The fishing industry brought only about $150 million in the 1990s and $100 million in the 2000s. In Monterey, the local catch topped out above $10 million in 1981, when

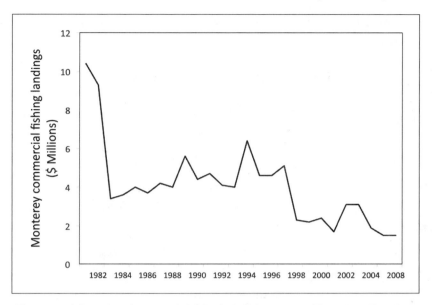

Figure 11.3. The value of commercial fisheries in Monterey and Moss Landing. Data from 1980 to 1990 are estimated from the value of the statewide commercial landings. (Data from the National Marine Fisheries Service.)

the statewide fishing picture was rosy, but as the fishing industry of coastal California waned between 1980 and 2008 (Figure 11.3), the local catch dropped to $4 million, then $2 million a year.

In the face of lackluster fishing, the entrepreneurs of Monterey finally admitted that future economic development would not just swim up to the dock. They turned instead to other industries, especially tourism, because across the United States tourism revenues had built a reputation for strong annual gains.

Of course, a focus on tourism echoed the efforts of Samuel F. B. Morse, operator of the Del Monte Hotel, and compatriots from 60 years earlier. But this new tourism was different. Instead of an industry built on grand resort hotels catering to tycoons and presidents, the new tourism of Monterey would center on families arriving for the day in packed station wagons. These middle-class visitors might stay a night in a motel, or they might just cruise up and down

Cannery Row and stop for a meal at a seafood restaurant on Fisherman's Wharf.

Here was born a new relationship between marine industries. Previously, tourism and fishing had been bitter foes. But fishing in the 1980s would not be allowed to obviously damage tourism, and the fishing lifestyle morphed into a cultural icon that was required to coexist with visitors who wanted to breathe the air and touch the water.

The Aquarium Opens

The first ballpark plan for the Monterey Bay Aquarium was a 10,000-square-foot facility built for about $7 million. Steve Webster does not remember when the floor plan or the budget was first exceeded, except that it was "early on."

"We had some pretty wild ideas—like a ring-shaped tank that would have all the different underwater habitats in a circular row, where the fish would know where they belonged and stay in their section."

"Obviously that wasn't going to work. The fish would never cooperate."

Another exhibit, the beach habitat, showed a typical progression of complexity and cost. First it was a simple strand of beach in a big flat tank. But then they decided it had to have waves, and David Packard designed that machine too. Then he said, "What about the birds? It has to have shorebirds."

So the simple flat tank with sand became an aviary with rolling wavelets and scuttering shorebirds of many species. "As long as we were true to our vision, we kept getting the go-ahead from David and Lucile," Steve Webster explained. The key was the basic aquarium mission: bringing the marine life and ocean habitats of Monterey Bay to people in a way that helped them see it scientifically and accurately but also captured their hearts. The three ingredients—science, accuracy, and passion—had to be mixed together.

The party the night before opening featured a sit-down dinner for 600 among the tanks. It featured the wildlife just getting used to their new homes and the clink and scrape of fine silverware on china. Among the gliterati of board members and VIPs and the builders and family friends, David Packard wandered away to stand wistfully at the rail of a small bar, built ironically atop the old sardine tank where his daughter Nancy and her friends had once had their Friday night parties. The view was the same, angled north toward Monterey's neighboring towns of Marina and Seaside, but the surroundings were much improved.

"You know," David Packard told the bartender that night, looking out at the view before returning to his dinner guests, "This is the most expensive bar I've even been to."

David Packard never hinted to anyone that the cost of the Monterey Aquarium was high. His restraint might have been based on success: The aquarium result was a stunning revolution in environmental education and entertainment.

What They Were There For

Julie Packard remembered the parade when we talked about opening day at the aquarium. Early that morning, the centerpiece of the event had marched down Cannery Row: a parade of high school bands and school kids dressed as starfish and other ocean creatures. The street, packed with people anxious to be among the first to see the new aquarium, could no longer pass any traffic whatsoever. Cars backed up for miles in every direction. David Packard's favorite music rose from a grandstand. Turk Murphy's San Francisco Dixieland Jazz Band played all day. Two mayors (Monterey's and Pacific Grove's) helped cut the ribbon, along with Julie. There was a speech by David Packard and a prepackaged proclamation from President Ronald Reagan. And then it was time to open the doors.

Too early.

It turned out that the speeches had finished 20 minutes ahead of time. Inside the doors, the animals and tanks were ready, but the cash registers and ticket booths were not. The aquarium was an educational tour de force, but it also was a business, and the business side was not quite ticking along yet.

What did they do? With the crowd ready and the ticket booths not? Julie said matter-of-factly, "We let them in. That's what they all were there for."

Chapter 12

The Century to Come

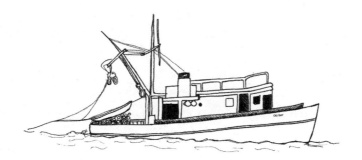

ONE OF THE things that fishermen like best about the sea is its rhythms. The tides. The phases of the waxing and waning moon. The marching waves that set across the ocean in packs. The sea's creatures have rhythms too, often tuned to the ebb and flow of light and currents and food. In Jean-Françoise de La Pérouse's time you could tell the season in Monterey by the animals that crowded the bay. Gray whales in fall and spring, dense salmon schools in May. Balls of mating squid in March and April. Schools of sardines in summer. These clocks still tick in Monterey Bay, though the signs of the seasons are softer than in La Pérouse's century.

Over the years, people have come to control some of the sea's rhythms. Fishermen still bow to the will of the deep, braving storms and chasing fish. But now human industry can change the oceans themselves, driving some species to near extinction and altering whole estuaries, bays, and seas. The story of Monterey shows how our actions, when out of sync with the natural rhythms of ocean life, can ruin that life. But it also shows that synchronizing with nature's patterns can help restore a bay.

The Phases of the Moon

Sardine fishermen have always adapted to the rhythms of their catch. Sardines display an ingrained aversion to bright light, cruising deeper in the sea when the moon rides high in the night sky. Fishermen soon learned that the harvest was best when only the tiny stars or the thick fog stood watch above the sea. When the moon was full, their boats could stay home.

So in 1933, when a group of Sicilian fishermen's wives began planning a festival to honor their patron Saint Rosalia, they decided to have it near her official saint's day, September 4, but not precisely on it. Instead, they "wanted to do it on the full moon so the men could participate."

Historian Carol Lynn McKibben describes the Festa Santa Rosalia as a particularly Sicilian event, conceived to bring together this community of Monterey fishermen and the wives who labored in the canneries. Santa Rosalia was the patron saint of Palermo, Sicily, someone whose intercession was invoked by a hundred wives as their husbands steered small boats toward a dangerous sea. The community used her feast day to celebrate the local fishermen and their catch. In 1952 the festival committee "rode in a decorated purse seine skiff." The sardine still reigned then, though they no longer rained on the canneries.

As fishing slipped in economic power, the festival slowly became a broader community event and changed its name to the more inclusive *Festa Italia*. It soon commemorated not only the people who fished but the fishing endeavor itself, and then the entire Italian community. Fishing is not absent from the Festa, but now the event attracts thousands of visitors to Monterey, and in the parade, the queen no longer rides a boat.

In September 2008, the queen of the seventy-fifth Festa Italia, a beautiful teenager, grandly entered Portola Plaza in a golden robe and a silver Lamborghini. The sun beamed down a smiling heat that lifted spirits all around fog-weary Monterey. Waving a bit sheepishly at the crowd of family, well-wishers, and tourists, she was followed a few minutes later by the statue of Santa Rosalia herself, clutching a skull and offering a wooden blessing. By then, there was only one boat in the parade, a small blue rowboat filled with smiling children and pulled on a trailer by a tiny tractor.

Across from Portola Plaza, named for the general who couldn't find Monterey Bay, a line of restored cars from the 1940s, 1950s, and 1960s proudly bounced the powerful sun off of chrome and polish. Everything about the scene was historical—the cars, the parade, the plaza, the former rail line that killed Ed Ricketts, now turned into a bike path—yet it was also updated, renewed.

The plaza teemed with visitors. The Festa featured traditional morning Mass, food, music, and dancing; with bocce bowling during all three days in Monterey. As always, among the tourists, the Festa brought out some of Monterey's traditional fishing families.

Gaspare Aliotti was avidly watching the bocce tournament when I was introduced to him. A solid, energetic man, he'd arrived in Monterey in 1951 in order to fish sardines and make a life here. I was puzzled by this: How could someone arrive so late in the fishery and still be welcomed in, with the boats going bankrupt, the canneries closing, and the fishing way of life in crisis?

Gaspare just shrugged and said, "Family. I came from Italy to help my father. I had family here on the boats." That's what it took, of course, the connection to family that opened a door for a new, young fisherman in 1951.

But there was perhaps another reason too. The 1949–1950 season was the last, great boom year for the sardines, a last flip of the tail. Nearly 131,000 tons were landed that year—maybe enough to lubricate a hope that the good times were returning. But in Gaspare Aliotti's first year, 1950–1951, the total catch was half that. By 1952–1953, the take for sardines all across the state was less than 300 tons, and it didn't get better for decades. Statewide, fishing was as poor an enterprise as it had ever been.

The boats still went out; some sardines could be had in Morro Bay a few hundred miles south. Gaspare said his boat had been based there, offloading the southern sardine catch into trucks. "I'd drive them north to Monterey in a truck," he said. "And deliver the sardines to the canneries here."

"And did you get full moon nights off?" I asked, joking about the legend of the Festa.

"Oh, yes," Gaspare said, to a chorus of general agreement from his friends. "Work five days from midnight to eight in the morning, then have Sunday off. But we got the two days before and after full moon off too. All the boats worked that way."

But no longer. "These new guys fish all the time—daytime, night time, full moon, whatever. They don't need to catch sardines close to the surface—they have deep nets—and those fancy fish-finders," said Gaspare. He wasn't criticizing, he was just a little wistful about how fishing had changed and how the rhythms of a lifetime had changed.

A roar went up from the bocce games, a surprise win that captured Gaspare's attention. This was now the heart of the Festa, the bocce tournament. There wasn't a sardine in sight.

Retrained in Restraint

The Festa parade was short and led directly to the national anthems of the United States and Italy. The festival celebrated an ethnic culture but also highlighted the history of Sicilian involvement in the fishing community. After the collapse of sardines, the Sicilian community persevered, and fishing remained a way of life. However, a change crept over the community during the decades in which the kelp forests bloomed in Monterey Bay, a change needed for the fishing industry to coexist with its stronger neighbor, tourism.

That change was restraint: Canneries could never again be allowed to destroy the environment because that environment was the heart of the new prosperity. Gone were the days when huge floating hoppers of dead sardines could sit anchored offshore or when tons of undersized fish could be dumped into the bay, or when a million pounds of fish could be pulped into fish meal in a single day by the intense heat of the reduction ovens.

It was not just the tides of overfishing that had come and gone. Gone too were the days the otters would be seen just as a fat profit in Canton. Gone were the summers when a half a hundred harpoon-hurling boats could plunder the gray whale along the California coast. Gone were the abalone hunters who could strip the coast of Monterey. Gone were the Monterey cannery owners who could thumb their noses at the stink in the air while fishing was good and then sell out the city and head south when the sardines fled.

Gone were the days that any fishery would be allowed to ruin Monterey Bay.

Today, no single industry can run roughshod over the environment that all industries share: the bay itself. Even tourism is shackled—by lack of fresh water for hotel rooms, lack of roads and parking, and a California Coastal Commission that withholds building permission from unsustainable tourist development. Fishing glowers under federal and state regulations that limit catches and control fishing grounds. Residents face increasing water use restrictions that frustrate plans for remodeling and new house additions. Agriculture has its own water use problems and must keep the groundwater free of pesticides and fertilizers. Even the military, given an environmental Get-Out-of-Jail-Free card in the form of immunity from most environmental laws, no longer maintains its biggest base (Fort Ord, now a California State University campus) near Monterey, going from supersized to absent landlord.

But these restraints, applied to all, also benefit all. At the same time that the ecological diversity and health of Monterey Bay have returned to the highest levels of a century, the economic diversity of the human community of Monterey also remains high. That economic diversity may well be a major factor in the current stability of Monterey's ocean life, because all the current economic players are currently in a rough, changeable balance.

The darkest days in Monterey were when one profitable business ruled everyone else's life: when a whale was worth a pound of gold, when the canneries could puppet the legislatures and the Fish and Game Commission. When economic might is too concentrated, it allows decisions to be made that benefit just one sector, to the detriment of others.

A Better Balance

Today, Monterey has achieved a better balance. That's not to say that juggling the needs of various industries, tourism, education, aquaculture, development, and fishing is easy. The current general plan for Monterey County was rewritten many times before competing interests were either satisfied or exhausted. But the tense conflict itself signals that none of the competing interests have overwhelmed the others, even though they want to.

Battles often play out in public meetings convened by the California Coastal Commission and the Fish and Game Commission. Starting in 2005, Fish and Game played a central role in creating a new set of marine protected areas. They have been so successful, in Monterey and around the world, that more are being planned all the time.

The protected areas also represent a balance between different uses of the same area, with decisions based partially on the biological reality of the way marine fish and invertebrates live their lives, but largely on the way people want to use the sea. Although the broad plans for California's new marine protected areas are firmly based in science, the details are tellingly human. And human points of view often differ.

Where Currents Clash

It was a pretty full room, a small auditorium in a nondescript California state office building that was nearly full of people with very different views of how to use small portions of Monterey Bay. The geography of the room was telling: Who you sat next to revealed a great deal about your point of view about restricting fishing in parts of the shoreline and the bay.

The Fish and Game Commission sat on stage, tasked with making the final decisions on what fraction of the bay (8 percent? 12 percent? 18 percent?) would face restrictions and, most importantly, what the restrictions would be. In 2006, two groups were vying for their own vision of the future of one tiny part of the bay. A long line of scuba divers faced a phalanx of fishermen over a plan to ban fishing off the Monterey Coast Guard jetty. Built in the center of the Monterey Harbor, in a place once oily with sardine offal and choked with oven fumes, the jetty had lately become a recreational magnet in the center of the city.

One by one, the scuba divers addressed the line of listening commissioners.

"Hundreds of divers get in the water there, every weekend."

"Dozens of scuba classes use that area, with the newest divers."

"I was on my first check-out dive when I got hooked by a fisherman casting from on top of the jetty. It's a hazard!"

The fishermen came next—just as numerous, just as passionate.

"It's the only place in the harbor you can fish—fishing everywhere else has been banned!"

"We only want 50 yards around the jetty to fish—the divers can have all the rest."

"Not many people get hooked, and no one has been hurt."

"You can't take it all!"

The commission was battered by these waves of opinion from both sides. Past commissions had sided with the strongest economic voice. And even longer ago, before commissions, the users of the sea had free rein to take what they wanted. This commission was trying to do something that had never really been done before: balancing very different uses of the same part of the ocean. Their problem was in how to decide.

Then one last, older fisherman stood and made his way slowly to the microphone, set off by itself in the back of the packed theater. Looking the commissioners in the eye as they sat on their tiny stage in front of the crowd, he said very slowly in a quiet room, "It's the only jetty with wheelchair access in the whole county. It's the only place that disabled veteran fishermen can go to fish."

As the man slowly made it back to his seat, the entire room erupted in applause; fishermen and divers alike knew when the winning card had been played. There was no arguing against disabled veteran fishermen. Fishing stayed.

But other arguments played out differently, and the Fish and Game Commission has been drawing maps of the California coast that change how people can use 10 to 20 percent of the coastal ocean. Fishing is restricted in about half of this 10 to 20 percent, and it is banned in the other half. Julia's marine refuge is now an official state conservation area, has doubled in size, and abuts a conservation zone named after Ed Ricketts. Open ocean conservation zones protect some deep canyons. Intertidal protection peppers the coast from the old Russian otter camp at Fort Ross down to the spit of land that Vizcaíno cited and named on the Feast Day of the Holy Conception: Point Conception. Every square yard has been argued over by citizens with different points of view. The process has taken years. It should not be done any other way.

The Next Battles

The sardine catch is controversial again in Monterey. In 2008, the state set short-term quotas and then stood back as the boats scrambled out of port to take them—20,000 tons here, 20,000 there. "Crab bait, that's all they're good for," was one complaint this year. "You couldn't wait till they were in better shape—you had to go get them when the quota was open."

The next controversy is likely to be fresh water, a resource that has been stripped from the coast as severely as whales or otters. When Portolà walked his 63 men and 200 livestock north from San Diego in 1769, he drove a pace that covered only 9–10 miles a day, but he stopped each night at abundant running fresh water. Today these fresh water sources have been co-opted by millions of California residents. The Carmel River, where Junípero Serra moved the Monterey Mission so that fresh water would be abundantly available, is now so overpumped by the local, private water corporation that the only trickle of water that runs in it in summer is squeezed from the old dams upstream for the sake of endangered fish and frogs. Would a return of fresh water restore this summer-dry landscape as dramatically as the return of otters? No one is sure, but water as a resource may be the next conservation frontier.

And the ultimate challenge to the life of Monterey Bay, and to the fragile balance between human economic uses, is the changing climate. How ironic it would be if Monterey Bay were brought back to life just in time for everything to be undone by warming water, acidic oceans, and raised sea levels (all the result of climate change). Already southern marine species are immigrating into the bay. Already the temperature has risen one degree, and sea level has gone up nine inches. A little to the north, in Oregon, climate changes have brought huge burps of deep water without oxygen to the surface, killing huge numbers of crabs and other sea creatures. And more change, faster change, is on the way.

The Heartbeat of a Living Bay

The history of Monterey has been built from the response of local people to such real challenges. They have summoned the nerve to see things the way they should be, not just the way they are, and to thumb their noses at obstacles.

Few of the heroes of Monterey felt that they were well suited to the task. Julie Packard was never trained as a marine biologist. Ed Ricketts solved the sardine problem as an extension of his personal philosophy.

Julia Platt had no real intention to ever be mayor of Pacific Grove. In Julia's case, the job fell to her because no one else would do the things she demanded be done. In the end, she shouldered the mantle and made the changes she saw were needed. She is known now for shooting chickens, breaking gate locks, and protecting the Pacific Grove shore. These efforts demanded a fierce dedication. As Julia wrote to her cousin Sue in Vermont, "It is a busy old woman who finds herself mayor of Pacific Grove."

What has made this place so special that it can grow in beauty and productivity despite the ravages of the past and the controversies of today? The answers lie in long-term fishing families who put down roots and hold to their way of life; pioneering efforts of unique people such as Julie Packard and Nancy Burnett, Ed Ricketts and Julia Platt; and the tremendous bounty and productivity of the bay. But success is mostly due to generations of residents, fishermen and tourists, poets and businesspeople, all those who looked out on Monterey Bay and saw a home worth saving. They labored to protect its diversity—both the sea and the economies that use it.

They labored to save something of themselves too. Their personal connection to the bay. Their personal connection to their family's past. Their personal options for the future. They did it for logical reasons and for emotional ones. They did it for economic benefits and for uncountable sunsets and beautiful vistas.

Saving Monterey Bay has been done not by equation but by people who love the sea and their tiny place in the ocean world. They have needed tools to save the bay, tools often forged by science and sharpened by politics and argument. But in the long run, people have mostly needed passion and a sense of duty to something bigger than themselves. When the fishermen, scientists, hoteliers, and aquarists all get together and battle over the bay and its future, it's like a family fighting over something they all cherish. It's that passion that saved Monterey Bay.

On the roof of the aquarium, a heart beats the minutes into hours into days into decades. Every five seconds, the 10-foot-long piston moves up and down, driven by the wave machine that David Packard designed and built in the early 1980s. The same machine sits there still, working every day and every night since the aquarium opened. Beneath it swirls the tall, stately kelp forest tank, drinking in sunlight from its open surface and pushing gently and persistently on the kelp as the piston slowly rises and falls.

Down below, visitors stand entranced by the tank, parents and children staring into the kelp forest, unconsciously swaying with the surging water. This kelp forest has been plucked from the bay outside, plumbed and piped and displayed for millions to enjoy. But just beyond the walls lie mile after mile of real kelp forest, swaying to the heartbeat of nature's cycles, populated by protected otters, and nurturing a recovering ecosystem. In the aquarium, Dave Packard's piston pulses the kelp forest back and forth. In the bay, it is the ebb and flow of human action that sets the cycle of ecological health. The cycle is positive now, the forest has responded. It is the duty of those of us swaying to these cycles to learn the lesson of this recovery, celebrate it here, and create it elsewhere.

Acknowledgments

This book was the product of countless conversations, and years of poring over historical archives throughout the Monterey Peninsula. First and foremost to thank is Alan Baldridge, past librarian at Stanford University's Hopkins Marine Station, who with his twinkling eyes and encouragement shared everything he had discovered over generations of observing China Point and the bay and steered us in the right direction when we hit roadblocks. We also thank the dozens of faculty and staff at Hopkins and the Monterey Bay Aquarium, who shared their knowledge, enthusiasm, and support for the book: Joe Wible, Chuck Baxter, Chris Patton, Chris Harrold, Teri Nicholson, Freya Sommer, Dave Epel, Bill Gilly, Kris Ingram, Melissa Haber, and John and Vicky Pearse. Many people shared their stories with us, and we thank especially Joe and Doris Bragdon, Merilyn Derby Georgevich, David Greenfield, Izzie Abbott, Steve Webster, Nancy Burnett, Julie Packard, Chuck Baxter, and Jim Estes for the hours spent talking us through their own parts of the Monterey Bay story. Thank you to the guardians of Monterey's history, Tim Thomas, Dennis Copeland with the Monterey Public Library, Sandy Lydon, and many authors who have brought attention to the natural and cultural history of the region. Dr. Steve Zottoli provided Dr. Julia Platt a prime time debut in scientific literature this century. John Pearse looked at every niche of the bay. The book profited a great deal from reviews by John Pearse, Vicki Pearse, Susan Shillinglaw, Steve Zottoli, Jim Estes, Isabella Abbott, Ellie Maas Davis, Jim Watanabe, Chuck Baxter, Steve Webster, Nancy Burnett, Julie Packard, Randy Reeves, Sandy Lydon, Alan Baldridge, Joe Wible, and Mary Roberts. Lauren Palumbi provided the fabulous chapter line drawings, and Todd Baldwin and Emily Davis from Island Press were the perfect editorial team. Jonathan Cobb provided a keen early boost. Thank you to the photographers who provided incredible images featured throughout the book. Thank you, also, to the David and Lucile Packard Foundation for its early support.

About the Authors

STEPHEN R. PALUMBI is the Harold A. Miller Director of the Hopkins Marine Station and the Jane and Marshall Steele Professor of Marine Science at Stanford University. He teaches and does research in evolution, genetics, and marine biology and has long been fascinated by how quickly the world around us changes. Steve has lectured extensively on human-induced evolutionary change, has used genetic detective work to identify whales for sale in retail markets, and is working on new methods to help preserve coral reefs in the face of climate change. His laboratory work uses molecular genetics to help reveal the population biology of marine creatures. Steve helped research and write, and also appears in, the BBC series *The Future Is Wild* and the History Channel's *World Without People.* Other recent films appearances include *The End of the Line* and the Canadian Broadcasting Corporation series *One Ocean.* Major work continues on the microdocumentary project, the *Short Attention Span Science Theater.* Steve lives with his wife in Monterey, California and enjoys the adventure of two grown children out in the world.

After studying zoology at the University of Vermont, CAROLYN SOTKA earned an M.S. degree in marine policy from University of Miami's Rosenstiel School of Marine and Atmospheric Science. Over the last two decades, Carolyn has helped start ocean conservation programs at prestigious aquariums, universities, and nonprofits; authored reports, book chapters, videos, and podcasts on critical ocean issues; rehabilitated sea lions and monitored sea turtle nests; observed fishing activities at sea; and taught and instructed others on how to effectively convey information about marine science. Through her work at Stanford University's Hopkins Marine Station, she unearthed this book's protagonist, Dr. Julia Platt, whose passion helped secure a legacy of coastal preservation. Currently, Carolyn leads outreach efforts on behalf of the National Oceanic and Atmospheric Administration's Oceans and Human Health Initiative to Congress, government agencies, the media, and general public. She lives with her family on James Island in South Carolina.

Notes

Chapter 1

PAGE 4

Reports of Julia's funeral derive from the *Monterey Herald*, May 31, 1935: "She wished to be buried sailor fashion in the water of Monterey Bay," report from Chief of Police Sam Bashline, September 1935, in the records of the Pacific Grove Natural History Museum.

PAGE 5

The *Monterey Herald* (April 1931) described Julia's house as having "a room with big windows, commanding a broad expanse of bay."

Chapter 2

PAGE 12

Numerous early gray whales: Charles Melville Scammon, *The marine mammals of the north-western coast of North America and the American whale fishery* (Riverside, CA: Manessier Publishing Company, 1969), 23.

La Pérouse's entry into Monterey: Jean-François Pérouse, *Life in a California mission*, ed. M. Margolin (Berkeley, CA: Heyday Books, 1989), 54.

The description of Monterey Bay is based on the eyewitness accounts in La Pérouse and Scammon and the diaries of Costansó, augmented by the modern natural history of the bay and its common species. Detailed narrative natural histories of Monterey Bay from the 1700s are not available, as far as we know. Throughout the book, we occasionally provide a narrative description of scenes or produce dialogue that remains faithful to available material but has not been handed down verbatim. In such cases, we have been conservative about our interpretations of the past and have not included any facts that cannot be verified. But in these cases, we signal that the scene is more detailed than can be discovered from historical records by calling these accounts fictionalized.

Vizcaíno wanted pearls: I. R. S. Engstrand, "Seekers of the 'Northern Mystery,'" in *Contested Eden: California before the Gold Rush*, eds. Ramón Gutierrez and Richard Orsi, 78–110 (Berkeley, CA: University of California Press, 1998), 91.

"The best port that could be desired": p. 92 in Engstrand.

PAGE 13

"Sheltered from all winds": p. 92 in Engstrand.

The description of Monterey Bay is based on current natural history, the material in Engstrand, and the later commentary by Costansó and La Pérouse.

Description of Junípero Serra: p. 17 in La Pérouse.

Description of Junípero Serra's beliefs: Mary Trotter Kion, "Father Junipero Serra: Franciscan missionary to California Indians," *Suite 101*, April 13, 2007, http://colonial-america.suite101.com/article.cfm/father_junipero_serra (accessed June 13, 2010).

"He would pound his breast with a stone while in the pulpit, scourge himself, or apply a lighted torch to his bare chest": *New Advent Catholic Encyclopedia*, s.v. "Junípero Serra" (by Zephyrin Engelhardt) http://www.newadvent.org/cathen/13730b.htm.

PAGE 14

Costansó's description of Monterey Bay: Miguel Costansó, *The Costansó Narrative of the Portola expedition*, ed. Ray Brandes (Newhall, CA: Hogarth Press, 1970), 98.

H. Dallas, Gary S. Breschini, eds. *Archeological Investigations of Some Significant Sites on the Central Coast of California*, Archeological excavations at CA-MNT-108, Fisherman's Wharf, Monterey County, California, eds. Gary S. Breschini and Trudy Haversat no. 29 (Salinas, CA: Coyote Press, 1989), 40.

PAGE 15

Serra's hopes about the future promise of the missions: Frederick J. Teggart, ed., *The Official Account of the Portola Expedition of 1769–1770*. Academy of Pacific Coast History, Vol. 1. (Berkeley, CA: University of California Press, 1910), 27.

Junípero Serra's death: Grace McFarland, *Monterey, Cradle of California's Romance: The Story of a Lost Port that Was Found Again and a Dream that Came True* (Monterey, CA: Press of Weybret-Lee Co., 1914).

PAGE 16

Description of the natives: John Walten, *Storied Land: Community and Memory in Monterey* (Berkeley, CA: University of California Press; 2001), 53.

Good intentions of the priests: p. 53 in Walton.

"No country is more abundant in fish and game of every description": p. 64 in La Pérouse.

"Sea is covered with pelicans": p. 55 in La Pérouse.

"It is impossible to describe either the number of whales with which we were surrounded or their familiarity": p. 54 in La Pérouse.

La Pérouse refers to sea otters as a new branch of commerce: p. 63 in La Pérouse.

"For which China is a certain market": pp. 63–64 in La Pérouse.

Native otter hunting methods: p. 102 in La Pérouse.

PAGE 17

Sea otter skins common: p. 99 in La Pérouse.

PAGE 18

La Pérouse refers to sea otters as a new branch of commerce: p. 63 in La Pérouse.

Value of furs: p. 101 in La Pérouse.

Price of a house in San Diego in 1847, $96: Marvi S. Blanco, "Allen B. Light. African American mariner in Mexican California," San Diego Biographies (San Diego, CA: San Diego Historical Society, n.d.) http://www.sandiegohistory.org/education/light8/biolight.htm (accessed June 13, 2010).

Otter market in China: Adele Ogden, *The California sea otter trade 1784–1848.* (Berkley, CA: University of California Press, 1941).

"Style of the day for Chinese Mandarins": p. 5 in Ogden.

Vasadre fulfilling the dream of Vizcaíno: pp. 15–20 in Ogden.

PAGE 19

Vasadre took 1,060 skins to Mexico: p. 16 in Ogden.

Vasadre's demands: p. 17 in Ogden.

Opposition to Vasadre's plan: p. 22 in Ogden.

Sale of seized pelts: p. 23 in Ogden.

"With little ceremony left for Spain": p. 24 in Ogden.

PAGE 20

Betsy in the San Diego harbor: pp. 34–35 in Ogden.

PAGE 21

Lelia Byrd story: Ogden pp. 37–38. The dialogue is fictionalized but the rest of the details are as in Ogden.

Otter pelt export: p. 141 in Ogden.

Captain John Rogers Cooper quote: p. 142 in Ogden.

Otters becoming scarce for Russians: p. 141 in Ogden.

"Far more demands on the military and treasury than could be met": p. 59 in Walton.

"Effective central government collapsed": p. 59 in Walton.

PAGE 22

Buying pelts from the missions: p. 60 in Walton.

Missions losing power: p. 62 in Walton.

Otter pups were no longer to be killed: p. 142 in Ogden.

"The ground appeared covered with black sheets due to the great quantity of otters which were there": p. 142 cited by Ogden.

Otter hunting restricted to Mexican nationals: p. 141 in Ogden.

"After two months obtained 300 sea otter skins!": p. 121 cited by Ogden.

"The owners will not lose or gain anything by the voyage": p. 121 cited by Ogden.

Chapter 3

PAGE 26

"Began to experience cold and violent North winds": Miguel Costansó *The Costansó narrative of the Portola expedition.* ed. Ray Brandes (Newhall, CA: Hogarth Press, 1970) August 5th entry.

PAGE 27

Whales on Captain Davenport's mind: H. Sayers, "Shore Whaling for Gray Whales along the Coast of the Californias" in *The Gray Whale: Eschrichtius Robustus* eds. Mary Lou Jones, Steven L. Swartz, and Stephen Leatherwood (Orlando, FL: Academic Press, Orlando, 1984) 132–134FL.

Historic gold prices: www.goldinfo.net.

PAGE 28

Discrepancy in number of ships whaling: Thomas Leo Nichols, "California Shore Whaling, 1854 to 1900" (master's thesis, California State University, Northridge, 1983).

Cattle ranching in Monterey: P. Johnston, *A Pictorial History of Old Monterey County* (Monterey, CA: Monterey Savings and Loan, 1970).

PAGE 29

"The whales were plentiful and easy to approach": p. 132 in Sayers.

Oil production meager: pp. 132–133 in Sayers.

Bomb lances: p. 133 in Sayers.

Charles H. Townsend, *Present Condition of the California Gray Whale Fishery* (U.S. Fisheries Commission Bulletin 6, 1886), 346–350.

PAGE 30

Whales taken from Monterey after 1870: Sayers, "Whaling," 154; also from Randall Reeves, Tim Smith, "Commercial Whaling, Especially for Gray Whales (*Eschrichtius robustus*) and humpback whales (*Megaptera novaeangliae*), at California and Baja California Shore Stations in the 19th Century (1854.1899). *Marine Fisheries Review* (2010); Phillip J. Clapham, Stephen Leatherwood, Isidore Szczepaniak, and Robert L. Brownell Jr., " Catches of Humpback and Other Whales from Shore Stations at Moss Landing and Trinidad, California, 1919–1926," *Marine Mammal Science* 13(3)(1997):368–394.

"Rolled around in the surf": Charles Melville Scammon, *The marine mammals of the north-western coast of North America and the American whale fishery* (Riverside, CA: Manessier Publishing Company, 1969).

Whale numbers taken: interpolated from Table 1 in Sayers and Table 2 in Reeves and Smith.

Fraction of whales that were gray whales: estimated from Sayers, Table 1.

PAGE 31

Three main breeding lagoons: Table I in D. A. Henderson, "Nineteenth Century Gray Whaling" in *The Gray Whale: Eschrichtius Robustus* eds. Mary Lou Jones, Steven L. Swartz, and Stephen Leatherwood (Orlando, FL: Academic Press, Orlando, 1984) 169. See also Randall R. Reeves, Tim D. Smith, Judith N. Lund, Susan A. Lebo, and Elizabeth A. Josephson, "Nineteenth-century Ship-based Catches of Gray Whales, *Eschtichtius robustus*, in the Eastern North Pacific," *Marine Fisheries Review* 72 (2010):26–65.

Scammon's marine mammal biology: see Scammon, 1874.

Chasing southerly moving whales: p. 168 in Henderson.

PAGE 32

Whaling station in Crescent City: p. 127 in Sayers, and in Reeves and Smith.

Walked away from the Baja hunt: see Figure 3 in Reeves et al.

PAGE 33

"Must have far exceeded a sustainable kill": p. 175 in Henderson.

"Still well in excess of that sustainable by a rapidly declining population": p. 175 in Henderson. Note that the value in Reeves et al. (Table 4) is 114 whales killed on average between 1863 and 1873 in Baja.

Average whale hunt in Baja from Table 4 in Reeves et al.

Gray whale declines: Angliss, R. P. and R. B. Outlaw. 2007. Alaska marine mammal stock assessments, 2006. U.S. Dep. Commer., NOAA Technical Memorandum NMFS-AFSC 168, 244 p.

Gray whale killing without threatening population: Angliss and Outlaw.

Kill reports of gray whales in 1845 to 1854: p. 169 in Henderson. Another 150 or so are estimated by Reeves et al. as an annual aboriginal hunt.

Gray whale hunting summary in Reeves et al.

"Whaleships had abandoned most of the gray whaling grounds": p. 173 in Henderson.

PAGE 34

"Undoubtedly high": p. 176 in Henderson.

Discrepancy in Scammon's count of boats whaling: p. 34 in Nichols.

Scammon's estimate of surviving whales: p. 176 in Henderson.

Twentieth-century population growth model estimates: J. R. Brandon, and A. E. Punt. "Assessment of the Eastern Stock of North Pacific Gray Whales: Incorporating Calf Production, Sea-ice and Strandings Data," (Document SC/F09/CC5, submitted to the Scientific Committee of the International Whaling Commission, Cambridge, UK).

PAGE 35

DNA estimate of gray whale numbers: S. Elizabeth Alter, Eric Rynes, and Stephen R. Palumbi, "The Once and Future Gray Whales: DNA Evidence for Historic Population Size and Past Ecosystem Impacts," *Proceedings of the National Academy of Sciences (USA)* 104(2006):15162–15167.

Chapter 4

PAGE 37

First child born to Chinese parents in the United States: Sandy Lydon, *Chinese Gold: The Chinese in the Monterey Bay Region* (Capitola, CA: Capitola Book Company, 1985).

Birth of Jone Yow Lee not reported to census until 1900: pp. 29–30 in Lydon.

Arrival of Chinese: S. Lydon lecture at the Hopkins Marine Station, 2007.

PAGE 38

The start of the Chinese fishing and merchant culture: pp. 29–30 in Lydon.

Landed at Point Lobos: p. 140 in Lydon.

Chinese start a small fishing camp: p. 33 in Lydon.

Permanent site occupied by Chinese families: p. 154 in Lydon.

PAGE 38

Robert Louis Stevenson's tour of China Point in 1879: pp. 154–155 from Robert Louis Stevenson's *Scotland*, quoted on p. 345 in Lydon.

PAGE 40

500 to 600 Chinese arrived in Monterey from San Francisco: p. 32 in Lydon.

PAGE 41

Abalone natural history is from many sources, including Robert Harding Morris, E. C. Haderlie, and D. P. Abbott, *Intertidal invertebrates of California*. (Stanford, CA: Stanford University Press, 1980). For relationship of abalone to coralline algae, see Daniel E. Morse, Helen Duncan, Neal Hooker, and Lloyd Jensen "γ-Aminobutyric Acid, a Neurotransmitter, Induces Planktonic Abalone Larvae to Settle and Begin Metamorphosis," *Science* 27 (1979):407–410.

PAGE 42

"Cleaned nearly all the [abalone] from the waters around Point Pinos": p. 33 in Lydon.

Abalone declared exhausted all the way to San Diego: p. 33 in Lydon.

Eating sea urchins with a spoon: p. 33 in Lydon.

PAGE 43

"From sharks to shiners": p. 36 in Lydon.

"Smaller fish were dried on the ground or spread flat on racks while larger fish were split, salted, and hung by the tail from poles": p. 36 in Lydon.

Dried algae shipped to San Francisco and China: p. 38 in Lydon.

"The village grows all the while and the business this people is engaged in seems to thrive": quoted by Lydon on p. 155.

"An American citizen claiming equal rights vouchsafed by our Constitution": p. 160 in Lydon.

Competition from other fishing communities: pp. 166–167 in Lydon.

PAGE 44

Description of the birth of Pacific Grove in 1875: Kent Seavey, *Images of America: Pacific Grove*. (San Francisco, CA: Arcadia Publishing, 2005).

PAGE 45

Lovers of Jesus Point got its name: Seavey.

Nearest neighbor to China Point: p. 169 in Lydon.

Robert Louis Stevenson quote from 1879, p. 345 in Lydon. Note that the Lydon quote has been altered here from referring to a "joss-stock" to a "joss-stick."

PAGE 47

Chinese try to prosecute their tormentors without success: p. 54 in Lydon.

Chinese community and China Point fishing fleet driven toward destitution: p. 54 in Lydon.

Nineteenth-century scientist George Cuvier found one of these arms still stuck inside a female paper nautilus (not a squid, but close). So befuddled was he by the pale twist of tentacle that he thought the arm was a parasitic worm, and he gave it a grand new name as its own species: *Hectocotylus octopodis* (Cuvier 1829). Although the mistake was soon discovered, the spermatophore-delivering arm of a squid is still called the hectocotylid arm. Cuvier discovered many other kinds of animals— mastodons, fossil mammals of all kinds—and so his reputation didn't break off like a squid's arm.

PAGE 48

Use of bright light to attract squid: p. 56 in Lydon.

Salt smuggling: pp. 57–58 in Lydon.

PAGE 49

Courting diphtheria: Connie Chiang, "Monterey-by-the-smell: Odors and Social Conflict on the California Coastline," *Pacific Coastal Review* 73(2)(2004):183–214.

1902 rainstorm ruins squid: p. 194 in Chiang.

The stench chokes Pacific Grove: Augusta Fink, *Monterey: The Presence of the Past* (San Francisco, CA: Chronicle Books, 1972), 174.

PAGE 50

John Steinbeck's early years visiting China Point: Tom Mangelsdorf, *A History of Steinbeck's Cannery Row* (Santa Cruz, CA: Western Tanager Press, 1986), 4.

"Dotting the bay off Pacific Grove on moonless Spring nights": p. 59 in Lydon.

Within 12 hours, "half the heart of the city" had burned to the ground: Jack London "The Story of an Eyewitness," *Colliers*, May 5, 1906.

PAGE 51

Lease troubles on China Point: John Walton, *Storied land: Community and Memory in Monterey* (Berkeley, CA: University of California Press, 2001), 179.

"Do whatever it takes": p. 179 in Walton.

Chapter 5

PAGE 56

Summer educational series: Kent Seavey, *Images of America: Pacific Grove.* (San Francisco, CA: Arcadia Publishing, 2005), 31.

Famous names of the series: p. 31 in Seavey.

PAGE 57

Description of society life: Lucy Neely McLane, *A Piney Paradise by Monterey Bay: The Early History of Pacific Grove*, 4th ed. (Baltimore, MD: Gateway Press, 2004), 74.

"You could hear the women changing their minds": p. 31 in Seavey.

Businesses during the early church camp days: p. 48 in Seavey.

"The largest on the coast": p. 48 in Seavey.

Description of Julia Platt's appearance: Augusta Fink, *Monterey: The Presence of the Past* (San Francisco, CA: Chronicle Books, 1972), 254.

"She had come, unchaperoned, to study zoology": T. J., "Julia Platt: Lady Watchdog," Game and Gossip (formerly What's Doing) (Monterey, CA: Monterey Public Library, California History Room), 16.

PAGE 58

Platt's summer research in Woods Hole, Massachusetts: Steven J. Zottoli, and E. A. Seyfarth, "Julia B. Platt (1857–1935): Pioneer Comparative Embryologist and Neuroscientist," *Brain, Behavior and Evolution* 43(1994):92–106.

Platt's research on the dogfish: p. 96 in Zottoli and Seyfarth.

Platt obtained her Ph.D. on May 28, 1898: p. 95 in Zottoli and Seyfarth.

Formation of the Julia Platt Club in 1998: "International Society for Neuroethology: March 1998 Newsletter," *International Society for Neuroethology*, March 1998, http://www.neuroethology.org/newsletter/news_archive/isn.news.mar98.html (accessed June 29, 2010).

Platt was one of twenty American women with a Ph.D. in zoological sciences: p. 100 in Zottoli and Seyfarth.

Platt was born in San Francisco and raised in Vermont: p. 93 in Zottoli and Seyfarth.

PAGE 59

Jordan sought a marine teaching laboratory patterned after Woods Hole: David Epel, "Stanford by the Sea. A brief history of the Hopkins Marine Station," the Stanford Historical Society, *Sandstone and Tile* 16(4)(1992):3–9.

Heath taught summer classes at Hopkins: J. D. Conway, *Monterey: Presidio, Pueblo and Port*. The Making of America Series (Charleston, SC: Arcadia Publishing, 2003), 160.

Julia's letter to Jordan: Letter from Julia Platt to David Starr Jordan, 2 June 1899. Department of Special Collections and University Archives, Stanford University Libraries, CA: Palo Alto. Also reprinted in Zottoli and Seyfarth, "Julia Platt," 102.

PAGE 61

"Without work, life isn't worth living": p. 102 in Zottoli and Seyfarth.

Platt's discussion of reproduction: p. 16 in *Game and Gossip*, 1946.

PAGE 62

"Among a group of men": p. 16 in *Game and Gossip*, 1946.

Booming tourist enterprise: pp. 78–80 in Seavey.

"With skirts of ample size to cover the buttocks": p. 73 in McLane, 2004.

No "corrupting" dance styles: p. 73 in McLane.

Igniting small town controversy: p. 254 in Fink.

"I am not an atheist": *The Grove at High Tide* (currently known as *Pacific Grove Tribune*), April 10, 1931, Pacific Grove Museum Archives.

Platt's gardening: p. 40 in McLane.

Pacific Grove Women's Civic Improvement Club: *Monterey Herald*, April 11, 1931.

Livestock in Pacific Grove: see Box 5.1.

PAGE 63

"People within their thin-walled cottages were not safe": "Julia Platt Wielded Mean Six-shooter. *Pacific Grove Tribune*, December 20, 1932. Monterey Public Library, CA: Monterey.

"You could call her an early-day conservationist": in *Monterey Herald*, May 11, 1968.

"Big windows, commanding a broad expanse of bay": in *Monterey Herald*, April 1931.

PAGE 64

"There was a packed house every time the council met": p. 16 in *Game and Gossip*.

Platt's revision of the city's operation: p. 16 *Game and Gossip*.

Protection of the sea in the hands of Pacific Grove: *Works Progress Administration 1937. New bill creates marine refuge at local station* (WPA Historical Survey of the Monterey Peninsula Project #4080 MS, File 41, May 13), CA: Monterey, Monterey Public Library.

PAGE 65

Julia "molested" by Mr. McDougall: in *Grove at High Tide*, January 17, 1931.

Original deed null and void: p. 17 in *Game and Gossip*.

Platt destroyed gate padlock and opened the beach: *Grove at High Tide*, January 17, 1931, Pacific Grove Museum archives.

"When the gate was nailed shut, resorted to the axe": in *Monterey Herald*, April 1931.

PAGE 66

"Somewhat timid": Pacific Grove Museum of Natural History archives, 2003; *Game and Gossip*.

PAGE 67

"Neither age nor sex can be considered important in these days of political, social and economic equality": in *Monterey Herald*, April 1931.

"It will take a good man to beat me": in *Monterey Herald*, May 11, 1968.

Chapter 6

PAGE 68

Chinese village fire in 1906: see Chapter 4.

PAGE 69

Norwegian canning expert Knut Hovden in Monterey: J. D. Conway, *Monterey: Presidio, Pueblo and Port*. The Making of America Series (Charleston, SC: Arcadia Publishing, 2003); also Tom Mangelsdorf, *A History of Steinbeck's Cannery Row* (Santa Cruz, CA: Western Tanager Press, 1986).

Spring salmon run in Monterey: Kent Seavey, *Images of America: Pacific Grove*. (San Francisco, CA: Arcadia Publishing, 2005), 80.

Reported sardine biomass in 1936 was about 3.5 million metric tons, or about 3.5 billion kilograms: "FishWatch—U.S.Seafood Facts: Pacific Sardine," National Marine Fisheries Service, NOAA, http://www.nmfs.noaa.gov/fishwatch/species/sardine.htm

PAGE 70

Photos showing fishermen dipping sardines out of the water with hand nets: R. Johnston, *Old Monterey County: A Pictorial History* (Monterey, CA: Monterey Savings and Loan, 1970).

Frank Booth started the second cannery and bought the Robbins operation: Connie Y. Chiang, "Novel tourism: Nature, Industry, and Literature on Monterey's Cannery Row," *Western Historical Quarterly* 35(3) (2004a.):309–329.

The hiring of Knut Hovden: Connie Y. Chiang, C. 2008. *Shaping the Shoreline: Fisheries and Tourism on the Monterey Coast* (Seattle, WA: University of Washington Press, 2008), 49.

"The rich juicy smell causes everyone to hold his or her nose": p. 23 in Mangelsdorf.

Market after World War I: Connie Y. Chiang, "Monterey-by-the-smell: Odors and Social Conflict on the California Coastline," *Pacific Coastal Review* 73(2)(2004b.):183–214..

PAGE 71

Adoption of the Chinese practice of processing the byproducts of the fishery: Sandy Lydon, *Chinese Gold: The Chinese in the Monterey Bay Region* (Capitola, CA: Capitola Book Company, 1985).

Fish oil in commercial products: Donal Fitzgerald, *The History and Significance of the Hovden Cannery: Cannery Row, Monterey, California 1914–1973* [submitted by Carroll L. Pursell Jr.] (Monterey: Monterey Bay Aquarium Foundation, Monterey, 1979).

Joe Bragdon (cannery worker) in interview with Stephen R. Palumbi, November 2006.

PAGE 72

"Fisheries are subject to depletion because of too intense exploitation": p. 37 in Mangelsdorf.

"We must be sure that we begin an era of scientific investigation of our fisheries in time to adequately guide and control the exploitation": p. 37 in Mangelsdorf.

1921 season map from Scofield, W. L. 1929. *Sardine Fishing Methods at Monterey, California*. Division of Fish and Game of California, Fisheries Bulletin #19.

PAGE 74

Battle between fishery scientists and the fishing and cannery interests: Mangelsdorf, *Steinbeck's*, 37.

"The catch has not increased in proportion to the fishing effort expanded": p. 39 in Mangelsdorf.

Lake Miraflores: p. 66 in Mangelsdorf.

PAGE 75

"You can't keep those people from reducing sardines on the open seas": p. 67 in Mangelsdorf.

"Give more employment to cannery workers": p. 68 in Mangelsdorf.

Shore-based canners complained and were awarded more reduction allocation: p. 82 in Mangelsdorf.

"Unmistakable signs of depletion," N. B. Scofield, 1938: p. 81 in Mangelsdorf.

PAGE 77

Canneries dumped waste in the nearby waters of Hopkins Marine Station: Alan Baldridge interview with L. R. Blinks, January 5, 1974, on file in Miller Library; Kate Davis in personal communication with Carolyn Sotka, December 2003.

"Foul condition of the water caused by the canneries discharge of sewage and waste": Chiang, 2004b, 203.

Cannery operators flushed water into the bay from machine cleaning: Alan Baldridge in interview with L. R. Blinks, January 5, 1974.

"The fumes from the scum floating on the waters of the inlets of the bay were so bad that they turned lead-based paints black": E. H. Rosenberg, "A history of the Fishing and Canning Industries in Monterey, California,"(master's thesis, University of Nevada, 1961).

10 percent of catch is lost in wastewater: "Recovery of Organic Matter in the Fish-meal Industry of Chile," UNIDO's *Cleaner Industrial Production*,

North Carolina Department of Environment and Natural Resources, Division of Pollution Prevention and Environmental Assistance, November 1998, http://www.p2pays.org/ref/10/09370.htm.

PAGE 78

"Large quantities of decayed and putrefied fish": p. 206 in Chiang, 2004.

"Nobody has died of fish odors yet, it's one of the healthiest things we have": p. 183 in Chiang, 2004b.

"You smell money": Carol Lynn McKibben, *Beyond Cannery Row: Sicilian Women, Immigration, and Community in Monterey, California. 1915–1999* (Chicago: University of Illinois Press, 2006), 40.

PAGE 79

Merilyn Derby swimming at Fisher Beach: Merilyn Derby Georgevich in interview with Carolyn Sotka, March 5, 2007.

PAGE 80

The stench and the Del Monte Hotel: p. 58 in Mangelsdorf.

"Beautiful surroundings made uninhabitable by such a terrible stench": p. 94 in Chiang, 2008.

"Though the conflict diminished, the smells . . . probably worsened": p. 212 in Chiang, C. 2004. Monterey-by-the-Smell: Odors and social conflict on the California coastline. *Pacific Historical Review* 73:183–214.

PAGE 81

Sea anemones grown up along the rock at Hopkins: G. Haderlie in personal communication Carolyn Sotka, November 2004.

Healthy shores in Pacific Grove if the Monterey problems were solved: *Works Progress Administration. 1937. New Bill Creates Marine Refuge at Local Station* (WPA Historical Survey of the Monterey Peninsula Project #4080 MS, File 41, May 13), CA: Monterey, Public Library), 4.

PAGE 82

Julia's new state law: see the Pacific Grove City ordinances, Chapter 14.04, "All the waterfront of the city, together with those certain submerged lands in the Bay of Monterey contiguous thereto, as set forth and particularly described in that certain act of the Legislature of the State of California entitled, 'An act granting to the City of Pacific Grove the title to the waterfront of said City together with certain submerged lands in the Bay of Monterey contiguous thereto,' approved by the Governor June 9, 1931, are hereby established as a refuge for the protection of certain kinds of marine life hereinafter mentioned and as a marine garden of the city and reference is hereby made to said act of the Legislature for a particular description of said waterfront and

said submerged lands" [Ord. 210 N.S. §5-401(1), 1952]. The date of the
California state law seems very close to the date of Julia's election, so it
is possible that the state law had been pursued by Julia beforehand. We
can find no record of this in Julia's writings.

PAGE 83

Julia gained legal authority to manage the Pacific Grove shoreline and police
its access: p. 4 in WPA, 1937a.

Julia's plan for the refuge to be the center for scientific research and nursery:
p. 4 in WPA, 1937a.

"From where the tiny larvae may swim": p. 4, WPA, 1937a.

PAGE 84

Julia crafted the Pacific Grove Marine Gardens: *Works Progress Administration. 1937. New Bill Creates Marine Refuge at Local Station* (WPA
Historical Survey of the Monterey Peninsula Project #4080 MS, File
41, March 24), CA: Monterey, Public Library), 1.

PAGE 85

"Civic dignitaries traditionally accompany the body of a Mayor to its last
resting place": T. J., "Julia Platt: Lady Watchdog," Game and Gossip
(formerly What's Doing) (Monterey, CA: Monterey Public Library,
California History Room), 16.

Charter of *The Two Brothers*: funeral records, Pacific Grove Museum.

Rough weather and "a few were seasick": interview with Chief of Police Sam
Bashline, Pacific Grove Museum archives.

"The pallbearers said that there were times they wished they could trade
places with her!": Helen Spangenberg, *Memorial Recollections of Pacific
Grove*, Pacific Grove Museum Archives.

Julia's burial at sea: *Game and Gossip*, 1946; Pat Hathaway Collection, n.d.;
Pacific Grove Tribune, May 3, 1935; *Pacific Grove Tribune*, May 31, 1935;
Sam Bashline comments in the Pacific Grove Museum archives.

Julia's legacy at Lover's Point: *Pacific Grove Tribune*, October 26, 1935.

Chapter 7

PAGE 88

Séance scene is recounted in John Steinbeck and Ed Ricketts, *The Outer
Shores, Part 1: Ed Ricketts and John Steinbeck Explore the Pacific Coast*, ed.
Joel W. Hedgpeth (Eureka, CA: Mad River Press, 1978), 12–.

Joe Campbell accomplishments: Eric Tamm, *Beyond the Outer Shores*. (New
York: Four Walls Eight Windows), 195.

PAGE 89

Steinbeck and Campbell move to Pacific Grove: p. 6 in Tamm.

PAGE 91

Tide pool descriptions are from personal observation and from Ed Ricketts and Jack Calvin, *Between Pacific tides* (Stanford, CA: Stanford University Press, 1939); and personal observation. The six-armed starfish is *Leptasterias* spp. and does not actually lose count but deliberately grows six arms. The description of hermit crabs waiting for shells comes from Dan Rittschof's work in North Carolina.

PAGE 92

For example, p. 7 in Hedgepeth.

Descriptions of Ricketts's training: p. 8. in Tamm.

PAGE 93

Exequial Ecsurra, untitled lecture (Pacific Grove Natural History Museum, Pacific Grove, CA, February 10, 2007). Ricketts's motto emphasizes the connections between all things, from the small to the large. To understand the small, look to the large, and to understand the large, look back at the small.

Allee writes about the role of cooperation in animal ecology: Warder Clyde Allee, *Animal Aggregations: A Study in General Sociology* (Chicago, IL: University of Chicago Press, 1931).

W. E. Ritter's ecological ideas about "superorganisms": Edward Flanders Ricketts, *Renaissance Man of Cannery Row: The Life and Letters of Edward F. Ricketts*, ed. Katherine A. Rodger (Tuscaloosa, AL: University of Alabama Press, 2002), xxiii–xxiv. See also Richard Astro, John Steinbeck and Edward F. Ricketts: *The Shaping of a Novelist* (Minneapois: Minnesota University Press), 67.

"Everything that has happened since was taking shape": p. 17 in Tamm.

PAGE 94

Face-slapping contest between Campbell and Lovejoy, "gaze each other's hearts out" from Campbell's journals, cited in Rodger, p. xxix.

Pursuit of "quietism" by Ed and friends: p. xxviii in Rodger.

Jeffers poem and the philosophy of breaking through: pp. 14–15 in Tamm.

PAGE 95

Campbell's talk with Steinbeck about Carol: quoted in Rodger, Renaissance, xxvi from Stephen Larsen, and Robin A. Larsen. 1991. *A Fire in the Mind: The Life of Joseph Campbell* (New York: Doubleday, 1991), 193.

John and Carol return after Campbell leaves for good: p. xxvii in Rodger.

PAGE 96

"Thoughts on my first (substantial) taking over the responsibilities of a parent": p. 31 in Rodger.

Fire at Ed's lab occurred November 25, 1936, destroying all of Ed's notes, books, and specimens: p. 30 in Tamm.

PAGE 97

Campbell leaves for good: p. 17 in Tamm.

PAGE 98

Sales of *Between Pacific Tides*: see Katherine A. Rodger, "The Center for Steinbeck Studies: Collection Highlights," *Steinbeck Studies* 15(2) (2004):35–38. (doi:10.1353/stn.2004.0049).

PAGE 99

Huge windstorms ravage the Midwest in the 1930s: Zeynep K. Hansen, and Gary D. Libecap, "Small Farms, Externalities, and the Dust Bowl of the 1930s," (National Bureau of Economic Research Working Paper No. 10055, November 2003) available at http://www.nber.org/papers/w10055.

Whole picture of ecology: p. 247 in Rodger.

Chapter 8

PAGE 100

Ed plans to sell lab in 1945–1946: Eric Tamm, *Beyond the Outer Shores*. (New York: Four Walls Eight Windows), 148.

PAGE 101

In 1919, state legislation gave the department legal authority to regulate the sardine industry and establish a scientific monitoring program: Tom Mangelsdorf, *A History of Steinbeck's Cannery Row* (Santa Cruz, CA: Western Tanager Press, 1986), 36.

"Tampering with its abundance may result disastrously to many interests," "Sardines could not be exhausted": quoted in Mangelsdorf.

Frances Clark, ecosystem implications of the sardine fishery: Tim Thomas in a personal communication with Carolyn Sotka, October 13, 2003.

Clark says that the sardine population could not withstand the exploitation by Monterey fleets: p. 120 in Mangelsdorf.

Clark argued for a reduction in catch, although this remained controversial as late as 1955: Frances N. Clark, John C. Marr, "Population Dynamics of Pacific Sardine," CalCOFI Progress Report, July 1, 1953–March 31, 1955:11–48.

No catch limits were imposed: p. 120 in Mangelsdorf.

"The canneries are going strong—they will extract every single sardine out of the ocean": Edward Flanders Ricketts, *Renaissance Man of Cannery Row: The Life and Letters of Edward F. Ricketts*, ed. Katherine A. Rodger (Tuscaloosa, AL: University of Alabama Press, 2002), 32.

PAGE 102

Engines of prosperity so loud that they "shake the building": p. 32 in Rodger.

Playing phonographic records: Edward F. Ricketts, *Breaking Through: Essays, Journals, and Travelogues of Edward F. Ricketts* ed. Katherine Rodger (Berkeley, CA: University of California Press, 2006), 30.

Ecology took a back seat as canneries supplied canned fish to troops abroad: p. 146 in Mangelsdorf.

"The canneries started up as soon as war was declared, the first of the profiteers": p. 47 in Rodger, 2002.

PAGE 103

Sicilians return to their homes: Carol Lynn McKibben, *Beyond Cannery Row: Sicilian Women, Immigration, and Community in Monterey, California. 1915–1999* (Chicago: University of Illinois Press, 2006), 80–92.

Ed in the Army: p. 160 in Mangelsdorf.

Additional fishing efforts would return additional fish in equal proportion in the mid-1930s:

Radio fishing the last sardines: Edward Ueber, and Alec MacCall, "The Rise and Fall of the California Sardine Empire," *Climate Variability, Climate Change and Fisheries*, ed. M. H. Glantz, 31–48 (Cambridge, England: Cambridge University Press, 1992).

PAGE 104

"It's mostly about me": p. 126 in Tamm.

"Write something for us to read—we're sick of the war": p. 133 in Tamm.

"Sentimental glorification of weakness of mind": p. 132 in Tamm.

Cannery Row as superficial: p. 132 in Tamm.

Steinbeck scholar Susan Shillinglaw likens *Cannery Row* to a busy tide pool: *Cannery Row* Introduction, cited on p. 133 in Tamm.

PAGE 106

"For years the canners . . . and the fishermen have been warned they are taking too much fish": p. 246 in Rodger, 2002.

"Pulls down the high a little, tho not so much as it pulls down the lows": p. 243 in Rodger, 2002.

"Sudden plankton imbalances": p. 222 in Rodger, 2002.

"Published reports that red water in south California (dinoflagellates, but this time apparently not the poisonous type) was so intense that many shore invertebrates including even lobsters, were killed by suffocation— low O_2 content": p. 223 in Rodger, 2002.

PAGE 107

Connection between the collapse of Monterey's economy and Steinbeck's *The Grapes of Wrath*: p. 283 in Tamm.

"Investigator Blames Industry": Ed Ricketts's publication for the *Monterey Herald*, 1948. Reprinted on pp. 325–330 in Rodger, 2006.

"Reduce their numbers to the point of commercial extinction," especially by taking undersized specimens and fishing in spawning areas: p. 327 in Rodger, 2006.

"Listen to the . . . businessmen": p. 328 in Rodger, 2006.

PAGE 108

"If conservation had been adopted early enough": p. 330 in Rodger, 2006.

"Don't blame the motorman," Ed Ricketts gasped upon being pulled from the wreckage: p. lii in Rodger, 2002.

PAGE 109

"He was my partner for 18 years": p. 50 in Rodger, 2006.

Chapter 9

PAGE 114

"Stay hidden, it's not your time yet": scene and dialogue fictionalized from details in John Woolfenden, *California Sea Otter: Saved or Doomed?* 2nd ed. (Pacific Grove, CA: Boxwood Press, 1985), 11.

Mr. and Mrs. H. G. Sharp's startling discovery: Woolfenden, *Sea Otter*, 11; and Rolf L. Bolin, "Reappearance of the Southern Sea Otter Along the California Coast," *Journal of Mammology* 19(3)(1938):301–303.

PAGE 115

Rolf Bolin found the Sharps' estimated sea otter population "beyond belief": p. 301 in Bolin.

Game warden assigned to guard population: p. 303 in Bolin.

PAGE 116

Eating habits of otters: Terry M. Williams, J. Haun, R. W. Davis, L. A. Fuiman, and S. Kohin, "A Killer Appetite: Metabolic Consequences of Carnivory in Marine Mammals," *Comparative Biochemistry and Physiology A: Molecular & Integrative Physiology* 129(4)(2001):785–796.

Marine shellfish prey of otters: in Marianne Riedman, "A Smorgasbord for Sea Otters," *California Wild* 49(4)(1996).

"Resting on its back and holding the food with its front paws, it proceeds in leisurely fashion to nibble or gnaw at it": p. 302 in Bolin.

Otters using tools: C. D. Woodhouse, R. K. Cowen, and L. Wilcoxon, "A Summary of Knowledge of the Sea Otter, *Enhydra lutris L.* in California and an Appraisal of the Completeness of the Biological Understanding of the Species," (Department of Commerce Publication PB-270 374. Marine Mammal Commission, Washington, DC, 1977), 21.

PAGE 117

Monterey diver Ernie Porter observing otters: E. Ebert, "A Food Habits Study of the California Sea Otter *Enhydra lutris nereis*," *California Department of Fish and Game* 54(1968):37.

Catalogue of the condition of abalone shells: p. 37 in Ebert.

Description of otter behavior: p. 50 in Woolfenden.

Use of a bottle as an anvil: p. 21 in Woolfenden; use of a soda can, p. 24.

PAGE 118

Public meetings demand otters be stopped: Richard Boolootian in interview with Stephen R. Palumbi, Pacific Grove, July 19, 2007.

PAGE 119

Boolootian's observation of otters cleaning out sea urchin beds: James H. McLean, "Sublittoral Ecology of Kelp Beds of the Open Coast Area Near Carmel, California," *Biological Bulletin* 122(1962):95–114.

"One large invertebrate that might normally be expected was not found in the areas . . . the large sea urchin": p. 101 in McLean.

PAGE 120

"The subtidal rocks in Monterey Bay at Mussel Point at the depth of 10 to 20 feet are covered with urchins": p. 102 in McLean.

PAGE 121

Gleissberg Cycle: Caiming Shen, Wei-Chyung Wang, Wei Gong, and Zhixin Hao, "A Pacific Decadal Oscillation Record since 1470 AD Reconstructed from Proxy Data of Summer Rainfall over Eastern China," *Geophysical Research Letters* 33(2006):L03702 (doi:10.1029 /2005GL024804).

Spawning congregations in Monterey Bay: Francisco P. Chavez, John Ryan, Salvador E. Lluch-Cota, and C. Miguel Niquen, "From Anchovies to Sardines and Back: Multidecadal Change in

PAGE 126

Harry Andrews counted animals in the Monterey Bay kelp forest: in Andrews, H. L. 1945. The kelp beds of the Monterey region. *Ecology* 26:24–37.

PAGE 127

Steinbeck's sarcasm: "the rocks and beaches be stocked with artificial fish guts and scales," and "reproducing the billions of flies that once added beauty to the scene would be difficult and costly": Tom Mangelsdorf, *A History of Steinbeck's Cannery Row* (Santa Cruz, CA: Western Tanager Press, 1986), 197.

PAGE 128

Otters depleting resources in Monterey Bay: p. 41 in Ebert, citing Fisher.

From the otter's perspective: Jean-François Pérouse, *Life in a California mission*, ed. M. Margolin (Berkeley, CA: Heyday Books, 1989).

Large raft of otters take up residence in 1963 just off China Point: Paul W. Wild, Jack A. Ames, "A Report on the Sea Otter, *Enhydra lutris L.* in California," (Marine Resource Technical Report No. 20, California Department of Fish and Game, 1974).

PAGE 129

Otters stop moving north: James Estes in interview with Stephen R. Palumbi, November 2007.

PAGE 131

Abalone bonanza near Año Nuevo: John Pearse in interview with Stephen R. Palumbi, November 2007.

Chapter 10

PAGE 134

"The number of living creatures of all Orders, whose existence intimately depends on the kelp is wonderful": Charles Darwin, *Journal of researches into the natural history and geology of the countries visited during the voyage of H. M. S. Beagle*, Vol. 1. (New York: Harper and Bros., 1846), 309–310.

PAGE 136

First Pacific harbor seals in China Point in more than a century: A. Baldridge, personal communication with Carolyn Sotka, 2003.

Marine Mammal Protection Act of 1972 folded harbor seals into its protection of dolphins, whales, and sea lions: NOAA Harbor Seal Stock Assessment Reports, 2003; Jay Barlow, Steven L. Swartz, Thomas C. Eagle, and Paul R. Wade, "U.S. Marine Mammal Stock Assessments: Guidelines for Preparation, Background, and a Summary of the 1995 Assessments," (NOAA Technical Memo NMFS-OPR-6, U.S. Department of Commerce, 1995).

By 1979, more than fifty harbor seals were counted at China Point: J. Boal, "Haul Out Impact on the Rocky Mid-tidal Zone," *Marine Ecology Progress Series* 2(1979):265–269.

Seals needed quiet: Teri Nicholson in personal communication with Carolyn Sotka, November 22, 2004.

Seal numbers rising: Teri Nicholson in personal communication with Carolyn Sotka, November 22, 2004.

First pupping witnessed in Monterey since California belonged to Mexico: Teri Nicholson in personal communication with Carolyn Sotka, November 22, 2004.

PAGE 137

Harbor seal diet: S. J. Trumble, "Abundance, Movements, Dive Behavior, Food Habits, and Mother–pup interactions of Harbor Seals (*Phoca vitulina richardsi*) near Monterey Bay, California," (mater's thesis, California State University, Fresno, 1995).

Filter feeding organisms benefit from kelp: D.O. Duggins, C. Simenstad, and J. Estes, "Magnification of Secondary Production by Kelp Detritus in Coastal Marine Ecosystems. *Science* 245(1989):170–173.

Fish, algae, and corals: Terence P. Hughes, " Catastrophes, Phase Shifts, and Large-scale Degradation of a Caribbean Coral Reef," *Science* 265:1547–1555.

Seabirds guano and grasses: D. A. Croll, J. L. Maron, J. A. Estes, E. M. Danner, and G. V. Byrd, "Introduced Predators Transform Subarctic Islands from Grassland to Tundra," *Science* 307(2005):1959–1961.

Collapse of diversity and fisheries when estuaries are invaded and used up: H. K. Lotze, H. S. Lenihan, B. J. Bourque, R. H. Bradbury, R. G. Cooke, M. C. Kay, S. M. Kidwell, M. X. Kirby, C. H. Peterson, and J. B. Jackson "Depletion, Degradation, and Recovery Potential of Estuaries and Coastal Seas," *Science* 312(2006):1806–1808.

PAGE 138

Murre numbers from the Farallon Islands: David G. Ainley, and T. James Lewis, "The History of Farallon Island Marine Bird Populations, 1854–1972," *Condor* 76(1974):432–446.

PAGE 139

Cormorant numbers and history of Farallons: p. 433 in Ainley and Lewis.

PAGE 140

EPA Superfund designation near Los Angeles due to DDT: Franklin Gress, Robert W. Risebrough, Danial W. Anderson, Lloyd F. Kiff, and Joseph R. Jehl Jr, "Reproductive Failures of Double-crested Cormorants in Southern California and Baja California," *The Wilson Bulletin* 85(2) (1973):197–208.

Robin Burnett's thesis: Robin Burnett, "DDT in Marine Phytoplankton and Crustacea," (thesis, Department of Biological Sciences, Stanford University, Palo Alto, CA).

Metabolic byproducts of DDT build up to deadly toxins: William J. Sydeman, Richard D. Brodeur, Churchill B. Grimes, Alexander S. Bychkov, and Stewart McKinnell, "Marine Habitat 'Hotspots' and Their Use by Migratory Species and Top Predators in the North Pacific Ocean: Introduction," *Deep Sea Research Part II: Topical Studies in Oceanography* 53(3–4)(2006):247–249.

"All Brown Pelican colonies in the United States and north-western Mexico
produced thin-shelled eggs in 1969 and 1970": p. 198 in Gress et al.

PAGE 141

Double-crested cormorants decimated by egg hunters in the mid-1800s did
not recover: see Figure 2 on p. 433 in Ainley and Lewis.

PAGE 142

Anchovies did not venture near the Farallons: p. 443 in Ainley and Lewis.

Chapter 11

PAGE 144

"What would Monterey be like without a fishing industry?" demanded
Hovden Cannery manager W. O. Lunde: Connie Y. Chiang, "Novel
tourism: Nature, Industry, and Literature on Monterey's Cannery
Row," *Western Historical Quarterly* 35(3)(2004a.):314.

PAGE 145

"A working waterfront": para. 14 in Chiang.

"They fish for tourists now, not pilchards": quoted on p. 320 in Chiang.

They were looking "for Lee Ching's grocery, for Doc's Western Biological
Laboratory, . . . and the girls of the Bear Flag Restaurant": Margaret
Hensel, quoted on p. 24 in Chiang.

"Design something new in the world": p. 319 in Chiang.

Frank Booth proposal for a cannery in 1914: Tom Mangelsdorf, *A History
of Steinbeck's Cannery Row* (Santa Cruz, CA: Western Tanager Press,
1986).

PAGE 147

Nancy Burnett in personal communication with Stephen R. Palumbi,
December 12, 2009.

Steve Webster in interview with Stephen R. Palumbi, November 4, 2007.

PAGE 150

Julie Packard in interview with Stephen R. Palumbi, January 6, 2008.

PAGE 151

Oil spill: Carol Steinhart and John Steinhart, *Blowout: A Case Study of the
Santa Barbara Oil Spill* (Belmont, CA: Duxbury Press, 1972).

PAGE 152

Co-owner of a Fortune 500 company by age 50: David Packard, *The HP
Way: How Bill Hewlett and I Built Our Company* (New York: Harper-
Collins, 1995), 197.

"Their only responsibility was to generate profits": p. 166 in Packard.

Vacations with H. Hoover: in Packard.

Cost of $20 million during his 3 years in public service: p. 185 in Packard.

"There were some charities I wanted to help": p. 177 in Packard.

PAGE 153

Packard Foundation worth in the 1990s: Michael S. Malone, *Bill & Dave: How Hewlett and Packard Built the World's Greatest Company* (New York: Portfolio Publishers, 2007), 309.

Joint Chiefs do the dishes: in Packard.

PAGE 155

What kind of motion?: Chuck Baxter in interview with Stephen R. Palumbi, October 31, 2007.

PAGE 157

Spinning glasses: Steve Webster in interview with Stephen R. Palumbi, November 4, 2007.

PAGE 159

Fishing values in California can be found at the National Marine Fisheries Service Web site: www.st.nmfs.noaa.gov/st1/commercial/landings/annual_landings.html. See also statistics at the National Ocean Economics Program: www.noep.mbari.com.

Tourism posts strong annual gains: in Chiang.

PAGE 161

Bar cost story recounted by Steve Webster, interview with Stephen R. Palumbi, November 2007.

Chapter 12

PAGE 164

Festa Santa Rosalia "on the full moon so the men could participate": Carol Lynn McKibben, *Beyond Cannery Row: Sicilian Women, Immigration, and Community in Monterey, California. 1915–1999* (Chicago: University of Illinois Press, 2006), 103.

Festival committee "rode in a decorated purse seine skiff": p. 112 in McKibben.

PAGE 166

Fancy fish finders: G. Aliotti in interview with Stephen R. Palumbi, September 2008.

PAGE 170

"Crab bait": Joel Sohn in interview with Stephen R. Palumbi, September 2008.

PAGE 171

Portolà walked only 9–10 miles a day, but he stopped each night at abundant running fresh water. Miguel Costansó, *The Costansó Narrative of the Portola expedition*, ed. Ray Brandes (Newhall, CA: Hogarth Press, 1970).

Southern marine species are immigrating into the bay: R. D. Sagarin, J. Barry, S. Gilman, and C. Baxter, " Climate Related Changes in an Intertidal Community Over Short and Long Time Scales," *Ecological Monographs* 69(1999):465–490.

Climate change and its approach are chronicled in Anthony D. Barnosky, *Heatstroke: Nature in an age of global warming* (Washington, DC: Island Press, 2009).

PAGE 172

"It is a busy old woman who finds herself mayor of Pacific Grove": letter to Mrs. Edward G. Benedict, "cousin Sue," Pacific Grove Natural History Museum archives.

Index

About Island Press

Since 1984, the nonprofit Island Press has been stimulating, shaping, and communicating the ideas that are essential for solving environmental problems worldwide. With more than 800 titles in print and some 40 new releases each year, we are the nation's leading publisher on environmental issues. We identify innovative thinkers and emerging trends in the environmental field. We work with world-renowned experts and authors to develop cross-disciplinary solutions to environmental challenges.

Island Press designs and implements coordinated book publication campaigns in order to communicate our critical messages in print, in person, and online using the latest technologies, programs, and the media. Our goal: to reach targeted audiences—scientists, policymakers, environmental advocates, the media, and concerned citizens—who can and will take action to protect the plants and animals that enrich our world, the ecosystems we need to survive, the water we drink, and the air we breathe.

Island Press gratefully acknowledges the support of its work by the Agua Fund, Inc., The Margaret A. Cargill Foundation, Betsy and Jesse Fink Foundation, The William and Flora Hewlett Foundation, The Kresge Foundation, The Forrest and Frances Lattner Foundation, The Andrew W. Mellon Foundation, The Curtis and Edith Munson Foundation, The Overbrook Foundation, The David and Lucile Packard Foundation, The Summit Foundation, Trust for Architectural Easements, The Winslow Foundation, and other generous donors.

The opinions expressed in this book are those of the author(s) and do not necessarily reflect the views of our donors.

P9-AGU-021

praise for

focus on the family marriage series

This marriage study series is pure Focus on the Family—
reliable, biblically sound and dedicated to reestablishing family values
in today's society. This series will no doubt help a multitude of couples
strengthen their relationship, not only with each other,
but also with God, the *creator* of marriage itself.

Bruce Wilkinson

Author, The BreakThrough Series: *The Prayer of Jabez,*
Secrets of the Vine and *A Life God Rewards*

In this era of such need, Dr. Dobson's team has produced solid,
helpful materials about Christian marriage. Even if they have been
through marriage studies before, every couple—married or engaged—
will benefit from this foundational study of life together. Thanks to
Focus on the Family for helping set us straight in this top priority.

Charles W. Colson

Chairman, Prison Fellowship Ministries

In my 31 years as a pastor, I've officiated at hundreds of weddings.
Unfortunately, many of those unions failed. I only wish the *Focus on the*
Family Marriage Series had been available to me during those years.
What a marvelous tool you as pastors and Christian leaders have
at your disposal. I encourage you to use it to assist those you
serve in building successful, healthy marriages.

H. B. London, Jr.

Vice President, Ministry Outreach/Pastoral Ministries
Focus on the Family

Looking for a prescription for a better marriage?
You'll enjoy this timely and practical series!

Dr. Kevin Leman

Author, *Sheet Music: Uncovering the Secrets of
Sexual Intimacy in Marriage*

The *Focus on the Family Marriage Series* is successful because it shifts
the focus from how to fix or strengthen a marriage to *who* can do it.
Through this study you will learn that a blessed marriage will be the
happy by-product of a closer relationship with the *creator* of marriage.

Lisa Whelchel

Author, *Creative Correction* and
The Facts of Life and Other Lessons My Father Taught Me

In a day and age where the covenant of marriage is so quickly tossed
aside in the name of incompatibility and irreconcilable differences, a
marriage Bible study that is both inspirational and practical is desperately
needed. The *Focus on the Family Marriage Series* is what couples are seeking.
I give my highest recommendation to this Bible study series that has the
potential to dramatically impact and improve marriages today. Marriage
is not so much about finding the right partner as it is about being the
right partner. These studies give wonderful biblical teachings for
helping those who want to learn the beautiful art of being and
becoming all that God intends in their marriage.

Lysa TerKeurst

President, Proverbs 31 Ministries
Author, *Capture His Heart* and *Capture Her Heart*

the giving
marriage

Gospel Light

Gospel Light is an evangelical Christian publisher dedicated to serving the local church. We believe God's vision for Gospel Light is to provide church leaders with biblical, user-friendly materials that will help them evangelize, disciple and minister to children, youth and families.

It is our prayer that this Gospel Light resource will help you discover biblical truth for your own life and help you minister to others. May God richly bless you.

For a free catalog of resources from Gospel Light, please call your Christian supplier or contact us at 1-800-4-GOSPEL *or* www.gospellight.com

PUBLISHING STAFF
William T. Greig, Chairman
Kyle Duncan, Publisher
Dr. Elmer L. Towns, Senior Consulting Publisher
Pam Weston, Senior Editor
Patti Pennington Virtue, Associate Editor
Hilary Young, Editorial Assistant
Jessie Minassian, Editorial Assistant
Bayard Taylor, M.Div., Senior Editor, Biblical and Theological Issues
Samantha A. Hsu, Cover and Internal Designer
Carol Stertzer, Contributing Writer

ISBN 0-8307-3151-2
© 2003 Focus on the Family
All rights reserved.
Printed in the U.S.A.

table of contents

foreword

The most urgent mission field on Earth is not across the sea or even across the street—it's right where you live: in your home and family. Jesus' last instruction was to "make disciples of all nations" (Matthew 28:19). At the thought of this command, our eyes look across the world for our work field. That's not bad; it's just not *all*. God intended the home to be the first place of Christian discipleship and growth (see Deuteronomy 6:4-8). Our family members must be the *first* ones we reach out to in word and example with the gospel of the Lord Jesus Christ, and the fundamental way in which this occurs is through the marriage relationship.

Divorce, blended families, the breakdown of communication and the complexities of daily life are taking a devastating toll on the God-ordained institutions of marriage and family. We do not need to look hard or search far for evidence that even Christian marriages and families are also in a desperate state. In response to the need to build strong Christ-centered marriages and families, this series was developed.

Focus on the Family is well known and respected worldwide for its stead-fast dedication to preserving the sanctity of marriage and family life. I can think of no better partnership than the one formed by Focus on the Family and Gospel Light to produce the *Focus on the Family Marriage Series*. This series is well-written, biblically sound and right on target for guiding couples to explore the foundation God has laid for marriage and to see Him as the role model for the perfect spouse. Through these studies, seeds will be planted that will germinate in your heart and mind for many years to come.

In our practical, bottom-line culture, we often want to jump over the *why* and get straight to the *what*. We think that by *doing* the six steps or *learning* the five ways, we will reach the goal. But deep-rooted growth is slower and more purposeful and begins with a well-grounded understanding of God's divine design. Knowing why marriage exists is crucial to making the how-tos more effective. Marriage is a gift from God, a unique and distinct covenant relationship through which His glory and goodness can resonate, and it is only through knowing the architect and His plan that we will build our marriage on the surest foundation.

God created marriage; He has a specific purpose for it, and He is committed to filling with fresh life and renewed strength each union yielded to Him. God wants to gather the hearts of every couple together, unite them in love and walk them to the finish line—all in His great grace and goodness.

May God, in His grace, lead you into His truth, strengthening your lives and your marriage.

Gary T. Smalley
Founder and Chairman of the Board
Smalley Relationship Center

introduction

At the beginning of creation God "made them male and female." "For this reason a man will leave his father and mother and be united to his wife, and the two will become one flesh." So they are no longer two, but one.
Mark 10:6-8

The Giving Marriage can be used in a variety of situations, including small-group Bible studies, Sunday School classes or counseling or mentoring situations. An individual couple can also use this book as an at-home marriage-building study.

Each of the four sessions contains four main components.

Session Overview

Tilling the Ground
This is an introduction to the topic being discussed—commentary and questions to direct your thoughts toward the main idea of the session.

Planting the Seed
This is the Bible study portion in which you will read Scripture and answer questions to help discover lasting truths from God's Word.

Watering the Hope
This is a time for discussion and prayer. Whether you are using the study at home as a couple, in a small group or in a classroom setting, talking about the lesson with your spouse is a great way to solidify the truth and plant it deeply into your hearts.

Harvesting the Fruit
As a point of action, this portion of the session offers suggestions on putting the truth of the Word into action in your marriage relationship.

Suggestions for Individual Couple Study

There are at least three options for using this study as a couple.

- It may be used as a devotional study that each spouse would study individually through the week; then on a specified day, come together and discuss what you have learned and how to apply it to your marriage.
- You might choose to study one session together in an evening and then work on the application activities during the rest of the week.
- Because of the short length of this study, it is a great resource for a weekend retreat. Take a trip away for the weekend, and study each session together, interspersed with your favorite leisure activities.

Suggestions for Group Study

There are many ways that this study can be used in a group situation. The most common way is in a small-group Bible study format. However, it can also be used in adult Sunday School class. However you choose to use it, there are some general guidelines to follow for group study.

- Keep the group small—five to six couples is probably the maximum.
- Ask couples to commit to regular attendance for the four weeks of the study. Regular attendance is a key to building relationships and trust in a group.
- Encourage participants *not* to share anything of a personal or potentially embarrassing nature without first asking the spouse's permission.
- Whatever is discussed in the group meetings is to be held in strictest confidence among group members only.

There are additional leader helps in the back of this book and in *The Focus on the Family Marriage Ministry Guide.*

Suggestions for Mentoring or Counseling Relationships

This study also lends itself for use in relationships where one couple mentors or counsels another couple.

- A mentoring relationship, where a couple that has been married for several years is assigned to meet on a regular basis with a younger couple, could be arranged through a system set up by a church or ministry.
- A less formal way to start a mentoring relationship is for a younger couple to take the initiative and approach a couple that exemplify a mature, godly marriage and ask them to meet with them on a regular basis. Or the reverse might be a mature couple that approaches a younger couple to begin a mentoring relationship.
- When asked to mentor, some might shy away and think that they could never do that, knowing that their own marriage is less than perfect. But just as we are to disciple new believers, we must learn to disciple married couples to strengthen marriages in this difficult world. The Lord has promised to be "with you always" (Matthew 28:20).
- Before you begin to mentor a couple, first complete the study yourselves. This will serve to strengthen your own marriage and prepare you for leading another couple.
- Be prepared to learn as much or more than the couple(s) you will mentor.

There are additional helps for mentoring relationships in *The Focus on the Family Marriage Ministry Guide.*

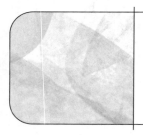

The Focus on the Family Marriage Series *is based on Al Janssen's* The Marriage Masterpiece *(Wheaton, IL: Tyndale House Publishers, 2001), an insightful look at what marriage can—and should—be. In this study, we are pleased to lead you through the wonderful journey of discovering the joy in your marriage that God wants you to experience!*

dealing with an
unfaithful *spouse*

Go, show your love to your wife again, though she is loved
by another and is an adulteress. Love her as the Lord
loves the Israelites, though they turn to other gods.

Hosea 3:1

In his book *The Marriage Masterpiece*, Al Janssen tells the story of a young pastor named Joe who found his long-lost childhood love, Georgine, living as a prostitute on the streets of a big city. Joe loved Georgine so much that he convinced her to leave her lifestyle and become his wife. Although Joe loved Georgine unconditionally, his church didn't accept her, and she felt the bitter sting of rejection. After a couple of years, Georgine began to long for her old, more exciting life, so she left Joe and their children to return to prostitution. This poignant vignette ends with Joe searching for Georgine and finding her once again in the city where he had found her several years earlier. Despite her unfaithfulness, Joe went to great lengths to free Georgine from her sinful life and bring her home.[1]

The word "unfaithful" arouses strong feelings in most of us. The following is the definition of "unfaithful":

> (1) not true to a promise, vow, etc.; (2) not true to a wife, husband, lover, etc., esp. in having sexual intercourse with someone else; (3) inaccurate; inexact; unreliable; untrustworthy.[2]

As you can see, sexual infidelity is only one aspect of being unfaithful. In this session, we're going to take a look at what it means to be unfaithful to your spouse and how Christ has set the ultimate example of faithfulness in all areas of marriage in His loving devotion to His Bride.

tilling the ground

The story of Joe and Georgine is a modern adaptation of Hosea's story in the Old Testament as recorded in the book of Hosea. Hosea was a prophet of God to the nation of Israel. His marriage and subsequent difficulties with his wife, Gomer, are a picture of God's relationship with unfaithful Israel.

1. If you were a member at Joe's church, what would you have thought about his decision to marry Georgine?

    What advice would you have given him?

2. Have you ever been criticized by other believers for doing something that was perceived as irresponsible, even though you knew you were doing what God wanted you to do? If so, what did it feel like?

3. Besides sexual infidelity, what are some other ways that a person could be unfaithful to his or her spouse?

    Let's explore more of Hosea's story and God's heart toward His people.

The book of Hosea relates an emotional and complex story of betrayal of a covenant relationship. Hosea was a prophet who lived during an era of extreme immorality and sinfulness in Israel (793-753 B.C.)[3] Hosea's marriage to Gomer paints a picture of God's love for His people, despite their unfaithfulness.

4. In Hosea 1:2-3, God instructed Hosea to marry an adulterous wife. Why do you think God asked him to do that?

5. According to Hosea 1:4-6,8-9, Gomer gave birth to three children: Jezreel, which means "to scatter"; Lo-Ruhamah, meaning "not loved"; Lo-Ammi, "not my people." Names in the Bible have significant meaning. Hosea means "salvation."[3] How do these names indicate God's feelings toward His people?

Notice the opening instruction to Hosea in 2:1: "Say to your brothers, 'My people,' and of your sisters, 'My loved one'"—the exact opposite of the names of the second and third child! He was addressing His beloved with words of affirmation. The rest of chapter 2 is God's indictment that He instructed Hosea to deliver to the Israelites.

6. What charges did God bring against Israel in Hosea 2:2-13?

What did God tell them He would do as a result of their unfaithfulness?

7. In verse 14, the tone of God's message changes. What does He promise to His Bride?

8. According to Hosea 2:19-20, what qualities should mark every marital union?

9. Why do you think God didn't give up on the Israelites?

10. What does His love for them reveal about His love for you?

11. In what ways is the Church today often unfaithful to God?

Get Outta Here, Satan!

Scripture has a lot to say about faithfulness in marriage. The apostle Paul urged believers to flee from sexual immorality. "All other sins a man commits are outside his body, but he who sins sexually sins against his own body" (1 Corinthians 6:18).

12. In 1 Corinthians 6:15-20, why did Paul point out that Christians are one with Christ in spirit? How does that relate to his command to "flee from sexual immorality"?

   How might this revelation affect an it's-not-hurting-anyone attitude about committing adultery or other sexual sins?

Satan's scheme is to gradually lower our standards and seduce us so that we spend less time with the Lord and other worthwhile pursuits, allowing more time to entertain tempting thoughts. It may begin by going to lunch with a coworker of the opposite gender or watching a movie that plants lustful thoughts in our minds.

Recent studies showed that Americans spend $8 billion on hard-core pornographic videos, peep shows, live sex acts, adult cable programming, computer pornography, sexual devices and sex magazines.[4] As a culture we are obsessed with sexual attraction. Is it any wonder that so many marriages are in trouble?

13. According to James 1:13-14, what happens when a person gives in to temptation?

To what does sin give birth (v. 15)?

14. What things tempt you the most?

15. How do you usually handle temptation?

Have you been honest with your spouse about your temptations?

16. Are you able to listen to your spouse talk about his or her temptations without being judgmental or disruptive?

Once you and your spouse are able to share your daily struggles and temptations with each other, you will experience a deeper level of honesty and openness. Any time a person admits his or her temptations, it pops the balloon, so to speak. The thought of that particular temptation becomes less exciting.

Pray often with your spouse that the Lord will help each of you walk uprightly before Him. Let this verse be your inspiration:

Whatever is true, whatever is noble, whatever is right, whatever is pure, whatever is lovely, whatever is admirable—if anything is excellent or praiseworthy—think about such things (Philippians 4:8).

Committing this verse and other similar ones to memory can be the first step in dealing with tempting thoughts or actions.

Adultery Hits Home

As you saw in Hosea, God is merciful. He forgives sinners, and so must we.

Hosea 3 describes Hosea's reconciliation with Gomer. Notice how Hosea's actions are a picture of God's reconciliation with us. Hosea sought out Gomer and paid the price to redeem her, but there was one condition on their reconciliation.

17. What was the condition Hosea put on Gomer's return?

   Was it a reasonable condition? Explain.

Hosea loved and married someone who did not remain faithful. By Jewish law, an adulterous spouse normally would have been sentenced to death by stoning (see Leviticus 20:10), but God used Hosea's experience to show how much He loves us who are so deserving of a death sentence for our sin.

18. Consider the biblical example of the woman brought to Jesus for committing adultery. "If any one of you is without sin," Jesus told the Pharisees, "let him be the first to throw a stone at her" (John 8:7). To the woman, he said with compassion, "Go now and leave your life of sin" (v. 11). How does that relate to the condition Hosea placed on Gomer's return to their marriage?

Sometimes it is easier to accept God's forgiveness than it is to forgive ourselves when we sin. Rather than *condemn* yourself for your sinful behavior, *change* your behavior. That's what God desires. He wants you to walk away from temptation and to experience true freedom.

If your spouse has been unfaithful to you by committing adultery, you have some decisions to make. Contributors to *The Woman's Study Bible* say "a spouse who is able to forgive adulterous behavior on the part of a mate is encouraged to remain within a marriage. [However,] adultery is regarded as such a severe breach of trust and fidelity that it is noted as *permissible* grounds for divorce"[5] (see Matthew 5:32; 19:9).

Likewise, Al Janssen states in his book that a spouse doesn't have to "endure endless infidelity. . . . Jesus Himself acknowledged that adultery was the one legitimate grounds for divorce, at least when the offender continues unrepentant."[6]

19. Why is adultery such a betrayal of trust in a marriage?

20. Do you know of someone who has dealt with the issue of adultery in his or her marriage? What were the consequences of unfaithfulness?

21. What can a couple do to guard against the temptation of having an affair?

22. What can we do to guard our hearts from lustful thoughts or sexual immorality?

23. Think about people you know who have committed adultery. What do you think led to their unfaithfulness?

Sexual immorality has wrecked numerous homes and created emotional turmoil for many families. If you have been faithful and your partner has not, you know how Hosea must have felt. In fact, you have a taste of how God must have felt—and still feels today. If you are presently in this situation, pray that you will hear clearly from the Lord. You may need to separate yourself from your spouse for a time to gain a fresh perspective on the situation. You should also seek outside help from a Christian counselor who can give you objective guidance in reestablishing a trustworthy relationship.

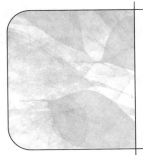

Note: *In additional to spiritual issues, there are some legitimate health concerns related to adultery. A woman I know is separated from her promiscuous husband. She is praying for God to restore their marriage. Her husband recently told her that he wanted to come back, and she wisely said that if he did, he would have to agree to be tested for HIV and other sexually transmitted diseases.*

Consider Susan's story.

> Susan works for a successful company and deeply respects her boss, Kent, who has built the company up from scratch. She is married, but he is single. They have a lot in common and their work requires that they spend a lot of time together working on specific projects. Kent is passionate about his work, and he regularly praises Susan for her work performance. Susan's husband, Phil, is quiet and reserved and finds it difficult to express his feelings and needs, but the two of them do share many of the same interests. In spite of her love for Phil, Susan has begun to feel more valued and appreciated at work than at home, and she especially enjoys her conversations with Kent. As she sat down one weekend and analyzed her situation, she realized she was becoming emotionally attached to Kent and could easily slip into an affair with him.[7]

24. In your opinion, how common is this scenario?

25. If you were Susan, what would you do?

If you were Kent and sensed Susan's emotional attachment, what would you do?

26. If Phil suspects that Susan is becoming emotionally involved with Kent, what should he do?

27. What safeguards can a couple establish to avoid work-related emotional affairs that might lead to adultery?

28. How do you think God views emotional affairs?

First, discuss your answers to questions 14 through 16 with your spouse.

29. Think of small ways in which you may have been unfaithful to your spouse. Did you recently say something negative about him or her in public? Have you been making more time for the kids' activities than you have been reserving for your spouse? Have you been spending too much time at work or with friends?

Ask your mate for forgiveness, and seek to be faithful in all ways. Give your spouse permission to tell you the next time you behave in a way that projects unfaithfulness—and don't be offended to receive the news. After all, unfaithfulness in seemingly small ways can easily lead to sexual infidelity.

To avoid lustful thoughts, guard your heart from sexually suggestive or explicit videos, movies, novels, magazines, radio and television programs and Internet sites. These items may cause you to stumble and lead you down the path of temptation into sin. Get rid of all questionable products in your home, and replace them with reading and viewing materials that will draw you closer to God and your spouse. Do you have a problem with Internet pornography? Ask your spouse to help keep you accountable. Install a filter to block inappropriate sites and related garbage. It might even require that you get rid of those things that cause temptation to enter your home and your thoughts.

Find an accountability partner of the same gender. An accountability partner should be someone who has a heart for serving the Lord and will keep matters confidential. Meet weekly, biweekly or monthly to pray for one another. Discuss and pray about all areas of unfaithfulness that are keeping you from enjoying a deeper relationship with God and your spouse.

Pray with your spouse, asking the Lord's help in staying faithful in your marriage. Keep short accounts of your sins with Him and with your spouse whenever you have a problem remaining faithful to your commitment to your spouse.

Note: *If you are experiencing serious problems with issues of trust and faithfulness in your marriage, we advise you to seek professional help through a reputable Christian counselor. Your pastor may be able to guide you in finding the right person, or you can call Focus on the Family's counseling department (1-800-A-Family or 1-719-531-3400) for a free consultation by a licensed counselor[8] and a referral to a national counseling service network of over 2,000 licensed counselors throughout the United States.*

Notes

1. Al Janssen, *The Marriage Masterpiece* (Wheaton, IL: Tyndale House Publishers, 2001), pp. 115-136.
2. *The Collins English Dictionary,* www.wordreference.com (accessed December 4, 2002), s.v. "unfaithful."
3. Dorothy Kelley Patterson and Rhonda Kelley, eds., *The Woman's Study Bible: Opening the Word of God to Women* (New King James Version) (Nashville, TN: Thomas Nelson, Inc., 1995), p. 1456.
4. Ed Young, *Fatal Distractions* (Nashville, TN: Thomas Nelson, Inc., 2000), p. 119.
5. Patterson and Kelley, *The Woman's Study Bible*, p. 1462.
6. Al Janssen, *The Marriage Masterpiece*, pp. 128-129.
7. This is a compilation of several stories. Any resemblance to an actual situation is purely coincidental.
8. Counselors at Focus on the Family are licensed in the state of Colorado.

living with an
unbelieving *spouse*

If any brother has a wife who is not a believer and she is willing to live with him, he must not divorce her. And if a woman has a husband who is not a believer and he is willing to live with her, she must not divorce him.

1 Corinthians 7:12-13

When I was a girl, my family went to church nearly every time the door was open: Sunday mornings, Sunday nights and Wednesday nights. I remember feeling sorry for the married women who attended without their husbands. At the same time, I admired them for their faithfulness. Some of them came with their children and sat by themselves as the children performed in the annual Christmas musical. Even then, I sensed how important it was to marry a believer, and if I was going to get married, I wanted a spiritual closeness much like my parents had.

Fortunately, I did marry a Christian. We attend church together and can relate on most spiritual matters.

For one reason or another, some of you may not be spiritually connected to your spouse. Don't give up the dream! God wants you to persevere, to keep believing for the salvation of your unbelieving spouse and to stay put in the marriage. You may be the only *Jesus* your spouse sees!

Whether your spouse is not a believer or is simply facing a time of spiritual rebellion, this study is designed to help keep you on track and stay committed to what God's Word says about this topic.

tilling the ground

Because God specially designed us with a body, soul and spirit, it's not surprising that spiritual matters play such a huge role in marriage. Think about it: Even people who don't claim to believe in God can become very emotional when spiritual topics are discussed.

1. Why might a person's religion be so important in a marriage relationship?

2. Why would unbelievers be attracted to Christians?

3. Why would a Christian be attracted to an unbeliever?

4. What characteristics attracted you to your spouse?

5. Even if both spouses are Christians, there might be areas where there is a spiritual mismatch. What, if any, spiritual concerns do you and your spouse differ on?

According to Dr. Fred Lowery, author of *Covenant Marriage*, if you are married to an unbeliever, you have *union* but no *unity*. "There is no agreement at the deepest level of the spirit," he writes.[1] Christ cannot be at the center of a marriage unless both parties put Him there.

planting the seed

God's perfect plan is for a believer to marry someone who loves and serves Him. The apostle Paul admonished us in 2 Corinthians 6:14: "Do not be yoked together with unbelievers. For what do righteousness and wickedness have in common?"

Sometimes in our disobedience, we ignore the voice of the Holy Spirit and give in to our own desires. Even Paul, one of the greatest evangelists of all times, experienced this internal struggle. "So I find this law at work: When I want to do good, evil is right there with me," he said. "For in my inner being I delight in God's law; but I see another law at work in the members of my body, waging war against the law of my mind and making me a prisoner of the law of sin at work within my members" (Romans 7:21-23).

As some may have discovered, there is often a price to pay for ignoring God's wisdom. But there is hope for those who have stepped outside of God's will.

6. What are the usual reasons that believers marry unbelievers?

7. What often happens when believers ignore God's mandate and marry unbelievers?

8. What advice would you give a Christian friend deeply in love with a seemingly *good* person who doesn't have a relationship with Christ?

Whether we are stepping outside God's will in choosing our marriage partner or in making wrong choices in other areas of our life, there will be consequences to our actions. When we return to God and repent, He is merciful and forgiving, but we must still live with the consequences of past choices. He will provide the strength and grace to live victorious in spite of our circumstances.

First Comes Love; Then Comes . . . Christianity?

The climate of a marriage can quickly change when two unbelievers marry and one later becomes a Christian. Consider the example of noted authors Lee and Leslie Strobel, who wrote *Surviving a Spiritual Mismatch in Marriage*. When Leslie became a believer, Lee said their fairy-tale marriage took a nose-dive—at least for him. He was afraid he was going to lose his wife to Jesus Christ.[2]

Leslie wisely heeded the biblical advice found in 1 Peter 3:1: "Wives, in the same way be submissive to your husbands so that, if any of them do not believe the word, they may be won over without words by the behavior of their wives."[3]

Leslie made certain that she was attentive to her husband and his needs. Although there were new conflicts that arose because of her newfound faith, she made it a point not to preach to him and instead focused on the activities they had in common. Ultimately, God used Leslie to point Lee to Christ.

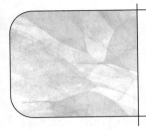

Note: *If an unbelieving spouse is involved in adultery or other wicked behavior, the situation becomes more complex. It is advised that you seek professional Christian counseling to deal with such a serious situation. (See p. 23 at the end of session 1 for further information.)*

9. What does 1 Corinthians 7:12-16 say about being married to an unbeliever who is willing to live with the believing spouse?

10. Look closely at verse 15. What do you think is meant by "God has called us to live in peace"? What should a believer do if he or she is married to a physically or emotionally abusive person?

11. One of the biggest obstacles in a spiritually mismatched marriage is how to raise the children. How might verse 14 be an encouragement to a believer married to an unbeliever?

12. What might a believer do if the unbelieving spouse asks him or her to do things that would displease God?

Show—Don't Tell

Those who try to evangelize and shove Jesus down the throat of their unbelieving spouse will likely encounter increased resistance—and may even make things worse. Have you heard the saying "Show—don't tell"? Sometimes it's best to demonstrate the love of Jesus through our actions, not just through our words—and that is exactly what Peter is talking about in 1 Peter 3:1.

Peter goes on to say in verse 4 that a woman's beauty "should be that of your inner self, the unfading beauty of a gentle and quiet spirit, which is of great worth in God's sight."

13. What are things that can be done to develop the inner beauty spoken of in 1 Peter 3?

14. Even in a marriage where both spouses are believers, the spouses still need to show Jesus' love to each other. List some practical ways that you can daily show the love of Christ to your spouse.

15. Read about the fruit of the Spirit in Galatians 5:22-23. Which fruit do you need to develop more fully in relation to your spouse?

16. Can you recall an occasion when your Christlike actions opened doors for you to share your faith with someone? Describe the experience.

How did that experience affect you?

17. Have you ever felt that you missed an opportunity to share Jesus with someone? Describe what happened.

Confront in Love

As we previously read in Romans 7, Christians do struggle with sin—and, unfortunately, we will have inner battles until Christ comes. Why? Because we are imperfect and live in an imperfect world. There may be times when even a believing, committed Christian will make bad choices and fall into a spiral of sin.

The Bible contains numerous examples of godly men and women who were disobedient and made wrong choices. Consider David, who committed adultery with Bathsheba. When she became pregnant, David had her husband, Uriah, killed in battle (see 2 Samuel 11). It's hard to imagine that a man who loved God so much could be caught up in such wickedness. None of us are immune to the influence of sin.

Nathan, God's prophet, confronted David about his sin. When David finally realized what he had done, he responded: "I have sinned against the Lord" (2 Samuel 12:13). But there were consequences. Despite his fasting and prayers, David's son by Bathsheba died. But God forgave David and continued to use him. In fact, he went down in history as Israel's mightiest king.

There may be times in a believer's life when a rebellious spirit takes over and a spouse heads down the wrong path. You might have to be a Nathan in your spouse's life and confront the sin. This is a situation that should be covered in much prayer and even fasting before a spouse (or anyone else for that matter) is approached and the sin is pointed out. When we do not know how to pray, "the [Holy] Spirit himself intercedes for us" (Romans 8:26).

If you are the one being confronted, how will you react?

18. What are some things a couple can do to foster spiritual growth and lessen the risk for spiritual rebellion?

Whether you are the confronter or the confrontee, you need to rely on the grace and power of God to see you through any time of testing or trial. "Blessed is the man who perseveres under trial, because when he has stood the test, he will receive the crown of life that God has promised to those who love him" (James 1:12).

 watering the hope

Consider the story of Louise and Paul Peppin.

Louise Peppin was married for 71 years to her unbelieving husband, Paul. He was a good provider and loved his family, but he wanted nothing to do with church. Year after year, Louise prayed that her husband would come to know God—but she never saw that happen.

Although she never saw the results of her prayers, they were not in vain. During the year before Louise's death, Paul suffered a series of strokes and ended up in the hospital in a partial coma. His grandson Bruce went to visit him the day before his grandmother's funeral and found his grandfather awake and listening intently to what Bruce had to share. Bruce prayed with his grandfather to receive the gift of eternal life through Jesus Christ. Bruce believed that "his grandfather had the experience of the thief on the cross next to Jesus. 'I believe my grandfather acknowledged all that he'd heard over the years and stumbled into the kingdom at the last hour. It's a legacy to the faithfulness of my grandmother.'"[4]

19. Why do you think it took Paul so long to acknowledge Jesus Christ as Lord and Savior?

20. What had he missed out on all those years that he had not followed Jesus?

21. Why do you think Louise did not give up on Paul and just divorce him?

22. How was the family sanctified by Louise's life (see 1 Corinthians 7:12-14)?

23. Do you know of someone like Louise who has prayed for an unbelieving spouse? Describe the effect that person's witness has had on others and, in particular, on you.

Because God has given each of us a free will, we can only pray that our loved ones will make a personal decision for Christ. James 5:16 says, "The prayer of a righteous man is powerful and effective." Consider keeping a prayer journal, recording your requests and the answers to your prayers concerning your spouse. Even if your spouse is a believer, he or she needs your prayerful support. You will be amazed to see how God hears and answers even the smallest of requests.

Ultimately, we all have to decide whom we will serve. Even if your spouse (or other loved ones) never comes to know the Lord, one thing is certain: By weathering the storms and diligently seeking the Father, you will certainly become more like Jesus.

 harvesting the fruit

If this study has touched a nerve in your marriage relationship, you and your spouse will need to deal with the issues it has brought up. That might require professional counseling with your pastor or a Christian counselor.

24. What is the benefit of staying with a spouse who has chosen not to follow the Lord?

25. What are the positive aspects of your marriage that encourage you to stay together?

26. If one of you (or both of you) is not a believer in Christ, what are some issues you need to deal with?

If you and your spouse are both believers, you can be a catalyst to help others who struggle in this area.

27. What would you tell a young person at your church who wants your opinion about dating an unbeliever?

28. Look around you. Are there any church members who come alone because their spouse won't join them? What could you do to encourage and uphold that person? What activities could you and your spouse invite them to if one of them isn't a Christian?

29. How can you strengthen your own marriage to avoid spiritual rebellion?

Be Prepared to Share Christ

Are you prepared to share God's plan of salvation with your spouse or other unbelievers?

What to Share About Christ

- God loves you and wants you to have eternal life (see John 3:16).
- Sin keeps us separated from God (see Romans 3:23; 6:23).
- Jesus paid the penalty for our sin by dying on the cross. Only His death on the cross can bridge the gap between God and people (see 1 Timothy 2:5; Romans 5:8).
- Our response is to receive Christ (see Revelation 3:20; Romans 10:9).

How to Receive Christ

- Admit you are a sinner—this involves confession.
- Be willing to turn from your sins—repent.
- Believe that Jesus died on the cross and rose from the grave.
- Invite Jesus to come in and control your life through the Holy Spirit.

Notes
1. Dr. Fred Lowery, *Covenant Marriage* (West Monroe, LA: Howard Publishing, 2002), p. 76.
2. Lee and Leslie Strobel, *Surviving a Spiritual Mismatch in Marriage* (Grand Rapids, MI: Zondervan Publishing House, 2002).
3. Ibid.
4. Al Janssen, *The Marriage Masterpiece* (Wheaton, IL: Tyndale House Publishers, 2001), pp. 132-133.

living with an incapacitated *spouse*

We also rejoice in our sufferings, because we know that suffering produces persever-
ance; perseverance, character; and character, hope.
Romans 5:3-4

Born in 1950, Joni Eareckson was the youngest of four daughters who grew up in a loving Christian home. Her close family was very involved in a wide variety of outdoor activities. Along with her athletic abilities, Joni was also blessed with creative talents, and having just graduated from high school, she looked forward to a promising future.

However, one July day in 1967 her life was irrevocably changed. When she dove into the Chesapeake Bay near her Maryland home, she immediately realized something was wrong. She had hit the bottom of the bay and broken her neck. As a result of the accident, she was paralyzed from the shoulders down and would spend the rest of her life in a wheelchair with others taking care of her most basic needs.

While dealing with her anger, severe depression, suicidal thoughts and the lengthy rehabilitation, Joni began to understand that God had a purpose for her life. With God's help and the aid and encouragement of family and friends, Joni's life is full and active. Despite her physical limitations, she is a best-selling and award-winning author of over 30 books, a highly sought after speaker, an advocate for disabled people and the founder and director of Joni and Friends, a ministry that serves disabled people all over the world. She also has a daily five-minute radio broadcast that is heard on over 850 outlets. She has also become known for her lovely singing voice and the beautiful pictures that she creates by holding the brush, pen or pencil in her mouth.[1]

Perhaps the most remarkable part of her story is her marriage to Ken Tada, which took place in 1982. Joni had resigned herself to remaining single all her days until Ken came into her life. They have been happily married now for over 20 years. A recently retired teacher, Ken now works full-time alongside Joni in the Joni and Friends ministry. Ken says, "I love working beside my wife in ministry that involves sharing the good news of Christ with disabled people. It's something I know a lot about!"[2] He was recently the honored recipient of the FamilyLife Ministries Robert McQuilken Award for "The Courageous Love of a Marriage Covenant Keeper."[3]

Most marriages may not experience quite so serious a disability as the paralysis of one spouse, but every marriage will have its tough times. A spouse might come down with a long-term illness (such as chronic fatigue syndrome) or experience a short-term injury or illness (such as a back injury or pneumonia) that requires an extended time of convalescence. Even clinical depression can have a negative impact on a marriage. Any difficulty or trial has the potential to adversely affect a marriage relationship, but God has made His power available to help any couple triumph over any adversity.

tilling the ground

When we plan our weddings, most of us do not anticipate trials or difficulties. However, if we said the traditional vows at our ceremony, we vowed to stay together through the good and the bad.

1. What do the vows "for better or for worse, for richer or for poorer, in sickness and in health" mean to you?

2. In what ways might a debilitating illness or injury impact a person's identity and self-worth?

How would damaged self-esteem impact a marriage relationship?

3. Have you or someone you know experienced a situation where a spouse has been temporarily or permanently incapacitated? How has that impacted the marriage?

Even situations such as the death of a relative or being passed over for a job can cause temporary setbacks in your life and affect your marriage. Knowing that trials are a part of every life and being prepared to deal them are important in building a strong marriage.

planting the seed

Refined by Fire

God never said it would be easy for us as Christians. In fact, Paul said we will experience trials but that these trials have a purpose: "We know that suffering produces perseverance; perseverance, character; and character, hope" (Romans 5:3-4). The apostle Peter wrote, "In this you greatly rejoice, though now for a little while you may have had to suffer grief in all kinds of trials. These have come so that your faith—of greater worth than gold, which perishes even though refined by fire—may be proved genuine and may result in praise, glory and honor when Jesus Christ is revealed" (1 Peter 1:6-7). God allows us to experience adversity and heartache, but He will bring out something positive when we are surrendered to Him.

4. How can suffering ultimately lead to hope, as Paul described in Romans 5:3-4?

5. Reread 1 Peter 1:6-7. Have you seen the evidence in your own life or in the lives of others where difficulties or troubles have resulted in a pure-gold faith? Explain.

The process of refining gold or silver requires very high heat. When the gold or silver is melted, the impurities rise to the surface where they can be skimmed off by the gold- or silversmith. That is a picture of what God does for us through adversity—He skims off those things that make us impure.

Built on a Strong Foundation

Matthew 7:24-27 relates the story of the wise builder and the foolish builder.

6. What is the requirement for a strong foundation in our lives?

Is it easier to build on rock or on sand? How does that relate to facing adversity?

7. How could a couple strengthen the foundation of their marriage?

8. What storms has your marriage weathered so far?

What has helped you weather these storms?

9. One of Joni Eareckson Tada's favorite verses is 2 Corinthians 12:9: "My grace is sufficient for you, for my power is made perfect in weakness." How has her life demonstrated this principle?

How does that verse impact you?

The words in 2 Corinthians 12:9 were stated by the Lord to Paul in answer to his prayers asking to have a thorn in the flesh removed from him. No one knows what the thorn might have been, but it caused Paul a great deal of suffering (see v. 7). What ever it might have been, the Lord did not remove it so that Paul might learn to rely on Christ's power to accomplish His plan. We might ask God to remove a difficulty from our own lives, but He does not always answer in the way we expect.

10. Reread 2 Corinthians 12:7-10. How have you experienced Christ's power in your weakness?

Where do you need Christ's power right now?

We need to realize that life will bring storms our way, and we need to be prepared for these storms by building our marriage on God's sure foundation, Jesus Christ. When we strengthen our relationship with Him, our marriage will be stronger and will hold up under the daily pressures no matter the circumstances.

Covered in Prayer

A woman wrote a letter to *Marriage Partnership* magazine asking how she could help her husband, who may have multiple sclerosis (MS). The symptoms, she said, have really taken a toll on him.

Gary and Carrie Oliver, who specialize in marriage and family issues, responded to her question. They suggested that "much of a man's identity is based on his ability to do 'manly' things: to provide, procreate, and protect."[4] It is normal for a man to feel a wide range of emotions in such a difficult situation, and they encouraged the writer to identify her own emotions so that she could interact better with her husband. The counselors also encouraged her to contact a local MS support group in her area.[5]

In conclusion they said it was essential to ask other couples to pray for her and her spouse daily and with them regularly. They referred her to James 5:16, which states: "The prayer of a righteous man is powerful and effective."[6]

The Olivers also wrote: "We're not being glib or 'spiritualizing' when we emphasize the power of prayer. It's transformed our own marriage and for more than 30 years we've seen what prayer can do in the lives of many other marriages and families."[7]

No matter what type of pain you or your spouse may be experiencing, be diligent to pray—together as a couple as often as possible as well as alone. Scripture promises, "This is the confidence we have in approaching God: that if we ask anything according to his will, he hears us. And if we know that he hears us—whatever we ask—we know that we have what we asked of him" (1 John 5:14-15). God loves us and hears our cries for help. He wants us to depend on Him for all things, big or small.

11. What difference would daily praying together make in a marriage?

    How often do you and your spouse pray together?

12. What prayers of yours have been answered recently?

13. How has prayer made a difference in your marriage?

    In the marriages of others that you know?

Not only can we turn to the Lord in prayer as a couple, but we can also turn to other believers for their prayer support. The Olivers suggested that the woman who wrote to them should seek out an MS support group to help her and her husband weather this terrible storm in their lives. Others who have gone, or are going, through similar circumstances can be of immeasurable help, encouragement and support. If you are going through this study with a small group, this is a great opportunity to build a support group for one another through prayer and encouragement. If you are not in a small group, look around for an opportunity to build a support group of fellow believers.

14. Who can you turn to—outside of your own family—for support, prayer and encouragement in difficult times?

If you can't name at least two other people to whom you could turn in times of trouble, what might you do to nurture supportive relationships?

The importance of prayer cannot be overemphasized. If you don't pray together regularly, decide on an action plan with your spouse now, and work toward making prayer a regular part of your daily schedule. In addition to your own personal needs, remember to pray for couples you know who are going through trials.

The creator made us and knows exactly how we are wired. If there were a problem with our house, we would go to the builder of our house, so why not go to God when an illness or setback impacts us spiritually, emotionally or physically?

Consider the story of Jake and Lil.

Jake had worked hard as an insurance salesman for over 30 years, and he eagerly looked forward to an early retirement at 57. He and his wife, Lil, had planned well and scrimped and saved their money to be prepared for this new stage in their lives. They planned on traveling around the country in their beautiful new motor home and had already mapped out their first journey. Just a few weeks before his retirement, Jake answered his office phone one afternoon and heard Lil's tear-filled voice on the other end.

"Jake," she began, but then her voice broke. After a moment to collect herself, she continued, "The doctor just told me that my X rays show a suspicious shadow on my liver." She began to cry softly. "And he wants me to go in Friday for surgery."

Jake jumped up from his chair and told her that he would be right home.

Their retirement plans were put on hold while they made the rounds of doctors, hospitals and chemotherapy. Against Lil's protests, Jake sold the motor home and told her he really would rather stay home anyway. When Lil lost all of her hair, Jake shaved his own head so that the two could admire their matching heads. Their children marveled at how patient and kind their father had become in his care for their mother.

Finally the doctors told them they could do no more for Lil and that she would have a year or two left to live. Jake planned a short trip for the two of them to the cabin they stayed in on their honeymoon 37 years before. It was a heaven-blessed time for both of them as they fished, prayed, walked, sang and reminisced about their life together. Fifteen short months later, Lil died at home in Jake's tender embrace, surrounded by their children.

When asked how he survived the ordeal, Jake could only say, "She was never a burden to me. It was a blessing to be able to love and care for her the way she had loved and cared for me for 38 years. I know we will be together in heaven one day."[8]

15. What legacy did Jake and Lil's marriage leave for their children and grandchildren?

16. Often our dreams are not carried out the way we planned. How do you react when your plans are cut short or even shattered?

17. How could others minister to couples such as Jake and Lil?

18. Do you know someone like Jake who willingly serves his or her spouse? What have you learned from that marriage model?

Even if you or your spouse never experience a debilitating illness or injury, there will be times when one spouse must give more than his or her 100 percent to the other, such as during illness, grief, depression or other emotional or physical stress. Even happy times—a new baby, a relocation, the holidays, etc.—can put extra stress on a marriage. The deeper we build our marriage foundation on God's Word and a growing relationship with Him, the better we can withstand the storms of life.

19. What do you and your spouse need to do to strengthen your marriage foundation so that you can weather life's storms?

20. What are some of the happy times that have put stress on your marriage?

21. How has your spouse shown compassion, tenderness and love to you during a difficult time? Have you thanked him or her for that support?

22. In what situations do you need to show compassion, tenderness and love toward your spouse?

Do you need to ask forgiveness from your spouse for neglecting him or her during a difficult time? Write down your thoughts here to share later.

23. How could you and your spouse be a support to someone else who might be going through a difficult time in their marriage?

Paul instructed us to "be kind and compassionate to one another, forgiving each other, just as in Christ God forgave you. Be imitators of God . . . and live a life of love, just as Christ loved us and gave himself up for us as a fragrant offering and sacrifice to God" (Ephesians 4:32—5:2). Pray together, asking God to help you to practice kindness, compassion and forgiveness.

Notes
1. Women of Faith, "Joni Eareckson Tada," *History's Women Newsletter*. http://www.historyswomen.com/joni.html (accessed January 20, 2003); "About Joni," *Joni and Friends*, http://www.joniandfriends.org/tadabio.shtml (accessed January 20, 2003).
2. "Ken And Joni Tada: Twenty Years of Marriage and Serving Together" *Joni and Friends*, http://www.joniandfriends.org/root/ken_joni.shtml (accessed January 20, 2003).
3. Ibid.
4. Gary and Carrie Collins, "Couple Counsel," *Marriage Partnership* 19, no. 3 (Fall 2002), p. 21.
5. Ibid.
6. Ibid.
7. Ibid.
8. This is a compilation of several stories. Any resemblance to an actual situation is purely coincidental.

living with a hopeful *heart*

All these people were still living by faith when they died. They did not receive the things promised; they only saw them and welcomed them from a distance.

Hebrews 11:13

I recently watched the interview of an amazing man named Garwin Dobbins on *The Austin Awakening*, a TV program that airs on several Christian networks. Garwin has a rare disease that causes his muscles to turn to bone. "It feels like two different people are twisting the inner core of your bones and putting them over an open flame," he explained.[1]

Despite his disease, Garwin said he is thankful for so many things. Referring to his appreciation of sight, Garwin said, "When I look about and see the color, I know He cares for me."[2]

I wasn't quite prepared for what happened after the brief interview. A few men helped Garwin get out of his wheelchair and propped him up to sing. As he stood leaning on a cane for support, he began to sing with a feeble voice the well-known chorus of "I Can Only Imagine" by MercyMe.[3] The lyrics expressed his anticipation of basking in all the glory of Jesus Christ in heaven. Although Garwin's body was racked with pain, he knew that all the anguish of this life would someday melt in the light emanating from Jesus' perfect face. The thought was overwhelming—his song was a natural overflow of the indescribable hope welling up within him.

Though his body is in pain, Garwin Dobbins isn't focused on this life—his hope rests in Jesus and what lies ahead! He isn't worried about his physical health because he knows he will soon have a glorified body in heaven. Garwin has the spirit of a champion.

Do you have Garwin's champion spirit when it comes to your marriage? Not many of us enter into marriage expecting to have an unfaithful, unbelieving or incapacitated spouse. But when wedded bliss turns into a wedded mess, we can turn to Scripture for comfort. In God's Word, we can begin to see the big picture unfold and can be reminded that those who have a personal relationship with Christ will spend eternity with Him in heaven, where there will be no sorrow or pain.

tilling the ground

For nearly 34 of her 37 years of marriage, Laura has served the Lord faithfully while her husband, Ken, has run from Him. They were separated once earlier in their marriage due to Ken's infidelity, but they got back together. Laura has suggested that they go to marriage counseling, but Ken thinks they have a great marriage and won't go.

Despite the circumstances, Laura is committed to hanging in there and making the most of their marriage. She knows her husband loves her and they do have a lot in common and enjoy doing things together. However, they have never experienced the spiritual depth that Christian couples can. Laura is hopeful that they will one day be spiritually united.

Has Laura found much happiness and fulfillment in her marriage? Probably not as she had planned, but she perseveres and continues to pray for her husband. Her focus is on God rather than her circumstances. She has been faithful to Ken and to God, and she hopes things will change. If they don't, she will at least have the assurance of knowing she obeyed God by staying in the marriage.

1. How can a couple who are not united spiritually still have a good marriage?

2. How might a person keep hope alive in difficult times?

3. Do you know someone like Garwin Dobbins who is an encouragement to others in spite of his or her severe pain or difficulty? How has that person encouraged or strengthened your own faith?

When your hope is in the Lord, the difficult circumstances will be easier to bear. Let's look at biblical examples of hopeful hearts for encouragement.

planting the seed

Hebrews 11 is a powerful, hope-filled chapter to read. In a nutshell, this chapter presents biblical heroes who served God, even when it was tough—men and women including Noah, Abraham and Sarah, Moses, Rahab, and the list goes on. Despite their obedience to God that brought on mistreatment, imprisonment, torture, etc., none of them received the full extent of what God had promised—at least not in their lifetime. Their faith was placed in the eternal Father, not on earthly comforts. They knew that God is sovereign and that He has an eternal plan.

By faith, Moses left his comfortable life as the son of Pharaoh's daughter to lead a group of grumbling slaves.

4. What is the definition of "faith" in Hebrews 11:1?

What does that mean to you?

5. Why is it impossible to please God without faith (see Hebrews 11:6)?

6. After reading Hebrews 11:23-28, list the ways in which Moses stepped out in faith.

7. According to Hebrews 11:25-26, what did Moses *choose* to give up and why?

According to verse 27, why did Moses persevere?

If you were placed in a situation such as Moses experienced, do you think you would have given up or persevered? Why?

8. How should the story of Moses give you hope?

9. Why do you think that people—even many Christians—do not put their hope in God?

As leader of the Israelites, Moses endured much hardship as he obediently endeavored to take God's people from slavery to freedom. And the people he was leading were not willing to be led! They whined; they complained; they rebelled; they questioned his leadership. After 40 years of wandering in the wilderness, Moses was not allowed to enter the Promised Land because of his own sin and lack of trust (see Numbers 20:12). Imagine the disappointment he must have felt when he climbed Mount Nebo, and the Lord showed him the land and told him: "This is the land I promised on oath to Abraham, Isaac and Jacob when I said, 'I will give it to your descendants.' I have let you see it with your eyes, but you will not cross over into it" (Deuteronomy 34:4).

Although Moses didn't get to see the Promised Land, God used him to prepare the Israelites for what was ahead. Scripture tells us that "no one has ever shown the mighty power or performed the awesome deeds that Moses did in the sight of all Israel" (Deuteronomy 34:12). Because of his enduring faith, he was included in Hebrews 11, which some people call the Faith Hall of Fame.

10. What does Hebrews 11:39 say about God's promises? What does that mean to you?

Think about the faith of Abraham and Sarah, who struggled with infertility, even though God had promised them a son. When Sarah was first told she was going to have a child past the normal childbearing years, she laughed. But her disbelief turned to faith when she found she *was* pregnant! She had an attitude change, and her faith grew as a result.

Abraham's faith was even more severely tested. According to Matthew Henry, "The greatest trial and act of faith upon record is Abraham's offering up Isaac"[4] (see Genesis 22:1-13). Can you imagine being willing to sacrifice the son you waited a lifetime to have—the son God promised over and over? And what do you think Isaac was thinking as his father laid him on the altar? Don't you know that both of them were relieved when the angel of the Lord told Abraham not to kill Isaac and provided a substitute sacrifice! Abraham was obedient beyond human reason, and God gave him back his son. More significant, He promised to bless Abraham and his descendants (see Genesis 22:17-18).

11. When Abraham died, most of God's promises to him—numerous descendants, possession of the land, all nations of the earth blessed— had not been realized. Does this challenge your faith in God's promises? Why or why not?

Faith has always been the mark of God's servants. As we look at the list of men and women included in Hebrews 11, however, we are reminded that none of them were perfect. Consider Rahab for example. She was a prostitute and a Gentile—a pagan—yet she demonstrated faith and risked her life for God's people (see Joshua 2) and she was rewarded for her faith (see Joshua 6:22-25; Matthew 1:5).

So how are faith and hope connected? In essence, faith means "trust or confidence in what God has promised."[4] "The same things that are the object of our hope," explained Matthew Henry, "are the object of our faith."[5]

An Eternal Hope

While some Bible characters had a happy ending to their stories (see Hebrews 11:5,31,33-34), many others didn't (see vv. 4,35-38). Men and women have for centuries faced persecution because of their faith. They have been put to death, stoned and left destitute for their faith. Yet it was worth it to them because their hope was in the Lord (see vv. 39-40).

12. What do the faithful receive (see Hebrews 11:6,40)?

Maybe you know someone like Laura who has been faithful to God regarding her marriage but hasn't yet experienced the fruit of obedience. It seems unfair, doesn't it? The truth is, even if we serve the Lord faithfully, Scripture doesn't promise believers an easy life, yet we do have hope in God's power and strength to help us endure victoriously until the end. Jesus even warned His disciples on His final night with them before His death: "In this world you will have trouble. But take heart! I have overcome the world" (John 16:33).

13. What did Jesus mean when He said that He has "overcome the world"?

14. What does Romans 8:24-25 say about hope?

What is one area of your life or marriage where you need to hope in the unseen?

15. Romans 8:28 is often quoted to encourage people who are dealing with problems. Does it encourage you? Explain.

Those in marriages where one spouse must give more than 100 percent have their hearts broken time and again. God rewards such faithfulness. The temporary unhappiness you experience on this earth will fade when He welcomes you into heaven and says, "Well done, good and faithful servant!" (Matthew 25:21).

16. Why do you think God allows Christians to suffer, or experience, unhappiness?

17. Have you ever seen something good come out of a marriage that seemed one-sided? Explain.

Whatever your circumstances, it's important to stay committed to God's plan. As Al Janssen stated in *The Marriage Masterpiece*, "If God can take Hosea's marriage and make it a means of ministry to the nation of Israel, then perhaps He can use any marriage where one partner is willing to let God work. Because God isn't willing to give up on His marriage to Israel and the church, I believe He won't give up on any marriage where just one partner is committed to Him."[6]

We've talked about several types of giving marriages throughout this study and concluded that even in times of unhappiness, God intends for us to honor our commitment to Him and our spouse. The hope of what lies ahead far surpasses anything we could ever experience on this earth.

Think about the following example and how you would deal with a situation like this. How would you remain hopeful?

> Seven years ago, Sheila's husband, Kevin, had a brain tumor. His health gradually deteriorated, and he had to quit working. Sheila had to keep her job because they desperately needed her health insurance. While she works, a nurse comes to make sure Kevin has everything he needs. Physically, his cancer has been devastating, but the worst part is the emotional side. The part of the brain that controls Kevin's emotions no longer functions properly, and he is unable to express his feelings. When Sheila hugs him, he doesn't even hug back. He has no idea that Sheila aches to be held lovingly in his arms.[7]

18. What steps can Sheila take to keep hope alive?

19. If you had a debilitating illness like Kevin's and still had your mental faculties, what could you do to keep hope alive?

20. How might a couple cope with the spiritual lows and sense of hopelessness that may accompany such an illness or other terrible circumstance?

21. How could the Church help couples in this kind of situation?

Unfortunately, some churches and many individuals do not know how to respond to couples that are living with difficult circumstances. More often than not, a couple struggling because one spouse is unfaithful, unbelieving or incapacitated—or other difficult family situations—is abandoned by many. The Church needs to respond in practical ways with compassion, love and encouragement.

 harvesting the fruit

When believers suffer, we have an ever-present hope in a loving God who sent His beloved Son to die for us. Even in unhappy or life-changing situations, knowing that God is pleased with our faithfulness to Him can bring hope and lasting joy.

Our prayer for you: "May the God of hope fill you with all joy and peace as you trust in him, so that you may overflow with hope by the power of the Holy Spirit" (Romans 15:13).

22. How has this study made you more aware of the need to be faithful to your spouse and to God in all circumstances?

23. On a scale of 1 to 10 (with 1 being hopeless and 10 being highest hope), how hopeful were you about your marriage before you completed this study? Has there been any change in your level of hope?

24. Now that you've completed the four sessions of *The Giving Marriage*, what steps will you take as a couple to build a stronger foundation for your marriage?

25. How could you help other couples who may need the hope of Christ in their difficult marriage?

Notes

1. Garwin Dobbins, interview by Randy Phillips, *The Austin Awakening*, Day Star Television, December 7, 2002.
2. Ibid.
3. Bart Millard, "I Can Only Imagine" © 2002 Simpleville Music.
4. Matthew Henry, "Commentary on Hebrew 11," *Matthew Henry Concise Commentary on the Whole Bible*, www.crosswalk.com (accessed November 3, 2002).
5. Ibid.
6. Al Janssen, *The Marriage Masterpiece* (Wheaton, IL: Tyndale House Publishers, 2001), pp. 135-136.
7. This is a compilation of several stories. Any resemblance to an actual situation is purely coincidental.

leader's discussion guide

General Guidelines

1. If at all possible, the group should be led by a married couple. This does not mean that both spouses need to be leading the discussions; perhaps one spouse is better at facilitating discussions while the other is better at relationship building or organization—but the leader couple should share responsibilities wherever possible.

2. At the first meeting, be sure to lay down the ground rules for discussions, stressing that following these rules will help everyone feel comfortable during discussion times.

   a. No one should share anything of a personal or potentially embarrassing nature without first asking his or her spouse's permission.

   b. Whatever is discussed in the group meetings is to be held in strictest confidence among group members only.

   c. Allow everyone in the group to participate. However, as a leader, don't force anyone to answer a question if he or she is reluctant. Be sensitive to the different personalities and communication styles among your group members.

3. Fellowship time is very important in building small-group relationships. Providing beverages and/or light refreshments either before or after each session will encourage a time of informal fellowship.

4. Most people live very busy lives; respect the time of your group members by beginning and ending meetings on time.

The Focus on the Family Marriage Ministry Guide *has even more information on starting and leading a small group. You will find this an invaluable resource as you lead others through this Bible study.*

How to Use the Material

1. Each session has more than enough material to cover in a 45-minute teaching period. You will probably not have time to discuss every single question in each session, so prepare for each meeting by selecting questions you feel are most important to address for your group; discuss other questions as time permits. Be sure to save the last 10 minutes of your meeting time for each couple to interact individually and to pray together before adjourning.

    Optional Eight-Session Plan—You can easily divide each session into two parts if you'd like to cover all of the material presented in each session. Each section of the session has enough questions to divide in half, and the Bible study sections (Planting the Seed) are divided into two or three sections that can be taught in separate sessions.

2. Each spouse should have his or her own copy of the book in order to personally answer the questions. The general plan of this study is that the couples complete the questions at home during the week and then bring their books to the meeting to share what they have learned during the week.

    However, the reality of leading small groups in this day and age is that some members will find it difficult to do the homework. If you find that to be the case with your group, consider adjusting the lessons and having members complete the study during your meeting time as you guide them through the lesson. If you use this method, be sure to encourage members to share their individual answers with their spouses during the week (perhaps on a date night).

Session One | Dealing with an Unfaithful Spouse

> *A Note to Leaders: This Bible study series is based on* The Marriage Masterpiece[1] *by Al Janssen. We highly recommend that you read chapters 12 and 13 in preparation for leading this study.*

Before the Meeting

1. Gather materials for making name tags; also gather pens or pencils, paper, 3x5-inch index cards and Bibles.
2. Make photocopies of the Prayer Request Form (see *The Focus on the Family Marriage Ministry Guide*, "Reproducible Forms" section) or provide index cards for recording requests.
3. Read through your own answers from the session and mark the ones that you especially want to have the group discuss. Also highlight any key verses you feel are appropriate to share.
4. Prepare slips of paper with references for the verses that you will want someone to read aloud during the session. Distribute these slips as group members arrive, but be sensitive to those who are uncomfortable reading aloud or who might not be familiar with the Bible.
5. Collect items needed for either of the ice-breaker options (see below).

Ice Breakers

1. If this is the first meeting for this couples group, have everyone introduce themselves and tell the group a brief summary of how they met their spouse, how long they have been married and one interesting fact about their spouse. Be sure to remind them not to reveal anything that the spouse would be uncomfortable sharing him- or herself.
2. **Option 1:** Find examples of how unfaithfulness is glamorized by our culture. These might include promotions for movies or TV shows, magazine or newspaper headlines, or magazine or TV advertisements.

Display the examples and invite discussion on how and why our culture glamorizes sexual infidelity.

3. **Option 2:** Bring visual aids that might represent things other than sexual infidelity that might cause spouses to stray away from their marriage commitment. Examples of things to bring might include money, sports equipment, family picture, church calendar or other calendar, a laptop computer, a cell phone, etc. These might be the actual objects or pictures of the objects. Hand one item or picture to each couple (or person if you have enough items) and ask each to explain how that item might relate to a form of infidelity. For example, the money might represent how a person hides money from a spouse or it might represent a spouse who is too wrapped up in work and making money, ignoring the family. The cell phone might represent spending more time with friends than the spouse.

Discussion

1. **Tilling the Ground**—Discuss questions 1 through 3. If you did not do the option 2 ice breaker, you could use that activity instead of merely discussing question 3. If you did do the option 2 ice breaker, skip question 3.
2. **Planting the Seed**—Invite three volunteers to read Hosea 1 through 3 aloud—one volunteer for each chapter—before discussing questions 4 through 11. Continue discussing the remainder of the questions, except questions 14 through 16, which will be discussed by the individual couples during the Harvesting the Fruit time. If some members are willing, invite them to share their answers to question 15 about how they handle temptation. This might be an encouragement to those who don't know how to handle temptation.
4. **Watering the Hope**— The case study and questions in this section will help members bring the Bible study into the reality of their own expectations versus God's plan. Don't neglect this part of the study, as it brings the whole lesson into the here and now, applying God's Word to daily life.

Divide the group by gender to discuss questions 24 through 28. Have the two groups share with the whole group their answers to question 26 about how to safeguard a marriage against affairs.

5. **Harvesting the Fruit**—This section is meant to help the individual couples apply the lesson to their own marriage and can be dealt with in several ways.

  a. Allow the couples one-on-one time at the end of the meeting. This would require space for them to be alone, with enough space between couples to allow for quiet, private conversations.

  If couples have already answered the questions individually, now would be the time to share their answers. Give a time limit, emphasizing that their discussions can be continued at home if they are not able to answer all of the questions in the time allotted.

  If couples have not answered the questions before the meeting, have them answer them together now. This works best when there is open-ended time for the couples to stay until they have completed their discussion and will require that the leaders stay until the last couple has finished.

  b. Instruct couples to complete this section at home during the week after the meeting. This will give them quiet and private time to deal with any issues that might come up and to spend all the time needed to complete the discussion. You will want to follow up at the next meeting to hold couples accountable for completing this part of the lesson.

  c. At times it might be advantageous to pair two couples to discuss these questions. This would help build accountability into the study.

  Allow time for the individual couples to meet together to complete this section of the questions. Encourage each person to find a partner of the same sex within the group to keep him or her accountable regarding faithfulness in marriage.

6. **Close in Prayer**—An important part of any small-group relationship is the time spent in prayer for one another. This may also be done in a number of ways.

  a. Have couples write out their specific prayer requests on the Prayer Request Forms (or index cards). These requests may then be shared with the whole group or traded with another couple as prayer partners for the week. If requests are shared with the whole group, pray as a group before adjourning the meeting; if requests are traded, allow time for the prayer-partner couples to pray together.

b. Gather the whole group together and lead couples in guided prayer.

c. Have individual couples pray together.

d. Split the members into two groups by gender. Have them pray over their marriages, asking that God would reveal any points where they might be acting unfaithfully toward their spouse.

After the Meeting

1. **Evaluate**—Spend time evaluating the meeting's effectiveness (see *The Focus on the Family Marriage Ministry Guide*, "Reproducible Forms" section).

2. **Encourage**—During the week, try to contact each couple (through phone calls, notes of encouragement, e-mails or instant messages) and welcome them to the group. Make yourself available to answer any questions or concerns they may have and generally get to know them. This contact might best be done by the husband-leader contacting the men and the wife-leader contacting the women.

3. **Equip**—Complete the Bible study, even if you have previously gone through this study together.

4. **Pray**—Prayerfully prepare for the next meeting, praying for each couple and your own preparation. Discuss with the Lord any apprehension, excitement or anything else that is on your mind regarding your Bible study material and/or the group members. If you feel inadequate or unprepared, ask for strength and insight. If you feel tired or burdened, ask for God's light yoke. Whatever it is you need, ask God for it. He will provide!

Reminder: In your desire to serve the members of your group, don't neglect your own marriage. Spend quality time with your spouse during the week!

Session Two | Living with an Unbelieving Spouse

Before the Meeting

1. Gather pens or pencils, paper, 3x5-inch index cards and Bibles.
2. Make photocopies of the Prayer Request Form, or provide index cards for recording requests.
3. Read through your own answers from the session and mark the ones that you especially want to have the group discuss. Also highlight any key verses you feel are appropriate to share.
4. Prepare slips of paper with references for the verses that you will want someone to read aloud during the session. Distribute these slips as group members arrive, but be sensitive to those who are uncomfortable reading aloud or who might not be familiar with the Bible.
5. Prepare a brief testimony of how you came to know Jesus as Savior and Lord of your life. Or call a member of the group and ask if he or she would share a brief testimony.

Ice Breakers

1. Invite couples to share how they applied to their marriage relationship what they learned in last week's session.
2. Ask volunteers to share one praise or good thing that happened during the past week. This is a good chance for those who might not always see the good in things to learn how to express gratitude and thanksgiving to God no matter what the circumstance.
3. Share your testimony or invite the member you contacted to share theirs.

Discussion

1. **Tilling the Ground**—Discuss questions 1 through 4 together as a group. Ask couples to briefly discuss question 5 on their own.
2. **Planting the Seed**—Have the group form at least two small groups to discuss questions 6 through 18. You might want to form groups by

gender. Another suggestion is to have couples pair up to form groups of four.

3. **Watering the Hope**—Discuss questions 19 through 23 with the whole group.

4. **Harvesting the Fruit**—Discuss questions 24 and 25 with the whole group. Then allow time for couples to share their answers to the remainder of the questions individually.

    Option: Invite members to pair up and practice sharing Christ. Encourage each couple to reach out to another couple in which one or both of them are not Christians and plan to do something together. Instruct them to focus on getting to know that couple and building a relationship and not merely looking at it as an evangelistic project.

5. **Close in Prayer**—Distribute Prayer Request Forms (or index cards) and allow time for couples to pray together for the requests of the couple whose form they chose. Close the meeting by praying that each member will have an opportunity to share Christ with someone during the week.

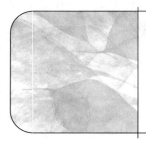

Note: Be sensitive to group members who might not know Christ as Savior and Lord. Be available after the meeting to answer any questions they might have concerning their relationship with God. Be open to the Holy Spirit's leading in asking if anyone would like to make a commitment or rededication to the Lord at this time.

After the Meeting

1. **Evaluate**—Spend time evaluating the meeting's effectiveness.

2. **Encourage**—During the week, try to contact each couple and ask them if they have had an opportunity to share Christ. If anyone accepted Christ during the meeting, follow up by making an appointment to meet with him or her. **Caution:** It is best for you and your spouse to meet with individuals together. Or you could meet one-on-one with the person of the same gender.

3. **Equip**—Complete the Bible study.

4. **Pray**—Prayerfully prepare for the next meeting, praying for each couple and your own preparation.

Session Three | Living with an Incapacitated Spouse

Before the Meeting

1. Gather materials for making name tags in addition to extra pens, paper, 3x5-inch index cards and Bibles.
2. Make photocopies of the Prayer Request Form, or provide index cards for recording requests.
3. Read through your own answers from the session and mark the ones that you especially want to have the group discuss. Also highlight any key verses you feel are appropriate to share.
4. Prepare slips of paper with references for the verses that you will want someone to read aloud during the session. Distribute these slips as group members arrive, but be sensitive to those who are uncomfortable reading aloud or who might not be familiar with the Bible.
5. Obtain a newsprint pad, white board, chalkboard or poster board and the appropriate writing instrument.

Ice Breakers

1. Hand a Prayer Request Form (or index card) to each member as he or she enters the room. Encourage them to at least fill in their name and address, even if they don't have any requests. Remind members that everyone needs someone to pray for them, even if there is no specific need.
2. Ask members if they know of any couples seriously impacted by a setback such as an illness, job loss, etc. (question 3). Invite members to share how that particular couple dealt with the situation.

Discussion

1. **Tilling the Ground**—Discuss questions 1 and 2 if there is time.
2. **Planting the Seed**—Discuss questions 4 through 14 with the whole group.

3. **Watering the Hope**—Have each couple pair up with another couple to discuss questions 15 through 18.
4. **Harvesting the Fruit**—Allow time for individual couples to share their answers.
5. **Close in Prayer**—Have couples rejoin the couple with whom they shared the Watering the Hope discussion. Instruct them to swap their prayer requests and spend a few minutes in prayer together. Encourage each couple to call their prayer-partner couple during the week and share any praises or further requests.

After the Meeting

1. **Evaluate**.
2. **Encourage**—During the week, call each couple and ask if they have called their prayer partners. Encourage them as they continue to complete the study.
3. **Equip**—Complete the Bible study.
4. **Pray**—Prayerfully prepare for the next meeting, praying for each couple and your own preparation. Whatever it is you need, ask God for it. He will provide!

Session Four | Living with a Hopeful Heart

Before the Meeting

1. Gather extra pens or pencils, paper and Bibles.
2. Make photocopies of the Prayer Request Form, or provide index cards for recording requests.
3. Make photocopies of the Study Review Form (see *The Focus on the Family Marriage Ministry Guide,* "Reproducible Forms" section).
4. Read through your own answers from the session and mark the ones that you especially want to have the group discuss. Also highlight any key verses you feel are appropriate to share.
5. Prepare slips of paper with references for the verses that you will want someone to read aloud during the session. Distribute these slips as group members arrive, but be sensitive to those who are uncomfortable reading aloud or who might not be familiar with the Bible.
6. If possible, obtain a CD of "I Can Only Imagine" by MercyMe, which can be found on MercyMe's *Almost There* and *Worship Project.* Make sure you have a CD player available to play the song.
7. Obtain a newsprint pad, white board or chalkboard and the appropriate writing instrument.

Ice Breakers

1. **Option 1:** Ask if anyone had an opportunity to share Christ with another person, and if so, invite at least one volunteer to share briefly.
2. **Option 2:** If you were able to obtain a CD of "I Can Only Imagine," play it now. Instruct members to close their eyes and imagine what heaven will be like. Invite volunteers to share what they "saw."

Discussion

1. **Tilling the Ground**—Discuss questions 1 through 3.
2. **Planting the Seed**—Read Hebrews 11 aloud. Discuss questions 4 through 17 with the whole group.

3. **Watering the Hope**—Discuss questions 18 through 21; then have members discuss how the group can do something practical to help a couple that is living in a difficult situation. Write their ideas on the board or newsprint and challenge the group to decide at least one practical way that they could serve that couple. For example, if they chose to help an elderly couple in which one spouse is bedridden, the group might decide to take turns once a week staying with the ill spouse so that the caregiver could enjoy a day shopping.

4. **Harvesting the Fruit**—Invite individual couples to discuss questions 22 through 25. Invite volunteers to share how the Lord has built their faith and given them a sense of hope as a result of this session.

5. **Close in Prayer**—Play the song (or read the lyrics) again. Invite sentence prayers of praise and thanksgiving. For the benediction, ask everyone to read aloud Romans 15:13: "May the God of hope fill you with all joy and peace as you trust in him, so that you may overflow with hope by the power of the Holy Spirit."

After the Meeting

1. **Evaluate**—Distribute the Study Review Forms for members to take home with them. Share about the importance of feedback, and ask members to take the time this week to write their review of the group meetings and then to return them to you.

2. **Encourage**—Call each couple during the next week and invite them to join you for the next study in the *Focus on the Family Marriage Series*.

3. **Equip**—Begin preparing and brainstorming new activities for the next Bible study.

4. **Pray**—Praise the Lord for the work He has done in the lives of the couples in the study. Continue to pray for these couples as they apply the lessons learned in the last few weeks.

Note
1. Al Janssen, *The Marriage Masterpiece* (Wheaton, IL: Tyndale House Publishers, 2001).

Welcome to the Family!

As you participate in the *Focus on the Family Marriage Series*, it is our prayerful hope that God will deepen your understanding of His plan for marriage and that He will strengthen your marriage relationship.

This series is just one of the many helpful, insightful, and encouraging resources produced by Focus on the Family. In fact, that's what Focus on the Family is all about—providing inspiration, information, and biblically based advice to people in all stages of life.

It began in 1977 with the vision of one man, Dr. James Dobson, a licensed psychologist and author of 18 best-selling books on marriage, parenting, and family. Alarmed by the societal, political, and economic pressures that were threatening the existence of the American family, Dr. Dobson founded Focus on the Family with one employee and a once-a-week radio broadcast aired on only 36 stations.

Now an international organization, the ministry is dedicated to preserving Judeo-Christian values and strengthening and encouraging families through the life-changing message of Jesus Christ. Focus ministries reach families worldwide through 10 separate radio broadcasts, two television news features, 13 publications, 18 Web sites, and a steady series of books and award-winning films and videos for people of all ages and interests.

We'd love to hear from you!

For more information about the ministry, or if we can be of help to your family, simply write to Focus on the Family, Colorado Springs, CO 80995 or call 1-800-A-FAMILY (1-800-232-6459). Friends in Canada may write Focus on the Family, P.O. Box 9800, Stn. Terminal, Vancouver, B.C. V6B 4G3 or call 1-800-661-9800. Visit our Web site—www.family.org—to learn more about Focus on the Family or to find out if there is an associate office in your country.

Strengthen and enrich your marriage with these Focus on the Family® relationship builders.

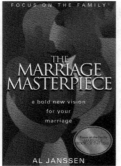

The Marriage Masterpiece

Now that you've discovered the richness to be had in "The Focus on the Family Marriage Series" Bible studies, be sure to read the book the series is based on. *The Marriage Masterpiece* takes a fresh appraisal of the exquisite design God has for a man and woman. Explaining the reasons why this union is meant to last a lifetime, it also shows how God's relationship with humanity is the model for marriage. Rediscover the beauty and worth of marriage in a new light with this thoughtful, creative book. A helpful study guide is included for group discussion. Hardcover.

The Love List

Marriage experts Drs. Les and Leslie Parrot present eight healthy habits that refresh, transform and restore the intimacy of your marriage relationship. Filled with practical suggestions, this book will help you make daily, weekly, monthly and yearly improvements in your marriage. Hardcover.

Capture His Heart/Capture Her Heart

Lysa TerKeurst has written two practical guides—one for wives and one for husbands—that will open your eyes to the needs, desires and longings of your spouse. These two books each offer eight essential criteria plus creative tips for winning and holding his or her heart. Paperback set.

• • •

STRENGTHEN MARRIAGES.
STRENGTHEN YOUR CHURCH.

Here's Everything You Need for a Dynamic Marriage Ministry!

Focus on the Family ® Marriage Series Group Starter Kit
Kit Box • Bible Study/Marriage • ISBN 08307.32365

Group Starter Kit includes:

• Seven Bible Studies: *The Masterpiece Marriage, The Passionate Marriage, The Fighting Marriage,*
The Model Marriage, The Surprising Marriage, The Giving Marriage and The Covenant Marriage

• *The Focus on the Family Marriage Ministry Guide*

• *An Introduction to the Focus on the Family Marriage Series* video

Pick up the *Focus on the Family Marriage Series* where Christian books are sold.

Gospel Light

Devotionals for Drawing Near to God and One Another

Moments Together for Couples
Hardcover • 384p
ISBN 08307.17544

Moments Together for Parents
Gift Hardcover
96p
ISBN 08307.32497

Moments Together for Intimacy
Gift Hardcover
96p
ISBN 08307.32489

Give Your Marriage a Checkup

The Marriage Checkup
How Healthy
Is Your Marriage Really?
Paperback • 140p
ISBN 08307.30699

The Marriage Checkup Questionnaire
An Easy-to-Use Questionnaire
to Help You Evaluate the
Health of Your Marriage
Manual • 24p
ISBN 08307.30648

How to Counsel a Couple in 6 Sessions or Less
A Tool for Marriage Counseling
to Use in Tandem with the
Marriage Checkup Questionnaire
Manual • 24p
ISBN 08307.30680

Complete Your Marriage-Strengthening Library

Preparing for Marriage
The Complete Guide
to Help You Discover God's Plan
for a Lifetime of Love
Dennis Rainey
Paperback • 170p
ISBN 08307.17803
Counselor's Pack
(3 books, I Leader's Guide)
ISBN 08307.21568
Couples Pack (2 books) • ISBN 08307.21576
Leader's Guide • ISBN 08307.17609

Communication: Key to Your Marriage
A Practical Guide to Creating
a Happy, Fulfilling Relationship
Dr. H. Norman Wright
Paperback • 244p
ISBN 08307.25334
Video Approx. 2 hrs.
UPC 607135.004639

Holding on to Romance
Keeping Your Marriage
Alive and Passionate
After the Honeymoon Years
Dr. H. Norman Wright
Video • Approx. 1 hr.
UPC 85116.00779